IMMIGRATION LAW AND SOCIETY

This one is for Gowan.

Immigration Law and Society

John S. W. Park

polity

Copyright © John S. W. Park 2018

The right of John S. W. Park to be identified as Author of this Work has been asserted in accordance with the UK Copyright, Designs and Patents Act 1988.

First published in 2018 by Polity Press

Polity Press
65 Bridge Street
Cambridge CB2 1UR, UK

Polity Press
101 Station Landing
Suite 300
Medford, MA 02155, USA

All rights reserved. Except for the quotation of short passages for the purpose of criticism and review, no part of this publication may be reproduced, stored in a retrieval system or transmitted, in any form or by any means, electronic, mechanical, photocopying, recording, or otherwise, without the prior permission of the publisher.

ISBN-13: 978-1-5095-0599-9
ISBN-13: 978-1-5095-0600-2 (pb)

A catalogue record for this book is available from the British Library.

Library of Congress Cataloging-in-Publication Data

Names: Park, John S. W., author.
Title: Immigration law and society / John S. W. Park.
Description: Cambridge, UK ; Medford, MA, USA : Polity Press, 2018. | Includes bibliographical references and index.
Identifiers: LCCN 2017040362 (print) | LCCN 2017043977 (ebook) | ISBN 9781509506033 (Epub) | ISBN 9781509505999 (hardback) | ISBN 9781509506002 (pbk.)
Subjects: LCSH: Emigration and immigration law--Social aspects--United States.
Classification: LCC KF4819 (ebook) | LCC KF4819 .P36 2018 (print) | DDC 342.7308/2--dc23
LC record available at https://lccn.loc.gov/2017040362

Typeset in 10.5 on 12pt Plantin by
Servis Filmsetting Ltd, Stockport, Cheshire
Printed and bound in Great Britain by CPI Group (UK) Ltd, Croydon

The publisher has used its best endeavours to ensure that the URLs for external websites referred to in this book are correct and active at the time of going to press. However, the publisher has no responsibility for the websites and can make no guarantee that a site will remain live or that the content is or will remain appropriate.

Every effort has been made to trace all copyright holders, but if any have been inadvertently overlooked the publisher will be pleased to include any necessary credits in any subsequent reprint or edition.

For further information on Polity, visit our website: www.politybooks.com

Contents

Preface		*page* vi
1	The Two Revolutions	1
2	The Kinetic Nation	11
3	The Immigration Act of 1965	28
4	The Multiracial State	49
5	Common Wealth	69
6	The Privileged Classes	86
7	Out of Status	106
8	Local, State, and Federal	125
9	The Great Divides	145
10	The Future of American Migrations	165
Epilogue		178
Notes		185
Index		211

Preface

Since 2002, as a professor of Asian American Studies at the University of California, Santa Barbara, I have offered every fall a lower-division course on immigration to the United States after 1965. I had focused on immigrants from Asia to the United States, as this was more in line with my early research interests, but then I revised the course to encompass a much broader cross-section of immigrants, if only to measure how Asian migrants were different from, say, Mexican and Central American migrants. The class is still evolving: over the last 15 years, many outstanding scholars have published work about immigration law and policy, as well as the impact of public law on immigrants and immigrant communities. It's been my pleasure to share that research with my first-year students, to introduce them to some of the best and most accessible works in the social sciences and the humanities, and to introduce familiar topics from a scholarly point of view.

In my class, I've tried to make a number of underlying arguments about the Immigration Act of 1965, the most important being that this law represented one of the most significant changes in American history ever. We still feel its overall demographic impact. There is a before and after to the rule: before 1965, persons of Asian ancestry comprised less than 1% of the population of the United States, and persons from Mexico, Central America, and South America comprised about 4%. In 1965, about 85% of Americans defined themselves as "White" in the national census. By 2010, however, there were about 18 million people of Asian ancestry in the United States, and 57 million people of Hispanic ancestry were, representing 6% and 18% of the American population, respectively. The proportion of "Whites" had fallen to about 60% by 2010. For persons of African descent, the Immigration Act of 1965 had surprising impacts, too: by 2010, more persons of African ancestry living in the United States were immigrants from the Caribbean and from Africa, and about 10–12% of all persons of African ancestry were immigrants. In so many ways, the immigrants who came after 1965 have had a profound and lasting impact on American society, and, if present trends continue, they and their children will reshape the United States even further.

★ ★ ★ ★ ★

This volume reflects upon the central themes in immigration law and policy in the United States after 1965, but by presenting, in some detail, the American experience, I've sought to explain to my own students why American legal institutions shaped immigration laws in specific ways, how those rules governed immigrants and immigrant communities, and then how all modern states have wrestled with similar problems and consequences. Immigration is quite the hot topic around the world. In the United States, President Lyndon Johnson promised that the Immigration Act of 1965 would not be a "revolutionary bill," but he was clearly wrong, and in ways that he and many other politicians and scholars could not have foreseen. Some members of Congress supported the Immigration Act of 1965 because they thought that this would be a race-neutral way of continuing to yield the same number and quality of European immigrants as before. Most Americans were of European ancestry in 1965, and a clear majority of leading colleges and universities were in Europe. Thus, some legislators thought that, by selecting immigrants with skills and family connections, the rule would yield mostly Europeans. Some 50 years later, though, persons of European ancestry were a far smaller proportion of the American population than since … well, ever. Combined with other developments around the world, the law resulted in a much more multiracial America than anyone could have predicted in 1965. Similarly, within Europe, few policy-makers thought that a European Union would produce such profound immigration consequences, and yet those consequences have caused many to reconsider the entire project.

Given the unpredictability of immigration rules, the field overall is suited to the "law and society" movement within the social sciences, as one of the main tenets among law and society scholars has been that the law often doesn't do what the legislators intended. Moreover, using methods in the humanities and social sciences, scholars in law and society didn't treat law and legal institutions as separate from political or social norms, and – perhaps most obvious of all – they did not take the law at face value. A law and society scholar might drive down a freeway and see a speed limit, 65 miles per hour, but she would never infer from that sign that people *actually* drove at or under that speed. Instead of just trusting the sign, the law at face value, this scholar might collect empirical data about speeds on the freeway, taking hundreds or thousands of measurements to see how the law shaped real-life driving speeds. A historian with a similar sensibility might study how the rule came to be, if just to understand why so many people tended to break it.

For scholars of the immigration law, a law-and-society approach has obvious intuitive appeal: for many years, American immigration rules have told some people not to come, encouraged others to live and work here, and threatened to remove a larger number of people who had come without inspection or who had misbehaved. Again, this book presents evidence from my colleagues that shows how these rules have never worked as intended; nor have they had consequences that the legislators themselves had foreseen or approved. The rules may provide some starting point for how things *actually* unfolded, but no one would conclude from the simple existence of rules prohibiting illegal immigration that there were, in fact, no illegal immigrants in the United States.

★ ★ ★ ★ ★

The first third of this volume lays out the historical context for the Immigration Act of 1965, drawing from several leading histories about the period before, during, and after. The first chapter outlines a theory for understanding everything else in the book: because of basic changes to our communication and transportation technologies, the world was a much, much smaller place than ever before, and so learning about distant places and then getting from one place to another was easier than ever. Federal immigration rules originated during a time when governments envisioned control of boundaries and territory and people. Governments passed these rules to regulate entry and exit, and yet with so much movement everywhere nowadays, all the time, it's no wonder that so many governments pass rules that so often don't work. Without question, many supporters of the Immigration Act of 1965 thought that persons of European descent would still dominate American immigration trends after the rule, just as they had before the rule. Instead, the rule resulted in millions of people immigrating from Asia and Latin America, and it's only in hindsight that we can understand how and why that came to pass. It turns out that many of the Asians and Latin Americans came from countries where lots of Americans had gone first, which might suggest that spilling yourself into the affairs of other countries may result in a lot of migration from there to here.

The middle third of this volume deals with some of the most difficult challenges arising from the new immigration law. The United States became far more multiracial, multiethnic, and multicultural within a very short period of time, and yet, as most professional historians know, the United States had never dealt well with this kind of diversity. In many instances, Americans continued to cope poorly with racial and ethnic diversity, and we focus here in this section on the persistence of hate crimes, hate speech, and then more disturbing instances of mass violence and social chaos. In the early 1990s, many Americans were watching entire cities fall apart through a combination of newer immigrant cacophonies layered over older, almost primordial, American racial tensions. In the aftermath of such recurring violence, many politicians and commentators proposed new and harsher immigration rules, ones designed to encourage "good," "productive" immigrants, and others to discourage and to expel anyone who might rely on public benefits, or who had committed a crime. Moreover, as the number of people migrating unlawfully rose from 1965 through 1986, and then into our current decade, more Americans demanded that the United States regain control over its borders.

The last portion of this book deals again with the unintended and unforeseeable consequences of these latest reforms. Nationally, after 1996, immigration policy was coming into a near-permanent deadlock – indeed, we have not seen a major, comprehensive revision to the immigration law since the Clinton Administration. Two presidents, each with two terms, both failed.

In the wake of these efforts, local governments, state governments, and the federal government have all pursued a mind-boggling range of policies, many of them completely contradictory. At the federal level, executive actions took the place of comprehensive legislation. States and local governments passed new rules that suggested profound disagreement about immigrants: were they public nuisances and threats to law-abiding communities, or were they integral members of communities and families? These conceptual disagreements were most obvious in the laws governing undocumented immigrants. In some states, young people who were out of status could attend public college and universities *and* get financial aid, while in others all the doors and supports were closed. In some jurisdictions, local police officers checked the status of anyone suspected of being "illegal," and yet, not 20 minutes away, in another city, political leaders told officers not to ask or to care.

At the national level, where immigration law was supposed to be supreme and over-riding of all state and local rules, both Presidents George Bush and Barack Obama did not get what they had wanted. Members of his own party refused to offer "amnesty" to undocumented immigrants when President George W. Bush proposed and pushed hard for that result. To appease members of his party, Bush said that undocumented persons would have to admit the error of their ways, pay a fine, and wait longer to vote or to be secure in the United States. This was not enough. Other leaders recommended instead that all levels of government should make life so miserable for undocumented persons that they themselves might "self-deport."

As these debates dragged on, there would be no "grand bargain," no immigration reform at the end of the Bush Administration in 2008. The next President, Barack Obama, began on such a hopeful note – hope and change everywhere – but he too did not get what he had wanted. There would be no comprehensive reform over the next eight years. Instead, as the grinding wheels of existing immigration rules continued to turn and turn and turn, Barack Obama's Administration ended up removing and deporting more people than any other Administration in American history. I am almost positive that he did not intend this to be a part of his legacy. There might be no mention of this in his Presidential Library back in Chicago.

In early 2017, the new President of the United States was blunt about what he had wanted in immigration law and policy. Even if he does get everything that he wanted, though, the readers of this book might, in the end, have a better sense of why he won't be as successful or as loved as he himself desired to be.

★ ★ ★ ★ ★

Throughout this work, and throughout my class, I've posed problems in immigration law and policy as though they remain "open" – open to debate, to moral and ethical considerations, to thoughts of how our present connects to our past. Of course, none of these problems is going away, and, at the end of my class, I've told my students that many of these issues are likely to dominate a huge portion of their lives, no matter what their professional or personal goals after college. Governments and states fell apart before 1965, and many are falling apart now, and we have in the world more refugees and displaced persons than ever before.

In addition, if the climate continues to change, if sea levels rise, if more violent weather events and droughts occur more often, the number of displaced people will increase ever higher, to figures that will dwarf our current crises. We thus leave the class having had a long and extended conversation about a vexing area of public law, and I do hope that my students might continue to cultivate a civic and scholarly engagement with the ideas presented over the term. We will all need that level of engagement as we approach even more formidable problems in human migration.

I am so deeply grateful to the hundreds of students at the University of California, Santa Barbara, for having taken my class. My students have come from all over the world in recent years, in all kinds of circumstances, and they've inspired me to design a class that speaks to as many of their experiences as possible. Rudy Guevarra, Malaphone Phommassa, Dusty Hoesly, and Philip Deslippe were among the excellent graduate students who have served as teaching assistants for this class, and they too helped me to think through improvements. Many of the class participants have said that they'd shared the class with their parents or roommates or friends, and so, with that in mind, I've tried for a prose that is free from academic jargon and as accessible as possible, so as to promote this kind of sharing. I hope that this volume can be useful for professional scholars, too, as an overview of the entire field, and for insights about how best to connect past and present migration problems. I hope that everyone will continue to read and to consider the scholarly authors I've relied upon for this work – I've been so grateful to have learned from the fine scholars working in immigration law and policy, in law and society, and in American ethnic studies, and my debts to them will be obvious to any reader. I am grateful to Jonathan Skerrett of Polity Press, because he reached out to me a few years ago to see whether I could recommend someone who could write about the Immigration Act of 1965 in a single volume. He managed to make me do it, and I've been thankful ever since. I would also like to thank the two anonymous reviewers for Polity, for their thorough read of my manuscript and for their helpful suggestions. My copy-editor, Leigh Mueller, caught many embarrassing errors, and she helped to produce a much-improved version of the final manuscript.

Finally, I've dedicated this book to my wife, Gowan Lee, because she's just the best. I'm inspired every day by her travels and by her constant and loving devotion to her family.

1

THE TWO REVOLUTIONS

Many politicians and citizens have repeated a truism when it comes to immigration law and policy in the United States over the last 40 years: the immigration system is broken, it doesn't work, and it needs to be "fixed." This book contains no "fixes." Rather, we begin with a set of basic observations that might help us understand *why* immigration law hasn't lived up to expectations, at least not since 1965. I propose that the problem might not be the immigrants, but with the dynamic shape of modernity itself: advances in technology allow us to see and to move faster and farther than ever before. In contrast, legislators and presidents and American citizens have shared an underlying premise – namely, that the United States is a stable, fixed nation, and that its legal institutions, representing the citizens of the United States, have the right to determine who may come, who may not come, and who must leave. Many Americans have still conceived their nation as a somewhat closed system with clear boundaries, as if the lines on the map can delineate what is within and what is without. Thus, they have been receptive to arguments about guarding those borders, the boundaries of the nation – perhaps even walling it off. They have believed that it's possible, that the very nation who drew the boundary can then enforce it, as though enforcement was just a matter of will.

But perhaps these expectations were too simple, or maybe way too optimistic.

The Two Revolutions

We live in the midst of two on-going revolutions that have shaped the modern world – the first in communication, and then the other in transportation. Together, they make the enforcement of national boundaries much more difficult, perhaps impossibly difficult. Since the mid-1970s, as these two revolutions have continued to unfold at a dizzying, accelerating pace, people who've expected stability, within a closed, bounded system of states, have been more frustrated than ever before. People around the world share new methods for *seeing* one another clear across the world, and they have access to new methods of transportation that can take them faster and cheaper and farther than at any time in human history. It's hard to imagine how any portion of the world can remain a closed system in light of the two revolutions.

Like all revolutions, no single person or entity can claim responsibility for the ease with which we can see one another across vast distances of time and space, nor can we even agree when exactly the transportation revolution began. But traveling anywhere around the world is not so difficult anymore. For people who travel a lot, across oceans and continents, the very mode of transportation is so connected to a set of interrelated communication networks that they don't have to miss much of anything, even when they're flying thousands of feet above the world. These methods of seeing and of traveling have become so common in the daily lives of many people that they can take them for granted. For the well-connected, as we shall see in this volume, being in one place and then flying to another clear across the world is not a problem – there are many thousands of people who *already* enjoy a borderless world with few meaningful restrictions.[1]

For poorer people, it's hard not to covet the life that the well-connected already enjoy. Through televisions, on computer screens, on their cell phones, or in mass print media, many of the poorest, displaced, and dislocated people can still *see* what Paris or London or New York looks like. Instead of staying around until their own homeland becomes somewhere that could be like one of those magical places, they develop plans to leave for Paris or London or New York. This is in large part because they can't fathom their own cities or towns ever becoming as gorgeous or livable, at least not in one lifetime. And for them, too, leaving is not so hard. Cell phones allow them to find out how to get from here to there; they can find boats for places with water, or trains to cross vast areas of land; and then they can pay to use trucks, tunnels, and shipping containers to cross an international border. Some can afford to pay for guides to avoid the public officials assigned to keeping them out. Of course, many of them won't make it, many will die trying – these crossings are dangerous. Moreover, in recent decades, there were more public officials trying everything to keep them out, as well as new and formidable physical obstacles, including walls, fences, and moats.

But some fraction of them will make it – this is why we can see them in Paris or London or New York – in every part of the world where things are marginally better. Because there are so many who wish to come, so many who try, even a small fraction of "success" can yield a large number. Wherever we have points of entry, places tied to the great circuits of global communication, commerce, and travel throughout the world, we also have "unwanted people," from Iraq, Syria, or Mexico, these poorer migrants who should not have come, at least not from the perspective of the states where they've appeared. That so many poorer people have risked their lives to make these journeys – this might well be the most shattering consequence of the two revolutions, unfolding as though, ideally, they should have made all of us more free rather than having condemned so many to premature death. Having underestimated the perils, or having so yearned for a better life, many migrants have perished in horrible ways: by drowning, through exposure, as the victims of predatory others. And yet still more will come.²

For that small fraction that do make it, American citizens have consigned them to a life on the margins of society. Thus, the immigrants often fall short of their dreams and expectations, their miseries rooted in the unmet (unrealistic?) expectations of the people who never wanted them at all. Because our governments have failed to keep you out, the citizens say, we will refuse to incorporate you. The frustrated expectations for a closed system, for a set of sturdy boundaries – these being unsatisfied – have led to strange forms of revenge, even petty forms of vindictiveness. We examine later in this book how millions of people live in this condition – here, and yet not supposed to be here. They are overwhelmingly poor, and they experience socially and legally constructed boundaries long after they've surmounted the physical ones that almost killed them. They have experienced an "illegality in everyday life." Thus, even when they make it across, the legal barriers *within* nations have become ferocious, too, as many migrants are routinely cast as criminals and wrongdoers, rather than people who were searching, like everyone else, for a better life.

For all of us, the two revolutions will unfold toward a future that we can only still imagine. Even our immediate ancestors might not fathom our present: in 1900, there was no commercial aviation – there was simply no aviation. People couldn't fly in metal tubes with wings attached to them at 10 or 12 kilometers in the sky. Trains and ships did take people across immense distances much more quickly than before, but nowadays, planes and airports move along millions of people every day, on a scale just inconceivable in 1900. To see why the United States has hundreds of thousands of "illegal immigrants," one needn't look at the southern border – instead, consider an average day at LAX or JFK. Count the international flights, and then imagine a small fraction of the "tourists" or other visitors who should leave eventually, but then don't. Again, small fractions will become, in time, very big numbers, for it was not hard to fly legally into the United States and then fall "out of status" in 2005 or 2010.

A few people grasp the scale of these problems, but their solutions tend to sound ridiculous, even totalitarian: in the presidential primaries of 2015, for example, the Governor of New Jersey, Chris Christie, suggested that everyone coming to the United States ought to be fitted with a bar code, rather like each package going through FedEx, so that we can keep track of everyone, coming and going. His solution sounded absurd, in a scary, Big Brother kind of way, and yet it's a real challenge, keeping track of everyone, if only because the numbers of people coming and going are so enormous. Another more serious problem might be that it's not hard to make excellent fake bar codes. It's a mind-boggling issue, mass migration; its scale is truly hard to fathom: in recent years, more people entered the United States through the international airports than the entire population of the country. Commercial aviation – this technology that did not exist in 1900 – made the United States much more porous than any public official might be willing to admit. A wall or another fence along the southern border will not help as much as some might promise, if only because walls and fences are ancient defensive technologies ill suited to the kinetic world in which we live.[3]

Similarly, in 1900, sending a message along a telegraph wire was an amazing advance in technology. But my cell phone (attached to nothing) can reach most other people with cell phones, too, in almost every urban area of the world, and, these days, the smartest of smart phones will become obsolete within two or three years. All of this is dizzying and disorienting: I myself admit that I'm unfamiliar with at least half of the computer applications on my own smart phone, and I don't use most of the social media tools that my own children have never not known. As of this writing, my children are teenagers, but they've become so familiar with these instantaneous forms of communication that they don't quite believe that their parents didn't have them when they were growing up. It's so easy for them, posting photographs and epigraphs for their relatives and friends in Asia, Europe, all over North America. And, like all children, they believe that they are at the end of the communication revolution, for what could possibly be better or more powerful than their own smart phones, right here, right now, right in their hands? We adults know, though, that by the time these children are middle-aged, they'll be as befuddled and disoriented with *their* latest communication devices as I am now. Again, these things never cease to evolve, exponentially so.[4] For hundreds of thousands – perhaps millions – of migrants, separated from their loved ones 30 or 40 years from now, we wonder whether the technologies yet to be invented will help them feel closer to their loved ones, or more pained by their absence.

Even in many of the poorest countries in the world right now, people are using their smart phones, their laptop computers, and other connected devices to see across vast distances, with a clarity and detail that was not possible in 1900. They can see how children like my children can have a decent life, where they do not worry about finding things to eat later that day or a place to sleep or clothes to wear. Through these ordinary miracles of modern communication, they see how another kind of life is possible in a place not so far away. Again, is it any wonder that we have so much migration? Is there anything more human than to want to try another place, another life, having seen that such things were possible?

For people who are not especially poor or disadvantaged, the two revolutions have also changed fundamentally how we relate to all that we know and love. In 1900, the University of California drew its students from within the state, and the campuses were located near the major cities of San Francisco and Los Angeles. After World War II, when the system expanded to serve a growing middle class, the new campuses matched the population growth of their regions – by 1960, parents in San Diego or in Sacramento could send their kids to campuses closer to them, rather than sending them to UCLA or Berkeley. Four decades later, however, the University of California drew students across the country and from all over the world. The University of California may have recruited and attracted students from out-of-state because of withering cuts in the state budget (which we will discuss later), but a student from China or Chicago can stay connected to their parents and fly back and forth and otherwise attend a UC campus without great difficulty. Again, to see this trend, one might visit SFO or LAX after final exams to see how many kids aren't staying in the state for the holidays. And students from San Diego have no problems attending Berkeley or UC Santa Barbara – distance is much less of an issue than it was for a similar student in 1900, in that time before interstate highways and cheap airfares. Many of my students text their parents every day, they post on sites where their loved ones can see what they're doing, every day – sometimes several times, every day.

When they graduate, they face a labor market that has spread everywhere, all over. We encourage students at the UC campuses to go abroad or go away as part of their undergraduate education, and many of them go and fall in love with Barcelona, Paris, Washington DC, or Seoul. They split after college. The University of California was once predicated on the idea that its graduates would be better citizens of California, and that they would support the economic and political development of this state. This may still be true, but a degree from one of these campuses is so valuable that companies and governments in New York or Shanghai or Tokyo offer jobs to these graduates, and these in turn can evolve into a lifetime away from Salinas or San Bernardino.

The two revolutions have let the privileged live farther away from the communities and the families that nurtured them as children – they can keep us connected through the internet or through cellular networks, even though we might live half a world away. Moreover, states and governments may regulate persons of this class and position, but nowhere near as severely as the people who are destitute. Many of my students and colleagues take vacations across an international boundary, and yet there are no police forces on the other end frisking or stopping them. In California, the great irony is that so many highly educated faculty members and students take vacations in Cabo or Cancun – going to Mexico and then coming back with a tan isn't a problem for these folks, and so they thus enjoy a freedom of movement unfathomable to a poorer Mexican person trying to cross somewhere near El Paso.

All of this freedom might suggest that life is fantastic for the highly skilled and the affluent – that the borders don't really matter much for them. There's certainly much to support this view. Still, it's not all great: many siblings and parents are spread across states, with perhaps a daughter in San Francisco, another in Vermont, and the parents in South Carolina. Getting together, even for holidays, can be a logistical nightmare, especially when everyone has small children, busy careers, and not enough time to handle the other time-consuming necessities of life. How often do we actually *see* the ones we love? Seeing someone through a screen is not quite the same as a loving embrace. Growing up in a tight-knit home, in a community where people know and care for each other, and then staying put well into adulthood – this is fast disappearing in the wake of the two revolutions. The highly educated, the highly skilled, the very affluent – it's true, for them, as we shall see, borders matter less, and their lives are fantastic. And yet they, too, can be scattered far and wide, and when the parents send their kids to a "good college," the odds aren't good that the kid will ever come back to the same town, or even to the same region or to the same state. They move away, and staying in touch is not a literal thing.[5]

The United States in the World, the World Coming Here

But because so many people in the United States have decent, good lives, a great many American citizens have regarded themselves as patriots who would die to defend this special place. To paraphrase President George W. Bush, Americans have had blessed lives. Some Americans might see the two revolutions working together to destroy everything that they've come to love, including a relatively homogeneous community – places where they were surrounded by familiar people, in a familiar setting, unchanging for the span of a lifetime. But it might also be true that the very goodness of a life lived here has drawn so many strangers from so far away – should the Americans admit everyone? It can all seem so overwhelming. American citizens might wonder how we could perhaps moderate or shape the two revolutions to stop the unraveling of the familiar, to keep things fixed for a while longer. So many students of immigration law and policy avoid that question or miss it altogether, and so I've foregrounded this discussion to give a sense of how the frustrations around immigration might have deeper, more profound existential roots.

The forces driving mass migration are too powerful for any one politician or party to stop, or perhaps even to manage – they appear to be inexorable, so that legislating as though the nation could ever be a closed system again just isn't plausible. The world has become too dynamic and interconnected, a fact that no politician or party seems willing to admit. Perhaps such an admission is too upsetting to the people who cherish stability or the familiar, to those political majorities who still insist, against all evidence, that they can protect the territory of an entire nation with better barriers or harsher rules. It (still) remains a matter of will, they say, and just another wall or a few million more deportations will do the trick. As for the people who promise these solutions – it's hard to know whether they themselves are the victims of a wishful thinking, or whether they're simply lying to people suffering from potent forms of political nostalgia. In this volume, we examine the continuing tenacity of nationalism in immigration policy, that nationalism often framed as if to advance the interests of citizens against waves and waves of new immigrants.[6]

The two revolutions have worked in multiple directions – it isn't just that people who want to move are coming to the wealthier countries, it's also that people from wealthier countries have been going to distant, not-so-well-off places. Because the two revolutions were well underway in the twentieth century, and because inventors in the United States developed some of the most ingenious new methods of transportation and communication, American citizens have been getting around a lot, for many years, to all kinds of places. And not just individual Americans: American government officials, American armies, and American corporations were some of the first large groups of people to leave the United States for places far away, and, through telegraph lines and radios and other nifty devices, they were able to keep in touch with their fellow-citizens back home. The Americans went to Korea, for example, the country of my birth, when the place was still just the Korean peninsula, not North or South Korea, and although they arrived in 1945, they're still there.

A lot of Americans are still there – public officials, entire armies, and many American companies are still there. The Americans introduced radios, televisions, and chocolate, as well as strange foods, like Spam and breakfast cereal. When she was a girl, my late mother listened to Elvis and Nat King Cole on a radio that her family got from the Americans. South Koreans took to many of these things, and with so many Korean kids trying toasted oats with cow's milk in the mornings, is it any wonder that a lot of these Asian kids shot taller than their parents? They grew faster than mung beans. Is it also any wonder that a lot of Koreans, including my mother, wanted badly to come to the land of Elvis, Nat King Cole, and chocolate? Alas, my mother's descendants still love Spam, just like thousands of English people who came to love Spam, too, when the Americans introduced it during and after World War II.[7]

Many thousands of immigrants who came to the United States in the twentieth century came this way – they were from countries where the Americans had appeared first. It wasn't as though, in 1945, Koreans wanted thousands of Americans to arrive – there wasn't a vote or a national referendum to bring canned pork and breakfast cereal to the peninsula – but for complex geopolitical reasons, the Americans came in a big way, as did the Soviet Union. When the Korean War erupted into a horrible civil war, the entire United States Eighth Army came, as did a million Chinese communist soldiers. The war ended in 1953, and then there were two Koreas, and, for a while, the two Koreas rebuilt from the ashes of war at roughly the same pace.

In the southern half, though, under American protection against the northern half, the transportation system and the communication system developed into some of the most advanced in the world. The South Koreans pulled away. They rebuilt with American help, and yet they built an infrastructure that was better than what many Americans might now enjoy. The New York City subways were amazing, but the Seoul subways were more amazing. Seoul was amazing, and anyone from New York might recognize the resemblance between the two cities right away, although the airports in Seoul were objectively better than the ones in New York. Through those airports, starting around 1955, Koreans started flying to America. There are now over 1.2 million persons of Korean ancestry in the United States. That was no accident: it was also no accident that Korean pop bands, Korean universities, Korean shopping malls, and the Korean government all bore striking resemblances to these institutions in the United States. The Americans had a White House, the Koreans had a Blue House. This was not a coincidence. Moreover, this was just one example, just one country – by 2015, the United States had about 1,000 military bases in at least five dozen countries throughout the world. Americans now might wonder why there were so many Mexicans, and Afghanis, and Iraqis, and Vietnamese – all of these people were here, too, and none of this was a coincidence.[8]

Alas, if Americans were sick and tired of strange foreigners showing up in big clumps in America, with their jars of kimchee and bowls of pho and kebab skewers, they should have avoided sending so many Americans to go to those foreign places first. But, for a variety of obvious reasons – study abroad, business opportunities, resistance to communism, regime change, leisure travel, the war on terror, and missionary work, to name just a few – it seemed unlikely that the Americans would ever stop leaving for distant places in coordinated, organized ways. They will take with them their newest electronic devices, these little miracles that help them stay connected with friends and loved ones while they're studying, or working on regime change. But then this will be how even more people will learn about the United States, thus cultivating again a demand for America itself.

Empathy and Exclusion

In the most optimistic versions of the two revolutions, all of us might become more aware of each other, seeing others and then being in places that we might never have imagined. Or, rather, we might find ourselves in places we *can* imagine because of the technological advances that allow us to see, and then the transportation networks that can take us anywhere. The two revolutions might work in curious ways, so that we can all see how our actions here in one place can have a profound impact on places we might never see in person. I drive a car, for example, and I know it spews carbon and other forms of pollution, and I'm also well aware that this isn't good for the planet, for entire ecologies sensitive to climate change, including, well, every part of the world. My own contribution might be tiny – insignificant really – but millions of people driving, just like me, can create massive ecological problems. I am much more prone, in light of that knowledge, to support collective efforts to shrink everyone's carbon footprint, especially the ones of hyper-privileged people like me, because our behavior can threaten the lives of penguins and polar bears that we may never see in their natural habitats. If we continued to do nothing, no one would ever see them at all.

Again, in the most optimistic future, the two revolutions might yield a better world, a place far more inter-connected than before, and where all of us can develop empathy for people and places unlike the ones with which we're most familiar. When a tyrant exploits his people, we can see and we can empathize with those who protest, and we ourselves might demand that our own government pay attention, perhaps to cut off aid or assist the rebels. When natural disasters destroy a region or cripple a country, we can see and send aid, too; we can deploy resources within a day to rescue the people in danger or help the survivors. In many instances, we see and experience these kinds of responses already, albeit in haphazard ways that are difficult to predict. (Sometimes we help a lot; sometimes we don't.) Those instances where we do help give us clues as to how greater cooperation might be possible across international boundaries, so that people can share their miseries and tend to one another through suffering, no matter how far apart they might be. When we see, say, an American soldier pulling a child from the rubble of an earthquake, those of us who are American citizens might feel pride for the life-saving work of that serviceman, half a world away.

However, in many places, in many countries, even as the two revolutions continue to unfold, governments have been busy building walls, fences, barriers, and obstacles, and offers of help are not always forthcoming, even for the people struggling *within* these places and countries. Fence-building has become especially popular: Israel, the United States, Saudi Arabia, and Thailand have had some of the more ambitious projects in recent years, but walls have become a routine part of many landscapes. In southern California, the walls and fences extend into the sea, and public officials use drones and cameras to see the most remote portions of the border. Vigilante groups have webcams and spycams at various spots, too, and when they see something, they call, quick, for Border Patrol agents to apprehend the unlawful migrants. The communications revolution allows for a surveillance that is mind-boggling in its intricacies – the vigilantes don't even have to confront the very people they attempt to block. Nationalism – of the kind that justifies all of the fencing and obstacles and drones – has experienced a resurgence in this global age, and even though the most prominent self-described nationalists in the United States insist that they're not *White* nationalists, their resemblance to older versions of racist, xenophobic nationalists can be unnerving.

Moreover, some forms of communication and transportation might seem innocent enough, and yet they may enhance self-absorption and selfishness, rather than a broader empathy. Many scholars have noticed that, even though various forms of social media may help people see across vast distances, most people use these to see people like themselves. The technology narrows the social field in which people exist, and many people can spend hours keeping up with "friends" whose lives are familiar rather than different. In politics as well, people might live in "echo chambers" – places on-line that enhance one's point of view but rarely ever offer any other. Our leading technology companies seem to know our preferences in creepy ways – they show what we prefer to see, they block what we've found objectionable. If a person finds undocumented children or Syrian refugees upsetting, she can click away from them, or she can click toward other people on-line who share her revulsion for them, for their pitiful condition. Exclusionists can better coordinate their paranoia to keep such persons out of *their* country. Although it might not be too difficult to find points of view that were the opposite of her own, it might be easier to confirm prejudices and to find places that strengthen convictions, however misguided they might be. And then there's "fake news" that confirms the worst – this has become very easy to find indeed, in a world that produces more information than any one person can possibly digest.[9]

Similarly, when privileged people travel, they might be able to see the misery of poorer people in exotic places, but they also might just as easily avoid paying attention. Routes from the international airport to a modern hotel can sometimes bypass the worst portions of a city. When wealthy, well-connected people visit other wealthy, well-connected people, professional and social courtesies might suggest that they avoid talking about the homeless people that they've just seen on the way from the airport or on the way to work. Many privileged Americans take vacations in Mexico or in Central America or in Central and Southeast Asia, and, quite deliberately, they can rest in resorts cocooned from the poverty endemic to many of these places. In Nepal, the local men can make a living by risking their lives to take climbers up on huge mountains that might kill all of them. We wonder about a building resentment between the guests and hosts. From the perspective of the people traveling to the most exotic locations, the world was full of adventure, fantastic, and open for exploration; but from the perspective of a tired, underpaid sherpa, it might take some restraint to avoid shoving the spoiled, insufferable foreigners.

Will the two revolutions make us all more interconnected, empathetic, and cooperative, or will they turn us into narrower beings, caring only about ourselves and people most like us, behind fences and barriers and obstacles that will become ever more fearsome and sophisticated? It's difficult to say. Nowadays, the people who've robbed from our checking accounts or interfered in our national elections did these things from abroad, with computers connected on-line. Words and phrases like "ransomware" and "keyloggers," and "misinformation campaign," suggested that using a gun to rob a bank, or stuffing a ballot box in a foreign country, were outmoded ways of committing crimes or interfering in another country's politics. Criminals and criminal governments had used high-speed ethernet connections, and so they didn't have to "invade" another country to engage in regime change, or break into a safe. In such a world, we may all want more control, enforcement, punishment, and prevention.[10] In this volume, where we examine the physical movement of people through immigration, we might also note in advance that the two revolutions have made the world smaller and more accessible to the highly skilled, the wealthy, and the privileged, while also inspiring new forms of repression and control over people who are poorer, abject, and less privileged. American immigration law and society have been full of such contradictions, and so we examine the immediate past so that it might tell us where we are going, and because it might give us clues to our further problems.

2

THE KINETIC NATION

The Migrating Nation

The two revolutions began well before the United States or the Immigration Act of 1965, and so this chapter connects past and present, if primarily to underscore just how unusual the Immigration Act of 1965 truly was, and to situate its consequences in light of a longer history. In the overview of the other America before 1965, I will propose that Americans have *always* passed rules encouraging the arrival of some people while discouraging the arrival of others, and they've also supported widespread policies of removal against people whom they'd considered unfit for full citizenship. We have ample evidence of how Americans thus attempted to manage the two revolutions long before the twentieth century. Moreover, immigration federalism is not new: local jurisdictions encouraged and removed certain kinds of people; state governments did the same, too; and the national government also had policies governing migration and belonging, some written into the Constitution of the United States. Indeed, many Americans developed their own distinctive conceptions of citizens and citizenship as they were considering with one another, in the public sphere, whom to encourage, whom to discourage, whom to remove. They communicated these decisions widely, so that people in Europe and in Asia learned whether or not they would be welcomed in the United States.

This chapter also explains how, in the modern era, the United States has been the most kinetic of nations, its citizens almost constantly on the move. American expansion was breathtaking: in the vulnerable, diseased, and weak outposts in Massachusetts and in Virginia, many Europeans did not survive the New World. In time, however, the immigrants from Europe dominated the landscape, and as they displaced the indigenous inhabitants, they also imported slaves from Africa, thus changing forever the very complexion of the New World itself. We should note that the Europeans were quite diverse: they were from every part of the United Kingdom, but then also from France and Spain, and Central, Southern, and Eastern Europe. A great many of these people were fleeing political and economic chaos, ranging from colonial policies in Ireland to the Napoleonic Wars of the early nineteenth century. Civil wars and wars to build nations brought many thousands to the United States throughout the late 1800s.[1]

Yet what did these Europeans have in common? They did not speak a common language, they practiced varieties of Christianity that were hostile to one another, and they varied widely in their traditions and customs. But Europeans became "White" in the United States, through politics, and then in public law. They rather invented – or socially constructed, as the sociologists might say – their common identity as "White people," because such an identity was nonsensical to the various Europeans from all over that continent who could not speak or practice anything in common. Through interactions with Native Americans and African slaves, Europeans of all varieties came to conclude that they were "White," and that definition grew so potent in law and politics that subsequent immigrants tended to measure themselves and their distance to whiteness. Many claimed whiteness by denying the status to others – the Italians and the Irish, "suspect Whites" on the East Coast – were some of the most ardent advocates for Chinese exclusion on the West Coast, and they claimed, with a straight face, that they were the defenders of Western civilization. Some of the most virulent segregationists of the twentieth century in the South had ancestors who were not quite White when they first came to the United States. It wasn't until 1965 that they rejected White supremacy in the immigration law – and yet everything before tended to support White racial identity as a prerequisite for full American citizenship.[2]

There was this time when the White people were the immigrants, and rather vulnerable, too. A century before the Revolution, the colonists of Massachusetts were mired in a mortal struggle with several Native American tribes, whose leaders called for the annihilation of English settlers, especially the ones encroaching further into their frontier. For native people, the colonists literally brought waves of death: European people, especially their children, harbored dangerous diseases to which the natives had no immunity, and so the death rate among native peoples was often staggering in the first decades of European colonization. Metacom, known to the colonists as King Philip, had called for his followers to kill as many European settlers as possible, and he compared these newcomers to a pestilence that would destroy all of his people.

For a moment, consider how traumatic the arrival of European settlers must have been to people like Metacom: the Europeans arrived on large, strange ships; they smelled, dressed, and sounded far more different than anyone had seen; and these pale people went from not knowing how to do anything to dominating everything, all in the space of one lifetime. The Europeans brought with them weapons and other instruments – especially objects made of metal – that must have appeared magical, otherworldly. Without meaning to, the Europeans also brought death: having lived among livestock for centuries, the Europeans had had exposure to horrible and contagious diseases with which Native Americans had had no experience. Entire villages died. The elders among the Native Americans saw waves of death unlike anything they had encountered.[3]

By 1676, the year of King Philip's War, the colonists were no longer struggling just to survive. Boston counted roughly 5,000 Europeans, with several hundred more in the outlying townships, and still more coming from England because of tensions between King and Parliament. The men who dominated politics in Massachusetts saw their colony grow and stabilize, even as the natives wasted away: not men of science, they imagined God "clearing the wilderness" of the natives, so that their civilization might prosper. Relations between the colonists and the natives took a more condescending tone. Once war erupted, the colonists waged a bloody campaign against all Native Americans, and they sometimes abandoned distinctions between the natives who were hostile and the ones who were not.[4]

Several hundred Native Americans had lived in "Praying Towns" founded by men like John Eliot, a preacher from England whose mission in life was to convert the natives to Christianity. Even though the war had been precipitated by the murder of a Christianized Native American, and even though converted natives had helped the colonists militarily against hostile tribes, the English colonists complained that all Native Americans were threats to Massachusetts Bay Colony. Colonial leaders had several hundred Native Americans on Deer Island imprisoned, and then they sold some of the prisoners into slavery in the West Indies when the war ended.

The war itself yielded new land for the colonists now that the Native Americans were defeated and "cleared," either as refugees fleeing west of their ancestral lands, or as slaves in the British colonies. Poorer colonists and White settlers in New England soon moved into those lands, supported by the clergymen who ran the Massachusetts Bay Colony, and many elites and new landowners saw these as fortuitous developments, as a spreading of the colonists' original "errand in the wilderness." Many people in Europe heard of these events, and many immigrants also saw the unfolding catastrophe in New England as an opportunity for them. They too could now acquire land in this wilderness.[5]

In time, they came to New England in larger numbers; they were encouraged to come. European newcomers and settlers alike – divided as they were, by region, class, religion, dialect, and language – well understood, through this experience of war, flight, and emigration, that they were somehow "White": that they also shared a common outlook despite their differences. The land should be divided and sold according to a legal regime from Europe; men of European descent, "good Christians," should be the landlords; and Native American tribes and political formations should never again dominate or threaten the regions in and around Boston. It was still possible in some cases for Native Americans who'd converted to Christianity to live among and assimilate into Christian settlements, but both the Europeans and the Native Americans wondered whether such persons were really "Native American" anymore. They were also "passing into whiteness."[6]

In the southern colonies, where the economies revolved around cash crops for export, especially tobacco, a dizzying array of Europeans tried to make a life in and around the Chesapeake. In the early seventeenth century, concerned that Native Americans could attack and massacre the small, starving bands of White colonists in the Chesapeake region, British policies from King and Parliament discouraged White "encroachment" on Native American lands. Yet, as tobacco production proved so alluring and profitable, perhaps irresistible, Catholics from Maryland and Protestants from Virginia attempted to gain as much land as possible, irrespective of whether Native Americans might also hunt or farm along those parcels now fenced and claimed by Whites. To grow tobacco, some European settlers brought with them White indentured servants and Black slaves. Some farms prospered. Members of the Pamunkey nation saw this success as a direct threat to their way of life, and also a violation of established agreements with the colonial governors not to send Europeans so far west of Jamestown.[7]

Perhaps armed conflicts were inevitable, and yet the outcome in Virginia and in Maryland clearly enlarged possibilities and opportunities for European migrants. For a time, White indentured servants and Black slaves had similar, equally atrocious conditions: in 1675, they rebelled together against the landed elite, for whippings and indefinite periods of labor, and then also over lands to the west, to the point of sending the Governor of Virginia into the sea in retreat. Bacon's Rebellion, led by Nathaniel Bacon, an immigrant from Suffolk and now a resident of Virginia, was one of the most significant uprisings in the late seventeenth century, as it marked a turning point for poorer White migrants, wealthier plantation owners, Native American tribes in the Chesapeake, and then African slaves. The Rebellion began as an armed struggle among poorer Whites, African slaves, and wealthier Whites over land and political corruption, but it resulted in a new regime in which all White persons would be elevated to full membership in Virginia, even as Native American lands would be taken to make this possible, and as the African slaves were reduced to perpetual chattel slavery. Contracts would govern relations between poorer and wealthier White men, but property rules would govern "White over Black."[8]

In the seventeenth century, in England, Catholics who'd not embraced the Church of England were forbidden from public employment, and could not own, purchase, or lease lands; nor were they free from searches and seizures of property at the hands of the King's officers. Maryland's very existence and growth was due, in part, to the persecution of Catholics in England, and yet, here in North America, Catholics were among the most prominent and powerful landlords, full citizens capable of owning extensive lands and slaves. Their Protestant neighbors relied on them when the Indians "encroached" on their plantations and farms, or when the African slaves attempted to revolt against their masters. Common racial fears again brought very different White people together: in 1640, the colonies had in place rules against slaves carrying firearms, and rules against Whites selling firearms to Native Americans. By contrast, 100 years later, by 1740, the colony had levied taxes to purchase firearms for any free White man serving in the militia, to make sure all able-bodied White men were well armed.[9]

In the Carolinas, in the early eighteenth century, the defeat and removal of Native Americans, the arrival of White settlers from England, from the West Indies, and from other North American colonies, and then the importation of African and West Indian slaves – these all continued the recurring pattern of settlement, exclusion, and removal. Tobacco was an important cash crop in northern Carolina, but in what became South Carolina, farmers grew rice for export as well, and they depended upon African slaves who sometimes outnumbered the Whites who owned them. Many of these White settlers were from other British colonies: unable to purchase larger sugar plantations in the West Indies, they brought themselves and their slaves to the lower Carolinas. Some flourished, and they purchased more slaves and land in an environment where European diseases had already killed roughly half of all the Native Americans. Contemporary anthropologists have described many of the tribes in the Carolinas as "extinct," having no surviving members, with no formal organization. They estimated that the mass wave of illness and death struck the Carolina tribes in the early part of the seventeenth century: weakened by disease, pushed further west by White settlement, the Native Americans were then replaced by an uneasy population of Africans and Europeans.[10]

White landlords had all the land and capital, but African slaves clearly outnumbered their masters in the Carolinas. White people were free, many owned land, and still others owned slaves – sometimes many dozens of slaves; the slaves themselves owned nothing, could not marry or legally form families, and were under the complete authority of these masters. Such circumstances were never stable, nor without violence. In 1739, a literate slave led about 60 other slaves in a rebellion that lasted over a month, resulting in the deaths of roughly 50 White people and many more African slaves. South Carolina's legislature authorized the creation of a standing militia to put down further rebellions, and other new rules in 1740 hardened the lines between White people and their African slaves. Under an "Act for the better ordering and governing of Negroes and other Slaves," slaves in the Carolinas were not allowed to assemble outside the presence of White people, even for religious meetings; they could not have weapons, especially guns; and the colony's government could "destroy" or sell incorrigible slaves.[11]

Many of the rules governed the behavior of White owners: they could no longer teach their slaves to read; they had to give written permission to their slaves if they wanted them to travel beyond their plantations; and if they emancipated their slaves, these freed people had to leave the colony. The authors of the Act criticized leaders in Spanish Florida for promising freedom to Black slaves fleeing from the Carolinas – they then offered bounties for escaped slaves who'd been found there, even detailing specific amounts for the recovery of their "scalps," with separate amounts for just "scalps," and then "for every scalp … with the two ears." The Seminole tribes of Florida also offered to help escaped African slaves, a practice that Whites in the Carolinas and then in Georgia found offensive to their interests. They complained that the Indian tribes had no respect for their private property.[12]

During this same period, however, the colony of South Carolina, like many colonies before the Revolution, attempted to stimulate the migration of people from Europe, even from places like Germany and Ireland. Lutherans from Salzburg, Austria, came to South Carolina, then migrated to territories that would become a new colony, Georgia – as would a substantial contingent of

Irish migrants after 1750. The colony approved rules and new taxes to set aside land and financial support for these immigrants, even though the steady importation of slaves and the natural increase of Africans born in the Carolinas would keep the colony's majority African well after the Revolutionary War. North of the Carolinas, in New York and in Massachusetts, as slave revolts endangered White people as well, many more American colonists supported policies to limit the importation of African slaves, while also attempting to enlarge their own population of White people. Distressed that slave revolts could inflame places like Boston and New York, anxious newer European immigrants moved farther west, and those who remained favored abolition to make sure that wealthier White citizens would not bring even more slaves to the North.[13]

"Free White Persons ..."

On the eve of the Revolution, the American colonies bonded not just over a common loathing for and aversion to British rule, but also over similar interests in lands to the west, as their populations settled and then prospered. During the French and Indian War, from 1754 to 1763, the British army and the American colonists fought side by side against France and its own colonists in New France. Both sides relied on sizable numbers of Native American fighters: the British and the Americans allied with the Cherokee and the Iroquois; the French fought with the Lenape, the Shawnee, and the Ottawa. Each sought to keep the other from the Ohio River Valley. The war proved a bloody, horrifying, and drawn-out struggle, and when the British and the Americans prevailed, they disagreed almost immediately about who should pay for the tremendous costs of the war.[14]

Over the next decade, the British Parliament imposed new taxes on the American colonies to help with the national debt, a policy that many people in London supported. After all, the British had financed much of the war in North America for the benefit of the British colonists there. Shouldn't they help to pay for it? Of course, the American colonists saw things very differently, and they complained throughout the whole decade that these novel and horrible British taxes – most approved without their consent – were reducing them to "slavery."[15]

Even as the Americans and the British were failing to work out their differences without further warfare, American colonists on the frontiers were taking advantage of the victory over the French to push further west. American colonists settled on lands that had belonged to the Lenape, the Shawnee, and the Ottawa, as well as the Potawatomi and the Chippewa. They were moving into the Ohio River Valley in significant numbers before the Revolution, and many native peoples themselves moved west to leave behind their ancestral lands. Their alliance with the French proved devastating, as the Americans came with all the brashness of conquerors entitled to the spoils of war. In the north, British and American forces deported about 80 percent of the French population of Acadia, a province of New France, sending away over 10,000 French settlers to Louisiana, France, and Haiti. Large portions of these territories came under the control of Massachusetts. In the South, settlers from North Carolina and Virginia moved so far west that many of them had no real contact with a functioning government – after the war, these territories would become Tennessee and West Virginia. Without question, English-speaking settlers solidified their dominance across several vast regions after the French and Indian Wars, much to the despair of the settlers of New France and their Native American allies. English-speaking settlers were even far outpacing the reach of their own colonial governments in their search for land.[16]

The Revolution itself was a kinetic affair, as British and American forces turned on one another with such hostility and suddenness, their animosity lasting well after the war had concluded. In the last war, the British and the French had relied on Native Americans; in this one, the British attempted to unleash African American slaves against their White American masters, and White people of all backgrounds found *that* policy one of the most offensive of all, designed specifically to destroy them where they lived. The list of offended Americans included George Washington, Thomas Jefferson, James Madison, Patrick Henry, and George Mason. They all complained of "losing" slaves after Dunmore's Proclamation in 1775, issued as it was by the fourth Earl of Dunmore, John Murray, the last Royal Governor of the Colony of Virginia. African Americans reacted immediately: over 1,000 ran from their masters to the British side within a month of the Proclamation, and many more thousands would run away during the chaos of war. Dunmore formed an Ethiopian Regiment, promising all Black Loyalists that they would be free men, no matter what the outcome of the war, and this was how Harry Washington, George's former slave, came to serve in an artillery unit on the British side. But, as the war dragged on, General Washington would also offer freedom to any Black slave who had fought for at least two years in the Continental Army, and he would also "deprive" White Loyalists of their slaves to reduce their strength, too, inspired in this policy by the Earl of Dunmore.[17]

By 40 years after the Revolution, the new nation was, literally, a different place. A year after the ratification of the United States Constitution, the first Congress, through the Naturalization Act of 1790, said that all "free white persons" would be eligible for naturalization, leaving to the states to determine who was "white." White settlers, including hundreds of thousands of new immigrants from Europe, now had strong legal incentives to claim a "White" racial identity. They encroached much more aggressively on Native American lands, unchecked by British or French or Spanish empires, and in spite of yet another bloody and disruptive war with the British in 1812, the Americans grew in population at a staggering pace. By 1830, the United States doubled the size of its territory, and its population increased from 4 million persons in 1790 to nearly 13 million persons. Because of technological innovations, Southern planters could exploit vast areas of land for cotton production. They favored "removing" Native Americans, they established a distinctive plantation economy in the lower Mississippi River, and they purchased thousands of African slaves from the Chesapeake Bay and removed them to the lower South, all with breathtaking speed.[18]

Prominent national politicians emerged from the frontier territories in support of these policies, including Andrew Jackson of Tennessee, whose advocacy of slavery, for Native American removal, and then for the "common [White] man" made him a folk hero long before he was President of the United States. In the Midwest, White settlers displaced all of the major tribes of the Great Lakes region, forcing the tribes from western New York to northern Minnesota to move farther and farther west, and thus precipitating lethal warfare *among* Native Americans in the first half of the nineteenth century. New state governments in the Midwest envisioned societies dominated by "White" people and free of all "people of color." In the Dakota territory, tribes and peoples that had been relatively untouched by Western influence saw their societies collapse, and not just under the push of Americans and immigrants from the United States, but also from well-armed Native American tribes from Minnesota and Wisconsin. The Sioux tribes had been migrating west in the face of White encroachment since at least 1700, taking advantage of the horses that the Europeans had brought to North America. As more White settlers pushed into their lands from the east, more and more Sioux people moved west. The entire Ohio River Valley and the regions around the Great Lakes were "cleared" of any significant Native American presence by 1840.[19]

Not wanting to share political space or citizenship with any people of color, state governments moved to discourage their migration, as New Jersey had done as early as 1786. Ohio's state government banned the settlement of any African Americans – slave or free – in 1802; Illinois passed similar rules in 1819; Michigan in 1827; Indiana in 1831; and Iowa in 1839. Oregon prohibited the migration of free Black persons in 1849; in California, the state legislature approved a rule in 1852 through which public officials could presume all Black migrants to be fugitive slaves, unless they could prove otherwise. Those who didn't have proper "papers" could then be held and sold "back" into slavery.[20]

"Aliens Ineligible for Citizenship ..."

We should recall that, in a nation that was expanding so rapidly, especially in the Far West, many American citizens were themselves the unlawful migrants, at least from another point of view. For Native Americans in the Southeast, when European Americans encroached upon lands that had been clearly marked by federal treaties as belonging to the Cherokee or to the Creek, the White Americans were the ones migrating and settling unlawfully. Although the United States had promised independence to many tribes, and thus the framers had referred to them as "Indians not taxed" under the federal Constitution, Native Americans found hundreds and then thousands of American citizens squatting and building permanent settlements on tribal lands. Yet under the Indian Removal Act of 1830, President Jackson legalized the settlement of White American citizens by removing the *Native Americans*. European Americans rationalized these kinds of policies as though God Himself had ordained them, as if their encroachment was a "manifest destiny," a triumph of (their) civilization against (Native American) "savagery."[21]

During this era, Christians settled on lands claimed by other Christians. In Texas and in California, the Spanish and Mexican governments had attempted to stop the encroachment of all outsiders. In the late eighteenth century, the Spanish government had forbidden American or Russian or British ships from landing in California; and in the first half of the nineteenth century, the Mexican government had prohibited the settlement of American citizens in Texas. Mexico had gained its independence in 1821, and its government had originally encouraged the migration of Americans. But then the Mexican government judged that there were too many such immigrants. In 1829, the Mexican government had abolished slavery, but the Mexican Foreign Minister observed that the Americans were also bringing their slaves to Texas and that they seemed in no hurry to emancipate anyone. By April 1830, President Anastasio Bustamante signed a set of rules that promoted the migration of Mexican citizens to Texas, while also prohibiting Americans from "colonizing" that portion of Mexico. Americans in Texas were incensed, but Mexican citizens and officials alike may have been puzzled as to why so many of these American slave-owners behaved as though they were morally superior to the Mexicans, or they had the better claim to Texas.[22]

Once these lands had been seized, in the wake of war, the new American citizens of the frontier united against Asian migrants. California's government pioneered restrictions against Chinese migrants during the Gold Rush, as governors, judges, and legislators alleged that Asians were "unassimilable," and that they would thus pose a perpetual, existential threat to the economic and political cohesion of the state if they were admitted to American citizenship. If California was to be a "white man's republic," "the Chinese Must Go." Hugh Murray was the second Chief Justice of the California Supreme Court, only 27 when he took that office – he embodied the fantastic opportunities available to educated White men on the frontier. As Chief Justice, though, he upheld the California Fugitive Slave Act in 1852 and also struck down the murder conviction of a White man, George Hall, in 1854, because some of the damning testimony came from Chinese witnesses. In this way, early public officials like Murray were not at all timid about imposing various forms of White supremacy upon yet another group of immigrants whom they considered non-White.[23]

The rules removing Native Americans, the rules legalizing White statehood and nation, the rules against the settlement of free Black persons, and the rules against Chinese migrants – these all reflected not just White supremacy, but another truth. People were on the move. African Americans were moving north *and* west, and Chinese migrants could come to California in significant numbers across the Pacific Ocean, sometimes getting to California faster than European Americans sailing from Boston or New York. Despite fugitive slave rules in the United States Constitution and in Congress that dated to the late eighteenth century, African slaves ran away, and so often that they kept inspiring more fugitive slave rules, including the infamous Fugitive Slave Act of 1850. By 1850, many African Americans in the North and in the Midwest were fugitive slaves and the sons and daughters of fugitive slaves, and as abolitionists spoke with greater vehemence about the horrors of slavery, African Americans and Whites alike were willing to evade federal and state rules to help people escape from slavery. This, in turn, provoked harsher fugitive slave rules. Thus, we see how the very existence and reinforcement of some rules suggest also their constant and recurring breach.[24] Similarly, the Chinese Exclusion Act of 1882 slowed, but did not stop, the migration of Chinese people across the Pacific, and so again, despite federal rules to prohibit the immigration of Chinese people, these made up the most obvious group of illegal immigrants on the West Coast at the turn of the twentieth century.[25]

The recurring truism – still taught in grammar schools – is that Abraham Lincoln freed the slaves, once through the Emancipation Proclamation and then again, with the Congress and the states, through the Thirteenth Amendment. But a more accurate description of events in this period might be that the slaves freed themselves, mostly by running away. That is, the fugitives themselves precipitated a deepening crisis between the free and slave states that led to the Civil War. Most slaves did not run away, but people like Anthony Burns, James Pennington, Frederick Douglass, Margaret Garner, and Dred Scott drew so much attention, and they so divided so many people, that they embarrassed the federal government and made relations between North and South hostile, and then irreconcilable. Many slaves became illegal migrants. White people helped them escape, and then often promoted their careers: William Lloyd Garrison, Levi Coffin, and Harriet Beecher Stowe were among the most prominent opponents of slavery. When the Civil War was over, the Great Emancipator himself said that men and women like Douglass and Stowe deserved more credit than he did for the abolition of slavery.[26]

The dynamic forces surrounding the war stimulated internal and foreign migrations well after it. The North would eventually end its military occupation of the South, and the North would leave to the South the fate of the newly freed slaves. As the Klan rose, as White supremacists took control of the Democratic Party in the Southern states, as they imposed segregation and unleashed violence against anyone who resisted, African Americans migrated north. At first, this migration was slow – the federal government investigated reports of African Americans moving to Kansas or into the lower Midwest in the 1870s and 1880s. Then, three decades after the Civil War, the trickles thickened, more people beyond government noticed, and, by 1910, tens of thousands of former slaves and their descendants were on the move. By 1920, African Americans lived in every major city in the East, Midwest, and the Far West, well beyond the Southeastern quarter of the United States, where over 90 percent of all African Americans had lived before the Civil War. White majorities approved ubiquitous forms of race-based segregation in response to the migration of African Americans – they used Jim Crow rules to separate and to disable African American residents politically and economically in the East, the Midwest, and the Far West, and, in many instances, they voted for segregation long *before* African Americans arrived, precisely to discourage their arrival.[27]

At the same time, European Americans, including immigrants from Ireland, Germany, Scandinavia, and Eastern and Southern Europe, also came to the United States in ever greater numbers from 1880 to 1930 – over 20 million during that period, so that the national population rose past 100 million persons by 1920. Many of these immigrants were fleeing from civil and religious strife in their home countries: in the late nineteenth century, "Germany" didn't exist as it does now: German-speaking people lived under several different states, often at war with one another, and large-scale efforts to "unify" Germany led to the migration of Catholics, political dissenters, and other displaced persons. We would consider many of these immigrants "refugees" under our own conventional definitions. And yet several state and local governments questioned the desirability of these immigrants, and they moved to exclude them. Public officials and cartoonists said that the Germans were way too fond of beer, that the Irish drank too much hard liquor, especially whiskey, and thus they were prone to fighting. Some Americans complained that the Italians gave their kids wine, and that they also turned on one another through organized crime. Oktoberfest, the Fighting Irish, the mafia – these stereotypes foregrounded notions that some Europeans were just not fit for American citizenship.[28]

In the eyes of many progressive reformers in the first half of the twentieth century, there were too many immigrants coming too quickly, and too many of them were drinking too much alcohol, to the point of eroding family life and making upright American citizenship impossible. The drinking – at all hours of the day – made regular work hours in the factories and farms unlikely or difficult, and so it generally rendered "those people" unfit for republican forms of self-government. Besides, none of these people spoke English, and they lived in strange ethnic communities within the major cities where they didn't need to speak English at all. They could go all day speaking Italian or Polish or German. Thus, during this period, states like Wisconsin and Nebraska objected to teachers in the public schools speaking and teaching in languages other than English, and they and other states passed rules declaring English their official language.[29]

The sum of these laws insisted that every child – especially the children of immigrants – should have their ethnicity melted away, as in a big pot or a smelter, so that they should become "American," and be molded into American citizenship. Federal and state officials promoted a flag salute at the beginning of every school day, within public schools where attendance was compulsory. Every child, no matter what their background (or maybe because of their background), had "to pledge allegiance to the flag of the United States of America, and to the republic for which it stands, one nation indivisible, with liberty and justice for all." This pledge made and reinforced an American identity, during a time when children from all over Europe were in their most impressionable years.[30]

From 1882 to 1934, the United States Congress moved toward exclusion, bookended by exclusions against Asian immigrants. The Chinese Exclusion Act of 1882 was in its title just so blunt – Chinese immigrants were not to come to the United States, or settle there, a principle repeated in subsequent rules in 1888 and 1892. When other Asian immigrants came, Congress replied with more restrictions, including the Gentleman's Agreement in 1907, against migrants from the Japanese Empire, and the Immigration Act of 1917. The Act of 1917 created an Asiatic Barred Zone, so sometimes it's called the Asiatic Barred Zone Act, this informal title again suggesting the widespread popularity of restricting all immigrants from Asia. Legislators in the United States were very open about their hostility toward Asians. In 1920, for example, James Phelan, the former Mayor of San Francisco, ran for re-election to the US Senate using a blunt campaign slogan, "Keep California White" – which for Phelan meant supporting immigration restrictions against Asians – and rules against "aliens ineligible for citizenship" (Asian immigrants) owning or leasing land in California. Phelan lost that year to Samuel Shortridge, a Republican, but this might have been because Shortridge was the more zealous exclusionist: "we of California are unalterably opposed to the further immigration of Japanese," he said to the *Sacramento Union* in 1921, and that "the two races will never live in peace and harmony on the same soil."[31]

Like many Democrats and Republicans, Senator Shortridge supported both of the Immigration Acts, in 1921 and 1924, as they created and then extended a national origins system. Thereafter, the admission of all new immigrants would be limited to the existing racial composition of the United States. The rules attempted to turn things backward: in 1921, Congress said that only 3 percent of foreign-born persons of each nationality should be admitted every year as immigrants, the figure tied to the Census in 1910. But in the Immigration Act of 1924, Congress dropped that to 2 percent, the target tied to the Census in 1890, when the United States had had far fewer Eastern and Southern Europeans (and Asians). Asians were special under the 1924 version: Congress barred completely these "aliens ineligible for citizenship." Even with regard to the Philippines, a most important American territory by 1902 – where American presidents had once promised to help these "little brown brothers" find their inner American – the United States Congress said that the nation ought to be independent, and that Filipinos should stop coming to the United States. Under the terms of the Tydings–McDuffie Act of 1934, Filipinos were also now "aliens ineligible for citizenship."[32]

In the wake of World War I, the United States had turned inward, and for three decades after, very few new immigrants from anywhere would be allowed to come. In 1910, about 1 million persons would arrive as permanent residents, but by 1938 that figure fell to about 80,000, and then to 24,000 on the eve of World War II. During a time of increasing political chaos in Europe and in Asia, the United States opposed immigration from anywhere, even for people fleeing under the most horrible circumstances. One instance underscored the enormous tragedy that would engulf the world: in 1939, the *St. Louis* carried passengers from Hamburg, Germany, to Cuba, where most of them had expected to petition for asylum in the United States. Almost all of them were Jewish, mostly from Germany, but also from countries in Eastern Europe. The Cuban government refused to admit nearly all of the passengers when the ship arrived in Havana, and when the ship departed and was within sight of Miami, the United States government simply refused permission for the ship to dock anywhere in the United States. The *St. Louis* went back to Europe, where, over the next six years, over a quarter of its original passengers would perish during the Nazi invasions of Western Europe. The experience of these and similar people would haunt American political leaders well after World War II.[33]

The United States in the World

A world at war drew in the United States at first, but then the United States became a global power, recovering from the Great Depression *through* the war to become not just a significant military presence throughout the world in the decades after, but also the most powerful country economically, ever. During the war itself, the United States sent hundreds of thousands of American citizens to Europe and to Asia – by 1945, American forces maintained a near-permanent military presence on both continents. They are still there. In the postwar period, American troops have continued a significant military presence in Britain, France, Germany, Italy, Japan, and then the Philippines and South Korea. After 1955, over 250,000 American soldiers were in Germany alone in any given year, for the next 30 years, and over 100,000 American troops were in Japan through 1960. At the height of the Korean War in 1952, over 300,000 American soldiers were fighting on that peninsula. Decades after the armistice there, tens of thousands of American troops lived in and guarded South Korea. During the Vietnam War, in the late 1960s, over half a million American soldiers were in Vietnam, and at least as many Americans were in support positions in the Philippines and in other countries in and around Southeast Asia. Indeed, since 1945, the United States has had an unusual and extensive military presence around the world, with no obvious end in sight.[34]

As we shall see in the next chapter, the presence of the United States explains why so many immigrants came from countries where the United States was already present. From Asia, immigrants from the Philippines, Taiwan, South Korea, and then Southeast Asia came in very large numbers – in the two decades after World War II, the military and political ties between the United States and these countries resulted in Little Manilas, resurgent Chinatowns, and the Koreatown in Los Angeles and Little Saigon in Orange County, California. The Cold War between the United States and the Soviet Union and communist China vexed every American President after 1945. As they pursued strategies of "containment," both to check the spread of communism and to enlarge the number of American allies, American political leaders deployed more troops in more places than ever before, on a scale unimaginable in the years after World War I. By the 1960s, American forces were not just in Asia, they were in the Americas, too: as Cuba "fell" to Fidel Castro and his communist allies, and as the new Cuban government built missile silos for Soviet nuclear weapons, American presidents were alarmed by the possible spread of Cuban-style revolutions in Central and South America. The civil wars in those regions would push hundreds of thousands of people to migrate to the United States, to the very country that supported governments who were fighting communist insurgencies in bloody, protracted civil wars.[35]

In this postwar period, the Soviet Union and communist China portrayed the United States as a hegemonic bully, pulling poorer countries into brutal forms of capitalism while also denying equality and human rights to many of its own citizens. When Nikita Khrushchev and Fidel Castro agreed to meet in New York in September 1960, they chose to see each other at the Hotel Theresa in Harlem. Many (White) American reporters and politicians mostly avoided Harlem, which was the center of African American life in New York, but both men drew the world's attention to racial segregation in the United States, on purpose. Castro met with Malcolm X, he sympathized with the plight of African Americans, and he promised that communism in Cuba would be the best thing for race relations on that island. His presence, his embrace of Khrushchev – these were clearly meant as a rebuke to the United States, and a not-so-subtle appeal to people of color around the world. Castro and Khrushchev wanted to show them that the United States was really not their friend, that deep down inside, the (White) Americans were racist, segregationist, and uninterested in improving the lives of poorer people even within their own country, let alone around the world. Just look at their history, the communists said. Communism would be much better for poorer people everywhere, and so this was why Castro and Khrushchev agreed to spread it everywhere. The communists said that if capitalists and other wealthier people didn't like communism, they could leave – perhaps go to America, as did many Cuban elites before, during, and after the revolution there in 1959.[36]

Indeed, after 1965, when the migrants from Cuba, South America, and Central America thus came to the United States, their migrations were also the results of civil wars and American military involvement in those regions. By 1980, the United States was supporting, and had been supporting, military regimes and dictatorships on multiple continents. The Americans financed Ferdinand Marcos in the Philippines, Ngo Dinh Diem in Vietnam, and Park Chung-hee in South Korea, but then also Anastasio Somoza Garcia in Nicaragua, Efrain Montt in Guatemala, Carlos Romero in El Salvador, and François Duvalier, and then his son Jean-Claude Duvalier, in Haiti. These political leaders and their allies did not practice regular electoral politics – they assassinated their political opponents, rigged elections, and unleashed death squads against anyone or any group that threatened their control. They were prone to seeing labor unions or appeals for land reform as evidence of communist infiltration. They varied greatly by religion and temperament, but the one thing that they had in common was that they were "anti-communist," they offered themselves as such in negotiations with the Americans, and this more than anything else was the basic reason – perhaps the only reason – why successive American presidents supported their regimes.[37]

It's a counterintuitive thing, to see how American involvement in these wars in such far-flung places then brought so many migrants to the United States. But the next chapter of this book relays primarily the story of American migration in the second half of the twentieth century, when so many people from South Korea, the Philippines, the Americas, and the Caribbean came to the United States. The United States military was engaged in so many places, all at the same time, that, in time, Korean war brides and military brides, Filipino military brides, refugees from Southeast Asia, and displaced persons from Central America, Cuba, and Haiti would make their way here. In a peculiar way, civil wars and endemic strife in their countries was pushing many of them *into* the United States. In academic circles, we tend to treat foreign policy and domestic immigration policy as though the two were unconnected, but in a profound way, on a global scale, they were more related than ever before in the decades after World War II.

Immigration law – so racist and White supremacist for so long – changed in this moment. In response to communist charges that the United States was hopelessly racist and hostile to people of color, successive American presidents, the federal courts, and then Congress moved to make federal law less racist and hostile. Scholars of legal history have framed the American Civil Rights Movement as part of the broader Cold War: the United States could not present itself as a beacon of freedom and liberty for the rest of the world, nor could it answer effectively communist propaganda about how it wasn't racist, when so many of its public law did reflect racist and segregationist practices. Cases like *Brown* v. *Board of Education* (1954) and *Loving* v. *Virginia* (1967) became landmarks because they were so unlike other federal cases that had gone before – for over 100 years, the United States Supreme Court and the highest state courts had *upheld* racial segregation and rules against miscegenation. The Civil Rights Act of 1964 and the Voting Rights Act of 1965 both enlarged federal powers to undo practices common in the states – private employers and businesses *did* discriminate on the basis of race, all the time, and the states had things like all-White primaries and grandfather clauses to deter people of color from voting. All that was being "reformed" in racially progressive ways. Civil rights activists and federal officials embarrassed by race-based restrictions folded the immigration law into this progressive turn. President Johnson embraced and pushed those reforms: from now on, the United States would not be racist, the United States was committed to equal opportunity, and so the United States would welcome everyone. In 1965, Congress and this President changed federal immigration law to make it do what it had never done before – to admit people from every country, irrespective of their race or national origin. The United States would never look the same again.

The Next American Nation

It's common to say the United States is a nation of immigrants, and yet it's more accurate to say the United States primarily welcomed people from Western and Northern Europe, not so much Central and Southern Europe, and definitely not from Asia or Africa. Europeans brought Africans, and then bought and used them, but Europeans certainly did not "welcome" Africans. European immigrants and their descendants created and supported a body of public law that favored them over others: only "free white persons" could become citizens under the Naturalization Act of 1790. Free White persons could own and dispose of property; African slaves *were* property. The Bill of Rights was the enlightened inverse of the darker slave codes: free White persons had the right to speak and assemble; they had the right (and they were given the resources) to bear arms; they had the right to due process of law, to be free of cruel and unusual punishment, as well as the right to just compensation for their property and labor. Slaves, on the other hand, were to be kept illiterate; they were forbidden from assembling outside the presence of White people; they could not have guns; there was no due process of law or freedom from cruel and unusual punishment; and there still has been no compensation for their labor, let alone the loss of their freedom. The American law of slavery, the American Bill of Rights – they were mirrors of one another. And if we date the extent of formal White supremacy from the start of chattel slavery in Virginia in 1619, to the dismantling of Jim Crow segregation in, say, 1965, that's over 340 years.

In the space of that American history, though, we can find so much that is instructive for our present, as Americans. For example, Europeans waged endemic warfare against non-Christians, especially Native Americans, who were then removed, and removed again, and then removed farther. Deportation from the United States was a common theme in immigration scholarship after 1965, but we should note that many people experienced removal and criminalization well before the twentieth century. Even the words – "deportation," and then "removal" – have a history, and as Americans continue to remove other people, they might consider again a strange and perhaps tragic resemblance to their ancestors.

Similarly, we may see now "undocumented immigrants" in our towns and cities, but we might consider how people who were out of place, people who could be removed and taken back, were also a troubling part of the American experience, and for most of American history, too. Many American citizens faced profound moral dilemmas when confronted with fugitive slaves: if, for example, you were a farmer in Pennsylvania, and you saw across your field a family of African Americans, running with knapsacks, might they be fugitive slaves? Would you turn them in? Imagine another dilemma in the early twentieth century – what if you discovered in passing that the Chinese guy living next to you in San Francisco was an illegal immigrant, a "paper son," and thus someone who had created a fictive persona to settle in the city? He had lied to get in. Would you tell the immigration authorities? Would you have him deported? Later in this volume, we will consider again how rules governing fugitive slaves and early Asian immigrants back then looked an awful lot like the rules we have governing illegal immigrants now. They govern the immigrants, but they also tend to govern us as well.[38]

In so many ways, the United States has had an unusual history – it was a special case. No other place had gone from thirteen disassociated colonies to a major global superpower in the space of 150 years. The American Civil War was devastating, but the two world wars were even more devastating and catastrophic, although both spared American infrastructure and industrial production. Asian and European states had crippled each other through 1945. By 1965, the United States was becoming the most prosperous country in the world, perhaps ever. More Americans were serving in the military in more places than ever before; more Americans owned their homes; and more Americans were going to college and sending their children to college. Plenty of Americans still remembered the Great Depression, but perhaps this simply enhanced their appreciation of American prosperity in the 1960s. During and after World War II, the great research universities propelled both the communications and transportation technologies so vital to American success in war and in everything else. By 1965, commercial aviation was well underway, President Eisenhower had organized the construction of an amazing interstate highway system that was as ambitious as the transcontinental railroad, and aircraft carriers fitted with sonar and radar had proven that huge ships could travel vast distances, projecting American power and commerce everywhere. Sonar and radar, radio and television and movies – they are familiar now, but quite revolutionary, still revolutionary. The United States has always been a kinetic nation, always accelerating, and in the second half of the twentieth century, the Americans would further revolutionize those technologies that had propelled them to distant places. People in the United States would thus help to develop the very means through which the world would become more interconnected and more kinetic than ever before.

3

THE IMMIGRATION ACT OF 1965

Cold War Civil Rights

As most students already know, after World War II the United States faced decades of turmoil, challenged by a rising communist threat in Europe and in Asia, and then by more vocal forms of dissent among people of color. The Soviet Union was no longer an ally against fascism – it was, rather, promoting and supporting communist governments and revolutions in Europe and in Asia, and eventually in the Americas, too. In 1949, when the Chinese civil war ended with a Chinese communist government, many Americans were shocked. The shocks continued: less than ten years after, the Soviet Union put Sputnik, the first man-made satellite, into a low Earth orbit. As it passed over the United States several times, seeing who knows what, many Americans wondered and worried over how the communists were literally getting over them. Moreover, the Chinese communists and the Soviet communists were highly critical of the so-called "free world," saying that the Americans were less advanced in other ways: the Americans tolerated way too much material inequality, for example, and there were huge gaps between rich and poor in the United States. The communists said that the Americans were imperialists as well, imposing their ways on weaker countries.[1]

Worst of all, the Americans were racists, the communists said, and American public laws closely resembled the ones once approved by the Nazis. This may strike many Americans as a slur, but several scholars have noted how American Jim Crow rules had served as templates for racist, heinous public laws in Nazi Germany before World War II, and in apartheid South Africa after 1945. Communist heads of state had had a point – the Americans had inspired White supremacists, because they were some of the most thorough White supremacists of all. The communists thus pushed other countries not to follow the American example. If communist leaders often wanted to see places like Harlem, New York, if just to show the rest of the world that many Americans who were poor were also non-White, then American diplomats had related problems whenever they were visiting non-White countries. Be suspicious, very suspicious, said the communists. Just ask the diplomats whether Americans were, in fact, racists. In the Cold War, when the "free world" competed with the "communist world" for everyone in the "Third World," American politicians, especially those engaged in foreign relations, were prone to thinking of Jim Crow segregation as a new kind of liability.[2]

Activists and political leaders saw in these developments a unique opening for reforming American public law toward a less racist direction. The American Civil Rights Movement changed American public law. We now have many scholarly accounts of its many public figures – Martin Luther King, Jr., Rosa Parks, Linda Brown and her family, and Malcolm X, to name just a few. All of this scholarship shows us that, before 1965, racism and egregious forms of racial discrimination were common and widespread in American law, whereas after, they were much less so. Certainly, from 1619 to 1970, American law had aspects that could only be described as White supremacist – these were rules that demanded, even after the Equal Protection Clause of the 14th Amendment, incredible degrees of segregation, a cradle-to-grave segregation, always placing White over Black and other "colored" people.[3]

Many senior scholars have noted that the Immigration Act of 1965 was of this moment in American history, when American public law was, on its face, clearly racist, and then it wasn't, at least not on its face.[4] The change was jarring for people who had been devoted to race-based public law, including the architects of previous immigration rules. Here was Senator Pat McCarran of Nevada, in 1953, explaining why the immigration law should retain discriminations by race and by nationality: "I believe that this nation is the last hope of Western civilization and if this oasis of the world shall be overrun, perverted, contaminated or destroyed, then the last flickering light of humanity will be extinguished." To clarify who might do the perverting and contaminating, the good Senator suggested that it was "untold millions . . . storming our gates": "The solution of the problems of Europe and Asia will not come through a transplanting of those problems en masse to the United States." Pat McCarran was a staunch exclusionist and an unrepentant racist. He died the following year.[5]

Over the next ten years, many leading politicians, including President Harry Truman, pushed Congress to get rid of immigration laws tied to national origin, and to open immigration to the United States to persons from everywhere. Representative Emanuel Celler of New York and Senator Phil Hart of Michigan were the primary co-sponsors of the Immigration Act of 1965, or the Hart–Celler Act, and, together with President Lyndon Johnson, they persuaded their colleagues in the House and Senate that the new immigration rule would not change the dominant migratory flows into the United States. Their proposed law expanded and clarified both employment-based immigration visas for prospective permanent residents, and visas for the relatives of United States citizens and legal permanent residents. The bill listed eight distinct preference categories, the majority of them for family members. In addition, immediate family members of United States citizens were not subjected to any quota or limit, and "special immigrants," including religious workers and foreign health care workers, were exempt from the quotas, too. In the quota system and in the exemptions, the Act retained many of the basic ideas in the Immigration Act of 1952, which also privileged immigrants with skills and with family connections to citizens and residents already in the United States.[6]

But the most striking feature of the new rule was what it didn't do – for the first time in American history, *all* countries could send immigrants to the United States. The Western Hemisphere would have a ceiling of 120,000 preference-based visas; the Eastern Hemisphere would have a limit of 170,000. Countries in the Western Hemisphere would have no per-country limits for preference-based immigrants, but countries in the Eastern Hemisphere would be limited to 20,000 preference-based immigrants per year. President John Kennedy had supported these reforms before he was assassinated on November 22, 1963; his two surviving brothers, the Attorney General, Robert Kennedy, and the Senator from Massachusetts, Edward Kennedy, continued to advocate for the new law. "Our cities will not be flooded with immigrants," Edward Kennedy had said, and "the ethnic mix of this country will not be upset." There were good reasons for this opinion – most Americans with proximate family connections to people abroad were of European descent. In addition, skilled laborers would probably come from colleges and universities, and the best of these were still based in Europe.[7]

The new President, Lyndon Johnson, pushed his former colleagues in the House and Senate to approve the new bill, as it would show to the world that anyone could now come to the United States, and that anyone could become an American citizen. As the United States was involved in yet another war in Asia – in Vietnam – and as it was coming to rely on its close allies in Asia, including Japan, the Philippines, and South Korea, President Johnson insisted that the United States simply couldn't hold on to Asian exclusion in the immigration law while asking Asians to help the Americans. After all, he noted, the communists in China, North Korea, and now North Vietnam had all pointed to American rules against Asians as evidence for America's nefarious motives in Asia. Immigration reform was an opportunity to answer that "propaganda."[8]

But, as with other civil rights bills, Johnson knew that resistance to a race-neutral immigration law came primarily from the South and from the West. And so, especially for Senators and Representatives from those regions, Johnson stressed that the new immigration rule was a clever way to be race-neutral publicly, and to respond to international criticism, while producing much of the same result as before. There would be no tide of non-European immigrants, Johnson reassured his Western and Southern friends. "This bill that we sign today is not a revolutionary bill," he said, when he signed it on Liberty Island in New York, on October 3, 1965; "It does not affect the lives of millions. It will not reshape the structure of our daily lives, or really add importantly to either our wealth or our power."[9]

The predictions proved all wrong. In the first two decades after the Immigration Act of 1965, the majority of new immigrants to the United States would come from either Mexico, Central America, and South America, or from

Asia, especially the Philippines, South Korea, and Taiwan. Prior to 1965, the overwhelming majority of new immigrants came from Europe, in large part due to the race-conscious exclusions rules approved since the Chinese Exclusion Act of 1882. Congress retained the basic preference system within the Immigration Act of 1952, so that persons with family members already in the United States would have an easier pathway into the country, as would persons with college degrees or employable skills. These preferences would seem to favor Europeans, albeit in race-neutral ways. Thus, whether a majority in Congress saw so many non-Europeans coming (which is doubtful), many Americans were taken aback by the sheer scale of non-European immigration, and, as we shall see in subsequent chapters, many did not react in positive ways toward that development. The new law did affect the lives of millions. It did reshape the structure of daily life in the United States, and it did add to American wealth and power. It really was a revolutionary bill.

In hindsight, there were substantial signs that, after 1965, non-Europeans would in fact take advantage of the opportunity to come to the United States. Many Asians, for example, had had substantial contact with Americans over many decades before 1965. In the Philippines, for instance, the United States had had a continuous military presence dating back to the previous century, through President William McKinley's Administration. In Japan, the United States arrived to sign the peace treaty that ended World War II, and they, too, never left. In South Korea, American forces arrived in September 1945, and by 1953, at the end of the Korean War, the American military would build so many bases that it would be difficult to drive in any direction for any significant distance and not run into one. Between the East and the South China Sea, an area of great strategic importance, the United States had signed a formal defense treaty with the new government in Taiwan in 1955. Under the terms of the Taiwan Mutual Defense Pact, American advisers and soldiers would remain in Taipei for the next few decades – aircraft carrier groups would be nearby, watching always to deter a communist China. In its own hemisphere, during World War II, American officials went into Mexico, encouraging Mexican workers to come to the United States, year after year after year. And so Mexican immigrants came, too, again because the Americans had come to them first.[10]

Professor David Reimers has been one of the most prominent scholars to insist that the consequences of the Act of 1965 were unintended, and Professor Gabriel Chin has presented evidence to suggest that Congress knew that a race-neutral immigration law would have obvious race-based consequences.[11] To this debate, we might consider adding another possibility: the Americans had always had a hard time admitting that they were an empire. For at least the first third of the twentieth century, most Americans had not supported American involvement in European or in Asian affairs. To fight against fascism in Europe and in Asia, the United States drew itself into World War II, and, in the wake of that conflict, the United States military stayed in Asia and in Europe to oppose the spread of communism. The United States was a somewhat reluctant empire, a nation that had, by chance, been spared the horrors of two world wars at home in the twentieth century. When they kept the nation removed and apart from the troubles of the rest of the world, American political leaders did little or nothing to undo virulent, popular forms of American racism; when they became leaders of the "free world," however, they learned that they could not maintain such an indifference. The United States occupied a global stage, even though many Americans had opposed this global role in the world. By approving a race-neutral immigration law, without grasping fully how the nation had grown into an empire, they were perhaps unprepared to comprehend how so many parts of their imperial sphere were now coming toward them, in the form of hundreds of thousands of immigrants.

The American Empire and the American Family

We turn first to Asia, where the United States military often had a profound impact on several countries, in ways that were obvious as well as subtle. For instance, in the early years of the American presence in the Philippines, even before 1910, military leaders had to contend with alarming rates of tropical diseases, including malaria, yellow fever, and dengue fever. These ailments had other names that may have felt more accurate to their victims, like "black vomit" and "break bone" fever. Thousands of Americans lived in the Philippines by then, but so did billions of mosquitoes, not to mention several other disease vectors that can thrive when there is no plumbing. Because so many soldiers and sailors were sick at any given time, military hospitals were busy places, with not enough medical professionals and staff members to treat all of the sick. The Navy realized that doctors and nurses from the United States were not rushing to the Philippines to assist these patients, despite overwhelming demand for their services. Some Americans insisted from this experience that the Philippines just wasn't worth this misery, even though it was an obvious and important strategic gateway into China and Southeast Asia.

After 1910, the Governor General of the Philippines, William Howard Taft, and then his Secretary of Education for the Philippines, Professor David Barrows, had worked to prioritize medical training for native Filipino men and women, primarily to serve American soldiers and sailors. They demanded more investment in the Philippines, not less, and they persuaded Congress to finance primary and secondary educational institutions more generally throughout the Philippines during this same period. But top administrators gave special attention to medical and nursing schools, so that hundreds, and then thousands, of Filipino medical workers were available to the United States armed forces by 1930. Indeed, bringing an American medical staff to teach Filipinos proved much cheaper over time than importing health professionals from across the Pacific. After World War II and through the Vietnam War, the United States federal government vastly increased spending on institutions to support medical training and medical services in the Philippines, again to support American troops. In her book, the historian Catherine Choy noted that this policy was also creating a pathway – a very large one – through which hundreds and then thousands of Filipinos would *leave* the Philippines after receiving their medical training. They went to where their teachers had come from: in search of higher wages and better working conditions – topics that the Americans themselves must have brought up constantly – the Filipino and Filipina trainees came to the United States.[12]

After the Americans had abolished the race-based provisions of the immigration law, it was hard *not* to find them within American hospitals. Indeed, by 1980, visit any hospital in America and you'd be hard-pressed not to find at least a half-dozen Filipino American nurses or physicians, many of them born in the Philippines, and trained in institutions that the Americans had established. Many government officials and scholars observed that, after 1952 and 1965, when immigration rules created preferences for skilled workers, Asians would come in large, and then larger, numbers. The Americans themselves had planted the seeds for that migration in places like the Philippines. To care for American soldiers and sailors – to do that in a way that did not rely on steady, expensive imports of skilled labor from the United States – the American military and civilian governments in the Philippines built a set of institutions that (still) brought Filipino and Filipina doctors and nurses to American hospitals and clinics.

Tropical diseases could be fatal and debilitating, but so could venereal ones. Many American soldiers and sailors were contracting these diseases at astonishing rates in the early twentieth century, especially (although not exclusively) in Asia. In the late nineteenth century, several states had approved a series of public laws to promote morals and public health and to suppress "vice," whether this manifested in the form of erotic prints, contraception, or medicines and devices to induce abortions. Congress passed a national version of these rules in 1873, an "Act for the Suppression of Trade in, and Circulation of, Obscene Literature and Articles of Immoral Use," commonly known as the Comstock Act, named after Anthony Comstock, the United States Postal Inspector. Comstock knew better than most the strange and weird materials sometimes going across the country by mail. One imagines his horror, as he unwrapped a sex toy from San Francisco traveling to somewhere in South Dakota. Under the Comstock Act, sexual libertines, prostitutes, and their pimps were among some of the people who could face criminal penalties for using (and for making) condoms or erotica, which were, after all, designed to increase demand for their services. Mr. Comstock and his supporters, many of them religious leaders, believed that sexuality and sexual reproduction should be reserved for decent, married couples, and that sexual activity should be open always to the possibility of conception, so that people might have sex for procreation and not for recreation.[13]

American military leaders, though, noticed that whenever they took their men abroad, without condoms or other forms of contraception, the men had lots of sexual contact with the local women, despite repeated warnings, severe punishment, and threats about refraining from getting too close to the locals. Nothing worked. Officers were embarrassed when other officers violated prohibitions against fraternizing with the locals. In the Philippines, by 1903, American soldiers and sailors had so much sexual contact with the Filipino women that venereal diseases were a very common and ubiquitous problem, sometimes infecting thousands of men and overwhelming the thin medical staff assigned to treat them. Rape and sexual violence against women were also quite common, too, and very poorly policed. But commercial sexual transactions between Americans and Filipinos were far more common, to the point where military leaders came to accept this kind of "exchange." Indeed, the running joke was that, if all soldiers and officers were punished for consensual and commercial fraternization, American forces across the territory would cease to function.[14]

The American military gave up on prohibition and instead devolved toward controlling the by-products of that unrepressed behavior. Military leaders adapted new policies to address unwanted pregnancies, orphaned children, and enormous rates of venereal disease, because these problems were embarrassing and expensive. By 1930, after hundreds of thousands of American soldiers and sailors had contracted venereal diseases in Europe and in Asia, American military leaders throughout the world promoted policies that Anthony Comstock would have considered unthinkable. The private sector helped: in 1930, in Akron, Ohio, an enterprising American inventor had developed a way to mass-produce latex, vulcanized condoms, just at a time when the Great Depression was depressing everything, including public support for the enforcement of the Comstock law. Married couples persuaded religious leaders to reverse blanket prohibitions on contraception, and then, by 1931, military leaders went much further by distributing these very reliable, very durable mass-produced condoms free of charge – as many as their soldiers and sailors wanted. The American government became one of the biggest single buyers of condoms, and these became "general issue," as in GI, like a soldier's rifle, his helmet and his uniform, and his bullets. From a certain perspective, this policy might seem pragmatic; from another, it was horrifying. Either way, it was full of irony.[15]

After 1940, even though there was no discernible decline in commercial sexual activity, unwanted pregnancies and venereal diseases associated with American military units were much less common. This decline happened even though as many as a quarter of all latex condoms may have been leaky or defective. To be clear, many other armies gave away condoms: the Nazis and the fascist Italians and the Imperial Japanese gave their soldiers many thousands, although these governments had outlawed contraception within their own home territories, so that the women there might bear more Nazis and fascists and imperialists. But wherever the Nazis and Italians and Japanese invaded, their men behaved in dishonorable ways, in ways that were often criminal and horrifying to the communities that they occupied, and on a scale that was abominable. During World War II, the Japanese Navy transported "comfort women" great distances so that Japanese soldiers and sailors could have sex with them or simply rape them. The Americans and their allies, including the Soviets, insisted that they were not this way, and that their enemies were worse. But war debased all men, and the Americans and their allies in Japan and in Europe behaved in deeply unfortunate ways, too, both during and after the war. Indeed, when we consider the sheer level of sexual violence during World War II, committed by all of these combatants, we despair at the human condition.[16]

In the midst of that hostility, however, and after thousands of instances of gendered contact between American men and foreign women, much of it lacking any dignity, some people developed strong feelings for one another, to the point where they were willing to begin a life together even while everything around them seemed to be falling apart. The term "war bride" became more common in the language of the American military during World War II, when hundreds and then thousands of soldiers wanted to bring back home the women that they'd met overseas. Many of the Americans met these women in conventional ways – through welcoming ceremonies for American troops, for example – but many couples began their relationships through more commercial transactions, often over many visits. The lines between "sex worker," "sex partner," "girlfriend," and then "spouse" – these were blurrier than many people liked to admit. American military leaders had discouraged their soldiers from "contact" with foreigners, of course, but they also knew that so many soldiers had sacrificed so much, and that so many of them had become so attached to the women they'd met abroad.[17]

Collectively, the soldiers did not like that their officers were less than receptive to their plea for assistance, especially when a relationship moved toward talk of marriage. The officers were, in fact, trained to be discouraging: they reminded their soldiers that the foreign women were often desperate, that they would do or say anything to get out of their miserable conditions, and that the bride would probably abandon the soldier shortly after her arrival in America. Still, despite these warnings, American servicemen married foreign women at such rates that Congress was moved to acknowledge and legalize the flow of war brides, first in 1945, in the War Brides Act, and then in 1947, when Congress expanded the rule to allow for Asian women coming as the brides of American servicemen. Hundreds and then thousands of European women came to the United States under this rule. In time, as hundreds of thousands of American soldiers were meeting women in Asia, thousands of brides from Asia would come, too. Thus, again, we see the origins of a significant movement of family members across the Pacific, after the immigration rules in 1965 strengthened and legalized that migration. Family-forming migrations were the direct results of the increasing presence of the United States military around the world in the second half of the twentieth century.[18]

At the end of World War II, instead of dismantling practices that tied commercial sex, access to local women, and their own military presence, the United States armed services did little or nothing to diminish this phenomenon. In Britain, France, Italy, West Germany, and Japan, soldiers and sailors from the United States did not have a hard time finding sex or buying it for several decades after the war had ended. In Japan, the government itself braced for this reality from the beginning, working with prostitutes and local governments and police departments to "make available" large numbers of women to "service the conquerors." According to the historian John Dower, the government of Japan considered these prostitutes and sex workers as a kind of "buffer" to protect "respectable women" from the Americans. The officials even praised the women for being "patriotic," for protecting the honor of the rest of the "pure" Japanese people. Thus, brothels were common throughout the country, and sex was cheap, about $1, "about the same amount as a half a pack of cigarettes on the Japanese market." Moreover, "although these services did not prevent rape and assault, the incidence of rape remained relatively low given the huge size of the occupation force – much as the government had hoped."[19]

In time, just as in the Philippines, so many Americans contracted venereal diseases that the Japanese and American governments coordinated the creation of "prophylactic stations," and then they moved to abolish open, public forms of prostitution. Still, prostitution and commercial sex remained common; this market was more highly regulated and supervised by the 1950s, but it wasn't hard to find, and there were many willing consumers and providers. About 150,000 American troops were stationed in Japan in 1950, the year that the Korean War consumed that peninsula. During that war, over 350,000 Americans soldiers arrived in Korea and in Japan, and when the war ceased in 1953, the Americans stayed in Korea until, well, now.

And as the Americans remained, they stimulated again a large industry of commercial sex, too, with entire "camptowns" adjacent to American military bases, their transactions overseen this time by the American and South Korean governments. Thousands of Korean women worked as prostitutes for American clients for many decades after the Korean War, just as thousands of Korean women had worked in similar conditions to "serve" the Japanese Imperial Army and Navy during its occupation of Korea from 1905 to 1945. This parallel deserves some explanation, as we acknowledge its controversy: several scholars in Japan and in Korea have argued, for example, that the forced migration of Korean women to "comfort stations" throughout the Japanese Empire at the height of World War II represented an expansion of an already extant system of prostitution under Japanese colonialism. Korean nationalists condemn such an argument, insisting instead that the Japanese state and the Japanese military were singularly criminal in forcing Korean women into sexual slavery.[20]

Yet recent works by Ji-Yeon Yuh and by Katherine Moon, among other scholars, show that prostitution in South Korea was common, pervasive, and supported by an array of policies within the South Korean state, during a time when members of the United States military were among the key clients. In other words, the South Korean government knew that thousands of South Korean women were working as prostitutes for American servicemen. The South Korean government regulated that market instead of abolishing it. Perhaps, in the minds of Korean nationalists, it was different when the South Korean government made South Korean women available in this way, but such a position might unjustly diminish the shame of any government that had behaved in this way.[21]

In Britain, France, Italy, and West Germany as well, in the 1950s and 1960s, governments were gravely concerned about the rise of communist countries in Eastern Europe, as these regimes were supported or even created by the Union of Soviet Socialist Republics. In 1949, when the United States helped to form the North Atlantic Treaty Organization, their friends in western and southern Europe regarded the United States as an indispensable ally, and so they too "hosted" thousands of American troops in their own countries. Thus, in Europe, American soldiers and sailors had so much contact with the local women that this became a national issue in many countries, with heated debates about commercial sex, the sheer scale of prostitution near some American military bases, and then steep rises in unwanted pregnancies and rates of venereal disease. The Americans sometimes complained that the local women and pimps "attacked" their men, preyed upon the more gullible soldiers, and fleeced the Americans right through their pants. Nationalists in all of the European countries, including communists in Great Britain, complained back, saying that the sexual behavior of the Americans was as gross as that of any occupying army. The Americans didn't care, they said, whether a young woman was actually a young girl, whether there was money exchanged or the promise of money, or whether sexual contacts produced a child, or, collectively, many children. They noted that American soldiers made far more money than British soldiers, and American soldiers didn't suffer the same food rationing system that constrained British subjects until 1954, so that the two countries were allies, but not exactly equals. Some said that if the Americans were a necessary solution for an expansionist Soviet policy, this American cure could sometimes feel as degrading as the threat from the East.[22]

Again, prostitution in the postwar years was a common thing in Europe and in Asia, as were garden-variety affairs between American men and European and Asian women. For Americans, the phenomenon pre-dated World War II; during and after the First World War, at least half a million American soldiers had contracted venereal diseases in Europe. During World War II, American generals had affairs, American soldiers had affairs, brothels continued to be popular, and commercial sex was one of the most visible and most obvious forms of exchange between American and the locals, wherever they were. So, too, then, was marriage between American soldiers and foreign women. The pattern that had been obvious during World War II persisted after that war, and because the American military was now stretched across the Eurasian continent – including countries not exactly on the continent itself, such as England and Japan and the Philippines and Taiwan – Asian women were coming to the United States in significant numbers well before the Immigration Act of 1965.

As many Asian women married American soldiers, their presence within American military bases in the United States became more common. In time, like many immigrants before them, they made themselves anew: they often did not discuss how they'd met their husbands. After the couple had had children, they also experienced a desire to reunite with their own families, the siblings and parents left behind in their home countries. When the Immigration Act of 1965 provided the opportunity for this kind of reunion, the long-lost sister in America, the one who didn't talk about how she had been supporting herself or her family in Korea or the Philippines, became this important person in the future of the extended family. She was the anchor who could – through citizenship acquired from her American husband – bring her relatives to America. The outcast was now at the center. A surprising number of families in Europe and in Asia relied on such a sister to make their own lives anew here in the United States.[23]

And, since at least 1970, other women from Asia were coming to the United States in similar ways, through these "family-forming" migrations that also had postcolonial dimensions. Before the internet, for example, companies in Asia produced picture books that had listed prospective Asian women, rows and rows of them, so that men in the United States could write and get in touch, and perhaps develop a relationship that could lead to marriage. Some observers referred to these women as "mail-order" brides. It wasn't always clear which came first, the desire to live in the United States, or the desire to marry an American, but enough American men and Asian women found these arrangements desirable, and so these small-scale match-making services grew into much bigger operations. Hundreds of Asian women from Korea, the Philippines, and, to a lesser extent, Japan, came as the brides of American civilians through this pathway from 1965 through 1980. After the internet, thousands of women have still been coming this way every year, mostly from Asia, but also from Latin America, Russia, and other portions of the former Soviet Union.[24]

Several scholars have written extensively about this migration, including its origins, and then its transformation in the internet age, when by the mid-1990s, Americans could "shop" and find almost anything on-line. (I would recommend that the reader try, right now, a few on-line searches for "international brides," or "Asian brides," or "Russian women," just to get a sense of what this business looked like.) The social scientists examined the gendered dimensions of these international marriages, their class and status aspects, and their legal dimensions, too, as in cases where the bride divorced the American just after arriving, or when the husband proved abusive. New federal rules governed these marriages in those instances, from the 1980s through the 2010s. Over four decades, however, this migration has had consistent dimensions: the American men tended to be older, and many were divorced at least once; the men were more highly educated than average Americans; and yet they tended to complain that American women were not as "traditional" or as attentive as the women they were looking for. This aversion to women in the United States seemed to be the primary reason why many American men were looking abroad. As for the women, they tended to be significantly younger than the men they were marrying, and in many countries, including the Philippines, they also were more likely to be educated, too.[25]

Scholars estimated, by 2000, that about 5–10,000 women came to the United States through marriage to an American citizen every year. If we included women who came to the United States from abroad, then married an American citizen, those figures would be much higher, as this was becoming a more common pathway after 2000. That is, from the 1970s through the 1990s, Americans used to go all the way to Asia or Eastern Europe to meet and to date their prospective brides. Now, many more women from abroad can travel to New York and to Los Angeles for business or for tourism, and so it's not so hard to date those busy executives who can't always get away. The current First Lady, Melania Trump, was not a "mail order" bride – she came to New York in 1996 on a work visa, when she was in her mid-twenties – but other aspects of her courtship and marriage to Donald Trump would have been familiar to scholars in this field.

"The Dust of Life ..."

These international marriages were interesting because they revealed race, gender, and class-based patterns that have proven persistent over time. Arranging these marriages had turned into a big business – it was a multimillion-dollar industry by 1990, involving complex screenings, trips abroad, numerous dates, and lots of time and money. But highly educated, upper-middle-class White American women were not looking for men of color abroad in quite the same ways over this period, and that was itself revealing. Similarly, after 1950 and through 1965, families in South Korea or in China were not coming to the United States to adopt White American children, when the couples couldn't have children of their own, but the reverse pattern became very common after 1950, to the point where scholars were also studying this migration and noticing that the numbers were robust. By 1990, many thousands of children from Asia were living with middle- and upper-middle-class families throughout the United States. This was yet another set of family-forming migrations that Congress legalized and supported throughout the postwar period, even though it wasn't quite "new" – at least not for scholars familiar with nineteenth- and twentieth-century United States history.

Throughout the nineteenth century, when White settlers and Native Americans encountered each other in war and in peace on the frontier, they took one another's women and children. Oftentimes, the circumstances were traumatic, the "adoptions" and kidnappings coming in the wake of mass killings. In 1813, for example, Andrew Jackson adopted an infant named Lyncoya after the Battle of Tullushatchee during the Creek War, and thus the "Indian Killer" became the father of a boy that he'd purportedly wanted to send to West Point. Lyncoya was smart, but he died unexpectedly at the Hermitage in 1828, when he was about 16 years old.[26] Eight years later, in 1836, Comanche warriors massacred the adults of the Parker family in their settlement south of Dallas. They took Cynthia Ann Parker, about 8 years old, and five others as captives, and they gave her to a prominent Comanche family. The others were ransomed over time, but Cynthia Ann remained with the Comanche; she married Peta Nocona, a chief of the Quahadi band, and when she was "recovered" by the Texas Rangers in 1860, she had had three children with him. Having spent over two decades with the Comanche, Naduah did not respond to her English name, she spoke broken English and fluent Comanche, and even though her relatives did confirm that she was once Cynthia Ann Parker, she attempted to escape back to "her people" on several occasions until her death of influenza in 1871.[27]

By that time, though, after the Civil War, federal armies had moved to subjugate Native Americans on a much larger scale, and so hundreds of Native American families were lost or scattered. In the East, progressive reformers lobbied hard to stop the massacres and killings in the West, and perhaps also to save those children who were orphaned by war. In 1879, Richard Pratt, a United States Army officer, received federal support to establish the Carlisle Indian Industrial School in Pennsylvania, and, over the next two decades, government officials and religious leaders opened similar boarding schools across the United States. In a speech in 1892, Pratt said the mission of his school was in part "to kill the Indian in him to save the man." Teachers at these schools gave lessons in English, they provided religious instruction, and they forbade their students at these schools from wearing their native clothes, practicing their native religions, or speaking their native languages. Federal officials took hundreds of thousands of children from their tribal lands and put them under the guardianship of White teachers in these boarding schools. Once the children were fluent in English, many were sent to live with White families, to learn a trade or to live among White people. We should also note that many of these children were bi-racial – they had had White fathers, as many American soldiers had sexually assaulted Native American women during the Indian wars of the late nineteenth century.[28]

I've related this history because it bore, for me, such a striking resemblance to events in postwar Korea, when thousands of children were orphaned, when many of the orphans were bi-racial, when American missionaries were among the first to open institutions for these children, and then when those same missionaries organized the adoption of these children into middle-class Christian families in the United States. The circumstances of postwar Korea were devastating and horrifying, and although many American soldiers had behaved honorably, many others had not. News reports from Korea showed what the orphaned children looked like, and the miserable conditions that they faced in postwar Korea, where about 8 percent of the entire population had perished in the fighting. Some Americans were moved to act: Harry and Bertha Holt lived in a small town south of Eugene, Oregon; they were devoutly Christian, and they had already had six children. But when they saw these reports and images of children orphaned during the Korean War, they decided to adopt a few of the orphans, including ones that looked Korean and White and African American. In 1955, two years after the war, Congress passed An Act for the Relief of Certain Korean War Orphans, specifically in response to their repeated requests to take these children from South Korea. Although these children were born abroad, they looked sort of "American," and many observers agreed that their mothers may have abandoned them precisely for that reason.[29]

The Holts adopted eight children from Korea. The ensuing publicity was such that they decided to help others to do the same, and, in time, Holt International Children's Services became one of the most prominent international adoption agencies in American history. They placed Korean children not just with families in the United States, but also with families in Norway, Denmark, Belgium, Switzerland, France, and Germany. The Holt organization asked for prospective parents to be Christians, and to declare a willingness to raise their adopted children in Christian homes. From 1955 to 1959, about 3,000 children were adopted into families outside Korea, over 90 percent of them to families in the United States. In the next decade, over 6,000 children were adopted abroad. From 1970 to 1990, over 110,000 children from South Korea were adopted into mostly White, middle-class families in the United States, often the members of Christian congregations in the Midwest and in the South.

Around 1988, the year of the Seoul Olympics, international adoptions were so common and embarrassing to so many Koreans that the South Korean government moved to limit the number of adoptions per year. That proved rather difficult to do. During that period when South Korea was rapidly industrializing, many Korean women had had children out of wedlock, and many others had children in camptowns and in other circumstances that reflected the ongoing presence of the United States military. There were many more orphans and abandoned children than families in South Korea willing to adopt them.

And so, from 1990 to 2010, about 40,000 children continued to be adopted out of South Korea, despite efforts to encourage domestic adoptions and to regulate international adoptions more strictly. By 2010, Korean adoptees accounted for about 10 percent of all persons of Korean ancestry living in the United States.[30]

Many social scientists, artists, writers, and scholars have produced a voluminous literature about this distinct family-forming migration that emerged in the wake of war, one that amplified in that evolving alliance between South Korea and the United States. Korean adoptees themselves have written poignantly about their experiences, with emotions that have ranged from bitterness and rage to great sorrow and resignation. Many sought to reunite with their mothers and families in Korea – indeed, by 2000, there were so many of them attempting to do this that the South Korean government began supporting annual meetings in Seoul for Korean adoptees. In 2011, the South Korean government passed rules to extend dual citizenship to adoptees, so as to ease their travels back and forth, and to facilitate their "return" as Korean citizens. But just as Cynthia Ann Parker had become thoroughly Comanche, so, too, had many Korean adoptees become Americans, as they often discovered when they themselves returned to Korea after many years in the United States. Altogether, their stories were quite amazing.[31]

Of course, children from Korea were not the only adoptees from Asia and elsewhere coming to the United States after 1965. In 1975, during Operation Babylift, President Ford authorized the rescue of over 10,000 Vietnamese children in orphanages throughout South Vietnam, many of whom had American fathers. Other "Amerasian" children in the Southeast were left behind – they became the "dust of life" in a communist Vietnam, facing discrimination and poverty within a nation where many Vietnamese saw them as the living reminders of American imperialism and war. In 1987, Congress approved a set of rules to give these children and their immediate relatives the right to come to the United States. American government officials went back to Vietnam, to examine physically some of the claimants, and, in time, over 65,000 Amerasian children and their relatives came to the United States under these rules. These laws did not, however, offer the American government's support for children hoping to "reunite" with their American fathers, because some veterans' groups complained about that policy. It seemed that many American veterans of the Vietnam War did not want to be found. And so, less than 5 percent of Amerasian young adults have reunited with their fathers.[32]

In other contexts, as family reunification has become a standard feature of American immigration law, international adoptions have continued, even between countries that agreed on little else, if only because the underlying forces between weaker and wealthier nations could sometimes fix this pattern. For example, when the Soviet Union and its Eastern European allies collapsed, and when China abandoned communist economic policies, each country experienced chaotic economic and social transformations that resulted in hundreds of thousands of abandoned and orphaned children. As many as 1 million children in China were internally displaced between 1980 and 1990 – and after 1990, families in the United States had adopted at least 85,000 Chinese children. They were overwhelmingly girls. Deng Xiaoping's government had implemented the

One-Child Policy to control the overall size of the Chinese population, so that a sudden rise would not swallow the country's economic gains. Limited to one child, thousands of Chinese couples then abandoned their baby girls. Again, any society that has experienced sudden transformations tended also to produce orphans and abandoned children, as Charles Dickens and Victor Hugo both knew, but the unprecedented number of abandoned girls in China was the staggering result of many tragic factors converging all at once upon Chinese society in the late twentieth century.[33]

From the former Soviet Union and from its neighboring allied states, the number of children adopted into the United States was significant as well – about 45,000 since 1999 from just Russia alone, in a country with at least 700,000 children who had no parents or guardians. Many officials in Russia saw these numbers as embarrassing problems in a nation struggling to restore its prestige and place in the world. Russia and the United States developed a strained relationship, strained further after 2010, when the United States accused Russia of threatening and encroaching upon its neighboring states once again. From 2010 to 2012, many Russians were incensed by news reports of American parents abusing or even "sending back" Russian children that they'd adopted. Later that year, in 2012, the Russian government voted to ban all adoptions of Russian children into the United States, even though critics of the government said that the orphanages in Russia were completely and horribly overcrowded. Protestors there declared that Russia should lift the ban.

The Russian government discovered what the Chinese government had known since at least 2000, when it also tried to limit international adoptions: allowing eligible American families to adopt these children alleviated harsh conditions in China and in Russia, and so, despite whatever difficulties the governments may have had with one another, allowing this migration seemed more reasonable than banning it. Many American couples heard that the ban in Russia might be lifted, and they have since expressed strong desires to return to that country to look for a child that they might adopt. Legislators and others in Russia noted that the children in question were often "social orphans": one or both of their parents were still alive. They were sent to orphanages because these children had had physical or mental disabilities, and because Russia had inadequate public assistance for such children or for their families. Their parents had abandoned them. Some observers in Russia said that the Americans should just be allowed to take them away.[34]

"Braceros," "Wetbacks"

If the recurring truism is that American immigrants often come to America because the Americans came to their countries first, it was just true in Mexico as it was in Asia or in Europe. The Americans went to Mexico to look for laborers. After 1941, after thousands of men joined the United States military to fight in World War II, the United States government worked to bring agricultural workers from Mexico to the United States, especially to the Southwest, where agricultural producers were warning of serious labor shortages. Unless they received more field hands, the agribusinesses said, the United States would not be able to feed its own people, let alone its armies, as well as the armies of numerous allies in Europe and in Asia. And so, public officials turned south, to Mexico: the story of the Bracero Program is now well known, but it bears repeating here because so many Americans were (are?) still surprised by the number of people coming to the United States from south of the border, long after American officials stopped recruiting laborers. The Bracero Program also represents an interesting, instructive pattern: if a government establishes a way of doing things, even in another country, the people there will continue to do those things when the government frowns upon the very pattern that it helped to create.[35]

At first, the Bracero Program was a widespread effort. Several branches of the United States government negotiated and implemented the Program, and their discussions with the Mexican government began almost immediately after the United States declared war on December 8, 1941. The Department of State engaged in diplomatic outreach to the government of Mexico; the Department of Labor worked with producers in the United States to determine how much labor they'd need; and then the Department of Justice and its Immigration and Naturalization Service developed the legal mechanisms to process and to organize the migrant laborers. The Department of State framed the entire program as part of an important alliance between the United States and Mexico – the United States was sending men to fight fascism in Europe and in Asia, and Mexico would send its men to keep the fields and farms productive, to provide the material support for those Americans. Posters and official communications to prospective workers in Mexico emphasized the self-sacrifice of the bracero – he was going to use his arms, literally, to support democracy. As befitting an alliance, the Department of State assured the government of Mexico that all laborers would receive decent and fair wages (30 cents an hour in 1942), and basic housing and food. In portions of rural Mexico, where many people had endured poverty for many generations, recruitment moved at a clip after the formal agreements were signed in August 1942. No one expected the Program to last through 1965, nor did anyone predict in 1942 that about 5 million Mexican nationals would come to the United States under the Program, and perhaps just as many would come without formal labor contracts.[36]

Recent presidents have suggested that the United States has been addicted to oil, its economy driven by this one commodity that Americans had to get from someplace else. We observe here, through the Bracero Program, that the United States may have had other addictions, too – namely, to steady supplies of low-wage laborers willing to work in conditions that most Americans might shun. It wasn't just a trickle of Mexican nationals coming to America, it was a steady river of people, transported to California, Texas, and Arizona, aboard railroads and buses that the Americans themselves built or improved. In John Steinbeck's novel *The Grapes of Wrath* (1939), migrants from Oklahoma were the refugees from the Dust Bowl, and they worked in miserable poverty in the fields of California, where they did not enjoy decent housing, decent wages, or basic sanitation. This novel of the Great Depression reflected a basic truth – poverty in the late 1920s and early 1930s was horrible for many *White* Americans, and so people in Mexico did not necessarily think that their material conditions would improve simply by crossing the border. Poverty here was about as horrible as poverty there.[37]

The economy of war changed those equations. To finance the war itself, the United States government taxed, and then it borrowed from, its own citizens – by buying war bonds, American citizens were giving their own government a short-term loan, and the government then used this capital to wage a massive war on an unprecedented scale. War bonds helped to finance shipyards, steel mills, tanks, guns, planes, and the development of atomic weapons. War bonds drove basic advances in food technology – companies in the United States developed much better methods of preserving, storing, and transporting food, so that American soldiers could eat rations made months earlier. War bonds indirectly made many companies rich: for example, the Soviets, the British, the French resistance, and American forces in the Pacific – they all ate Spam. The Army bought lots of Spam from the Hormel Company, and so this was how Spam became a ubiquitous, global provider of American canned meat. Canned fruits and vegetables could be preserved and shipped over vast distances as well – how many of us now still open and eat vegetables and fruits preserved in this way? Before the war, Franklin Roosevelt referred to the United States as an "arsenal of democracy." In California, where fruits and vegetables were becoming as valuable as gold a century earlier, low-wage workers from Mexico were contributing to a pantry for democracy. They also helped many California growers make a fortune.[38]

However, not all Americans were pleased to see thousands of Mexican nationals working in agriculture in the late 1940s and throughout the 1950s. At first, aware that our own government had brought these workers at great expense across the border, local politicians and leaders of agribusiness worked with federal officials to put as many people to work as possible. The governors of California and Texas helped coordinate resources, and representatives of the Chambers of Commerce insisted that braceros would not be taking jobs from American workers. Quite often, though, given the sheer number of people involved, local officials and growers could not provide the basic infrastructure of housing and services that the federal government had promised. In 1948, for example, state and local officials complained that braceros were being "exploited," that they worked in harsh conditions with inadequate food and shelter, and with no obvious plans to remedy these conditions. The braceros themselves could not address these problems directly – the federal government contracts did not allow them to bargain collectively, nor were they allowed to go on strike. Shantytowns and migrant "camps" housed thousands of braceros, and, to make matters worse, state and local officials reported that thousands of Mexican nationals were migrating to the United States outside the Bracero Program after 1944, having heard that work was available, even plentiful. These reports suggested that the United States had advertised the need for labor so successfully that it was itself causing a significant unlawful migration from across the Southern border.[39]

In the immediate postwar years, the Bracero Program continued despite these problems, as did unlawful migration from Mexico. Thus, the pattern suggested a common by-product of many public policies: once groups of people start doing things, it's very hard to stop them from doing the same thing. The United States had established and supported the Bracero Program, but many Mexican laborers who were supposed to return to Mexico never did, and many who never signed on to the Program came, and they, too, never left. By 1950, leading politicians in California and Texas were complaining of a "wetback" problem – people were crossing at places like the Rio Grande without inspection. They said that hundreds and thousands of Mexican laborers were now living in a variety of communities in the Southwest, depressing wages for everyone and generally making these regions less livable.[40]

By 1952, about 200,000 persons were coming under the Program, and perhaps as many *outside* the Program, so that the population of Southern California, Arizona, New Mexico, and Texas had significantly more Mexican immigrants than before. Moreover, as Mexican nationals came to work, they inspired other Mexican nationals to do the same – during a time when the United States was enjoying an unprecedented economic boom in those postwar years, thousands of people were leaving Mexico and staying in the United States. In our current politics, as some political leaders have complained about Mexican nationals coming to the United States, illegally and otherwise, they often failed to grasp that it was the American government itself that helped to create and to sustain this pattern. Over one generation, as Mexican immigrants became Mexican Americans, they kept in touch with extended members of their family across the border. In time, as with Asian military brides, they petitioned for family members to join them here, under rules that allowed all Americans to enjoy family reunification.

Indeed, the immigration rules passed during this period reflected an ambivalence between the need to "control the border" and the need for cheap labor in agriculture, as well as a naïve faith that one could migrate "workers" rather than people with thick attachments to other people. The term "bracero" captured this naïveté – American growers wanted workers with good arms for picking. What they got instead were real-life people who wanted a better life for themselves and their loved ones. The growers wanted a steady supply of workers, but other Americans did not like seeing so many Mexican nationals in the United States. The law increasingly reflected tensions between these positions. For example, the Immigration Act of 1952 prohibited the "harboring" of anyone who came to the United States without permission or inspection – if an American citizen helped a communist infiltrator from the Soviet Union or from China, for example, that citizen would have been guilty of "harboring or concealing" an unlawful migrant. However, if that same citizen offered a job to an undocumented Mexican national, this was not to be considered "harboring and concealing," according to the "Texas proviso" included in the Immigration Act of 1952. Growers in Texas didn't want to be punished for hiring people who'd crossed into the United States illegally to work, even though those persons could themselves be punished and deported for arriving unlawfully.[41]

Other policies worked at cross-purposes as well: in 1954, the United States government spent a great deal of time and money deporting Mexican workers during Operation Wetback, a policy that was as racist as the name appears to us now.

Hundreds of American citizens were wrongfully removed under this program, as were thousands of "illegal aliens." And yet, in that year and in the ones that followed, the United States worked with growers to provide more braceros than ever before, so that 200,000 Mexican nationals were admitted in the year before Operation Wetback, and then over 400,000 persons per year, every year, from 1956 to 1959. As they saw braceros going to the United States to pursue work, many Mexican nationals also attempted to come for those same purposes, and as long as they could cross, American employers would have no trouble hiring them – no trouble with the federal law at all. Thus, again, thousands of Mexican nationals were becoming Mexican Americans even before the Immigration Act of 1965 – like other immigrants before them, they were settling in the United States, forming families, and then also retaining their attachments to family members back home. In time, they would petition for family reunification.[42]

For prospective migrants south of the United States, the Immigration Act of 1965 was supposed to "regularize" immigration from Mexico, so that Mexico would be just like any other country under the new immigration law. Because the Bracero Program had brought so many rural migrants from Mexico – and many thousands of unlawful migrants from Mexico as well – many prominent Mexican Americans were more than ready to support a more "regular" flow of immigrants from Mexico. Cesar Chavez in California and Hector Garcia in Texas were among two leading figures who said that the growers had always abused the braceros, that they paid them lower wages than they did American citizens, and that they degraded the overall conditions in this industry just at a time when agribusiness was booming. Each lobbied heavily for an end to the Program. Even though Cesar Chavez and his United Farm Workers had many members who were, in fact, "illegals," as Chavez himself once described them, they could not support programs like Operation Wetback, nor envision future versions of such draconian federal policies. And so they hoped for immigration reforms that would allow for orderly migrations, without the chaos of brutal and often racist enforcement.[43]

As we shall see later, however, migrations across the Southern border didn't fall into familiar patterns. Many people came legally under the family reunification provisions of the Immigration Act of 1965, but Mexican nationals continued to cross into the United States to look for work, often in agriculture but in other industries as well. Again, once a pattern is established, it's hard to undo. By the mid-1970s, states like California and Texas attempted to discourage the further migration of unlawful immigrants, either by cutting off jobs or by limiting access to essential services like public education. The tensions between growers who "needed" unskilled workers and other citizens who wanted them excluded would dominate immigration law and politics well into our time.

Postcolonial Migrations

Perhaps we should observe, in these trends, the hand of our own federal government, without whom this pattern and other migration patterns might never have emerged in quite the ways that they did. Migration from Mexico, migration from Asia – these were postcolonial or neocolonial migrations, the result of the new American position in the twentieth century, as a global leader for democracy, as a nation that fought communism everywhere, as a place that sent public officials to far-flung places all over the world, only to witness droves of migrants from those same places. By 1950, the United States Army and Navy were in Europe, of course, but they were also in Asia, in the Philippines, Japan, Korea, and off the coast of Taiwan. They are still there. The United States encouraged and organized the migration of hundreds of thousands of people from Mexico, a process that began during World War II, but grew and expanded to include even more Mexican workers *after* the war. In 1964 and 1965, when legislators and politicians debated the Immigration Act of 1965, they knew of these developments, and yet they seemed genuinely surprised when, a decade later, so many Mexicans and Asians arrived in the United States. Were the demographic impacts of the new law foreseeable? Perhaps they should have been.

That is, if the consequences of the Immigration Act of 1965 were "unintended," it might only seem that way because, in 1965, most American politicians were unwilling to admit to themselves and to their own constituents that the United States had, in fact, become an empire. American military officials, American diplomats, American corporations, American interests – they were everywhere, often guarding massive armories and firepower, just like any other empire. The Americans had developed much faster, safer planes in the middle of the twentieth century, and so American military leaders and Americans in general could get to Asia, to Europe, and to Mexico more quickly than ever before. They brought televisions and refrigerators to places like Seoul, and then the people living in Seoul, including my late mother, saw *I Love Lucy* and *Bonanza*, years before they took their flights to Los Angeles. In 1975, my mother purchased her first albums in America – it was a double record, *Elvis Presley's Forty Greatest Hits*. Many Americans, however, still considered people like my mother foreigners, even though she'd been long familiar with American culture, for the Americans had been in her country since she was 5 years old.

In the subsequent decades, as American citizens then saw in their own cities many more Asians and many more Latinos than ever before, to the point where they worried and considered restrictions against these trends, they sometimes behaved as though all of this had been unforeseeable, even surprising. They did not like what the Immigration Act of 1965 was doing to *their* country. Yet, had they paid more attention to American foreign policy – including American military deployments – and to American labor recruitment policy, they would not have been so surprised. By 1975, a clear majority of new immigrants to the United States were not from Europe. Europeans did migrate during this period, but Asians and Latinos dominated the migratory flows by wide margins, and over half of immigrants from Asia, and nearly 90 percent of immigrants from Mexico, came under family reunification preferences. In addition, American citizens themselves – including many middle-class and highly educated Americans – were choosing Asians and others to migrate them to the United States, through marriage and through adoption. In the absence of formal laws restricting these choices, American men chose Asian women and Asian children, far more than – say – African women or African children, and then they were marrying them and adopting them to form or to complete their families in the United States. Through marriage and through adoption, American citizens could confer American citizenship, as though it was a privileged status that many people around the world coveted.

In the first two decades after 1965, skilled migrants came to the United States, but family-forming migrations under the Immigration Act of 1965 quickly changed the complexion of the United States in much broader and more expansive ways. Approved during the Civil Rights Movement, this law now made the United States less White, less African American, and much more multiracial than it had ever been before. In most states, marriages between Whites and non-Whites had been illegal, at least until the *Loving* decision in 1967. For American soldiers and for many more American civilians, though, interracial marriages were common before 1967 and well after, as were international, transracial adoptions. In many churches, and near American military bases in the United States, many families were already multiracial. In this way, the Immigration Act of 1965 became one of the single most consequential rules passed in Congress in the second half of the twentieth century, because it enhanced the underlying patterns of migration that rather preceded the rule, and because it strengthened and amplified existing, persistent trends in migration arising from the south and to the east of the United States.

4

THE MULTIRACIAL STATE

In the first two centuries of the European Enlightenment, a surprising number of political philosophers did not think that a multiracial or multinational society was a good idea. John Stuart Mill was one of the most eminent political philosophers of the nineteenth century, and he had pointed to the Balkans to argue that multinational states were almost always a disaster. He noted how infighting there seemed to be endemic, the people couldn't get along across religious and ethnic and linguistic differences, and when they faced a national crisis or an international threat, they divided along ethnic and religious factions that made a broader cohesion impossible. In multiracial states, there was no *common* good. I first read Mill in college, in the early 1990s, when the Balkans were falling apart again, when Yugoslavia was disintegrating, and so it felt odd to read about the present in the past. Mill conceded that all states had had ethnic or religious diversity within them, including his own Great Britain. But he pointed to the Balkans to recommend that governments should try to *subsume* diversity as much as possible. Religious, linguistic, ethnic, and tribal differences in the public realm could be catastrophic, and fatal to nations.

John Stuart Mill and other English elites felt that all British subjects should speak English, that they should elect representatives to Parliament, and that they ought to fight for King and country when Parliament needed them to, even if they were Welsh, Scottish, or Irish. Especially if they *were* Welsh, Scottish, or Irish, Mill suggested, the King of England might just as well remove from their ancestral lands those very symbols of their tribal identities, to facilitate their devotion to King and country, to a *Great* Britain. In the classical liberalism of this English variety, tolerance meant an openness to *absorbing* "foreigners" into the state, and not necessarily tolerating foreignness to persist to the point where it might sow the seeds for perpetual faction and division, perhaps even secession and independence. Are multiracial states condemned to violence? Are they destined to fall apart? By 1980, in the United States, these were more than rhetorical questions – beginning around that time, 30 states would eventually pass rules declaring English their official language. Racial tensions and racial violence were common in cities and suburbs. In 1992, when Los Angeles fell apart over days of rioting, I remembered reading Mill, and then feeling a kind of despair as I watched the news. Perhaps Mill had been right. There was no common ground in Los Angeles in late April of 1992. This was not good at all.[1]

Violence Over the Land

On the one hand, it might seem obvious that the people of the United States had never dealt very well with racial diversity either, or any kind of diversity for that matter, and so it may not have been a surprise when, after 1965, old problems arose in new colors. Much of American history was violence, inflected with race and racial animus. Long before the United States was even a nation, conflicts between the colonists and the Native Americans were common. In the 1670s, in Virginia and in Massachusetts, the early colonists coveted Native American lands, fought one another over the right to settle the frontier, and they used coordinated, organized forms of violence to press their claims.[2]

Through slavery, White majorities in Virginia institutionalized racial violence: a White man who owned a Black slave had total control over his body and person, and many such men committed unspeakable acts against men and women held in bondage. Many Americans might have forgotten the intimacy of slavery – slaves were not unthinking beasts, as some White apologists had claimed for obvious, self-serving reasons. Slaves of African descent were people just like you and me. And so how might you behave, if some White man sold your brother or your mother or perhaps you for a profit, so that you would never see your loved ones again? What if that same man beat your loved ones in front of you, as both punishment and warning, and no other White men would regard that as an assault or battery? Consider these possibilities for just a moment and then ask whether it was surprising at all that Southern slave owners locked up their "property" at night, or that they proposed in their political assemblies a total ban on the sale of poison to any person of color, especially to slave women.[3]

Race-based violence appeared like a rolling catastrophe in American history – Native American dispossession and removal, the horrors of slavery, attacks against free African Americans in the North, and then race riots against Asian migrants in the decades after their arrival in 1850. After 1860, many towns, large and small, had had anti-Chinese or anti-Asian race riots, including several very large ones in Los Angeles in 1871, San Francisco in 1877, Denver in 1880, and Seattle in 1886. This might sound amazing to people familiar with San Francisco now, but this city was once the heart of an anti-Chinese movement so virulent and so popular that many of its streets still bear the names of famous anti-Asian figures, including Geary, Scott, Van Ness, and Phelan. These politicians ran for office using violent language, as though recommending forms of violence against Asians. Rather than acting as figures who might elicit empathy across diverse constituencies and people, men like Geary, Scott, Van Ness, and Phelan said that Asian immigrants were threatening, evil, and perpetually foreign. One might wonder what they would feel now, if, by some magic, they could see San Francisco in 2015.⁴

State officials and politicians were not race-neutral, and in those days before political correctness, many candidates for high office in the United States promised to pursue policies supporting slavery, or to clear Native Americans from their ancestral lands, or to block the arrival of "Chinese coolies." When he ran for President, Andrew Jackson was known as "the Indian Killer," a nickname that did not hurt him in the primaries or in the general election. When he ran for Governor of California in 1942, Earl Warren criticized his opponent for not taking a tougher stance against persons of Japanese ancestry. Warren promised mass internment, and he won that race. It wasn't just that Americans had had a hard time managing racial diversity – it's more accurate to say that they did it poorly, violently, in ways designed to terrorize people of color and to discourage their presence here. Imagine, for a moment, how you might react if the American government told you that it was building internment camps, in the middle of nowhere, where you and your family would be incarcerated indefinitely. Having heard stories of horror and death about similar camps in Europe, many Japanese Americans in 1943 wondered whether they would survive the experience. Many of them were terrified that the soldiers would shoot them in remote areas where no one else would see the mass murders.⁵

In 1952, after the former Governor of California Earl Warren became Chief Justice Earl Warren, many people were surprised that *he* was announcing the Supreme Court's decision in *Brown* v. *Board of Education*. Earl Warren had helped to overturn race-based segregation in the public schools, which was a major surprise for people who'd supported him for having supported Japanese American internment. Like other federal officials, however, Earl Warren thought that Americans should abandon race-based segregation, as it was now embarrassing for the United States on a global stage. Chief Justice Warren had read the *Brown* decision aloud, in front of both domestic and foreign news agencies assembled to hear the announcement. *Brown* represented at once a monumental shift. It thus became one of the most unpopular decisions in American history. Several governors and other leading politicians condemned *Brown*. They refused to acknowledge that it was binding. United States Senators wore buttons that said "Never," as in they would never comply with *Brown*. Leaders of several public school systems closed the schools rather than follow the decision in *Brown*. When school officials elsewhere noted that children of color and White children were too far apart to integrate without bussing, White mobs attacked the buses. Riots broke out across the country. Many families moved to the suburbs, and, in many instances, they formed new public school districts, these being as segregated as the school systems before *Brown*. Federal judges took over dozens of urban districts because local administrators had no political support to comply with *Brown*. These problems lasted decades, and desegregation and reverse segregation were all punctuated by violence.⁶

A few months before Lyndon Johnson signed the Immigration Act of 1965, Los Angeles exploded in riots, following an incident involving an African American motorist arrested for drunk driving. The California Highway patrol arrested Marquette Frye, but then they eventually arrested his mother and his brother as well, as witnesses saw the events unfolding in their neighborhood. Based on what they saw, they believed that the police were behaving in ways (yet again) that many recognized as a familiar pattern of racist, violent behavior toward African Americans in that city. For six days, Los Angeles burned. In 1965, as everyone watched these riots on television, it wasn't clear how the United States was going to handle the racial conflicts that it had already, let alone any significant waves of new people not from Europe. Throughout that period, racist politicians argued *against* diversity and *for* segregation: "Segregation now, segregation tomorrow, segregation forever," said the Governor of Alabama, who ran for President of the United States in 1968.[7]

George Wallace drew 10 million votes in that election; he carried 5 states and he collected 46 electoral votes. In subsequent years, as Mexicans and Central Americans and Koreans and Southeast Asians came to the United States, many of them were filled with great hopes and wonderful promises about a new life in this "beautiful country," which was what the Koreans had called America in their native Korean. Many of them did not know about, nor were they prepared for, the seemingly endless, chaotic cycles of violence that had plagued this nation from its very beginnings.

Hate Crimes

Indeed, after 1965, as more immigrants came to the United States, racial violence and tension persisted, and they formed one of the more depressing patterns from a time when White supremacy was ascendant. Many observers saw that, as more jurisdictions abandoned, repealed, or overturned race-based rules, unfortunate patterns of behavior outlived the end of formal White supremacy. White police officers still assaulted, and sometimes killed, unarmed African American citizens throughout the 1960s and well after (even now). Throughout the decade, as the Civil Rights Movement continued to unfold, racial violence in the United States was visible to anyone with a television. It happened over schools; it happened at schools. In the first ten years after the Immigration Act of 1965, as immigrants from Mexico and from Asia came to the United States in greater numbers, racist violence would fold them in, too, in deeply disturbing ways.

In 1976, in one particularly infamous case, a family of cattle ranchers caught three Mexican migrants along the Southern border near Douglas, Arizona. The migrants, Manuel Loya, Eleazar Zavala, and Bernabe Herrera, were attempting to enter the United States unlawfully; they were walking across a ranch that belonged to George Hanigan. His two sons, Thomas and Patrick, spotted the migrants, and, at gunpoint, the father and his two boys forced the three men to get into their truck. They drove into a field. For over an hour, after stripping them naked, the Hanigans robbed, beat, and threatened to kill all three men. They tied and hung the men from a tree. George Hanigan threatened to castrate them. One of the Hanigans dragged one of the migrants with a rope around the neck, while another burned their feet with a long iron that had been resting in a fire. After cutting the men loose, the Hanigans fired bird shot into their backs as the men ran away. The migrants somehow survived, and they eventually testified against the Hanigan family. Photographic evidence submitted at the trial showed clear evidence corroborating all of the tortures that the three men had endured.

Local prosecutors charged the Hanigans with several felonies, including one against torture, but George Hanigan died of a heart attack before that first trial, and then an all-White jury acquitted his two sons of the most serious charges against them. In that trial, when prosecutors insisted that the men had violated the civil rights of their victims, the judge replied that as "illegal aliens," the Mexican victims really didn't have any "civil rights." Many people in and around Douglas, Arizona, supported this view, as well as the jury's acquittal of the two Hanigan brothers, even as a Mexican official observed that this result was almost like a license for ranchers and others to hunt Mexican migrants along the border with impunity. When the state case failed, the federal government tried the Hanigan brothers again, in the federal courts, twice. The first trial ended in a deadlock, and then the second produced only one conviction against Patrick Hanigan, who was then sentenced to three years in prison. (His brother Thomas was convicted a few months later, in a separate case, for possession with intent to distribute almost 600 pounds of marijuana; he had kept most of this on his late father's ranch.) The Hanigan cases had dragged on for many years, from 1976 to 1981, and for Mexican Americans and immigrants of Mexican descent, memories of this case from Arizona still shock for their brutality.[8]

In 1982, two White men – a father and his stepson – bludgeoned a young Chinese American man in a suburb outside of Detroit. The three men – Ronald Ebens, his stepson Michael Nitz, and Vincent Chin – encountered each other on the evening of June 19, when they were all at the Fancy Pants strip club in Highland Park, Michigan. Chin was having a bachelor party with his friends, as he was getting married on June 27. Witnesses said that Ebens started the altercation by saying to Chin and his friends, "It's because of you little motherfuckers that we're out of work!" Nitz had been laid off from an auto plant in 1979. Chin and his friends reminded the White men that they themselves were not *Japanese* auto workers, and that Chin himself was working in an automotive supply company in the area. As might be common in these altercations, the men insulted each other in colorful language. Vincent Chin, his friends, Ebens, and Nitz were all thrown out of the strip club as a result. Incensed, however, Ebens and Nitz looked for Vincent Chin's car in the surrounding areas around Highland Park – they even paid $20 to another person to help them look. When they found Vincent Chin at a McDonald's, the two men grabbed him as he was attempting to escape, and, as Nitz held him, Ebens repeatedly bludgeoned Chin with a Jackie Robinson Louisville Slugger that he kept in his trunk. Ebens hit Chin in the head multiple times. When the paramedics arrived, Chin was unconscious, his head crushed, and he died in the hospital after four days.

In several profound ways, Vincent Chin's parents and his own life reflected the changing dynamics of the United States in that era. His father was a veteran of World War II, and he had met Vincent's mother in China, when he was an American soldier and she was his "war bride." She had migrated to the United States under the War Brides Act of 1947, that version of the War Brides Act that allowed American servicemen and their Asian brides to benefit from the rule, just like women in Europe. Lily Chin had had a terrible miscarriage when she was first pregnant; she could not become pregnant again afterward. The couple decided to adopt a child, and so they chose Vincent from an orphanage in Guangdong Province in 1961, when the boy was about six years old. The Chin family was at once unique, of course, and yet familiar in these ways – the Chinese American veteran father, the mother who was a war bride, and their son, an orphan and an adoptee. The Chin family was devastated by the sudden, violent death of Vincent Chin, and yet, during the trial of Ebens and Nitz, the judge seemed to express more sympathy with the killers than with the Chin family: "These weren't the kind of men you send to jail," Judge Charles Kaufman said. Ebens and Nitz served no time in a state penitentiary. Instead, the judge sentenced them to three years of probation, he gave them a $3,000 fine, and he ordered them to pay court costs – about $800.

Asian Americans, Asian immigrants, and other many American citizens were infuriated by Kaufman's judgment, or rather his lack of judgment. Some said that the defendants may as well have tortured and killed a dog, as the penalties would have been about the same. They asked federal prosecutors to sue to uphold Vincent Chin's civil rights (he was, after all, an American citizen), and so Ebens and Nitz were tried in the federal courts, twice, just like the Hanigans, although the second federal case even made its way through the Sixth Circuit Court of Appeals. Meanwhile, Lily Chin filed a civil action for wrongful death against the two men, which she won. Nitz was ordered to pay $50,000, Ebens was to pay $1.5 million. Ms. Chin never saw this money, as neither of these men was wealthy. Ebens himself lost both his job and his family during these four separate cases, stretching from 1982 to 1987. Ebens' stepson, Michael Nitz, was no longer his stepson after the divorce.

In some ways, the case has never ended: Vincent Chin's murder became the topic of two award-winning documentaries, and, in 2015, Ebens filed a petition requesting that his house in Nevada not be seized to satisfy the civil case, whose damages had ballooned to $8 million, as Ebens had never taken seriously his debts to Ms. Chin. The judgment had been sitting there, collecting interest. As of this writing, Ebens and Nitz are both free men, which might cause some people to wonder, even now, whether Vincent Chin received any justice at all.[9]

The Hanigan men, Ronald Ebens, and Michael Nitz – they too were familiar figures in American history – if, by "familiar," we mean the long list of White men who didn't suffer serious criminal penalties for harming and murdering men and women of color. There were turns, though, in these cases: by filing charges against the perpetrators, even after the state prosecutions had failed, federal prosecutors continued a legal strategy that they'd developed in the 1950s and 1960s during the Civil Rights Movement. They would use a wide range of new and existing federal civil rights statutes in attempts to punish defendants for violating federal laws and federal constitutional norms, when local juries and judges were unwilling or unable to empathize with the victims of senseless, racist acts of violence.

Many conservative commentators and scholars decried this development – federal authorities, they said, were interfering with routine criminal cases that had always been the province of local courts and local juries. The federal government was over-reaching, they claimed, and national civil rights groups, legal advocacy organizations, and other activists were turning federal prosecutors into politically motivated actors looking for "racist" causes and victims. The federal government was humiliating the locals. David Duke, the prominent Klansman from Louisiana, sympathized with the Hanigans and their supporters in Douglas, Arizona, and so he sent his fellow Klansmen to patrol the nearby border areas and to protest the federal prosecutions.[10]

But, during this period, yet another case illustrated the movement away from some of the more egregious forms of White supremacy that were so familiar in American history. The dispute arose over, of all things, shrimp: in the late 1970s, Vietnamese refugees who'd fled their homeland settled along the Gulf Coast, from Florida through Texas. Around Galveston, Texas, so many Vietnamese fishermen had gathered their shrimping boats in a specific area that the locals took to calling it "Saigon Harbor." In the early months of 1981, Vietnamese fishermen lost two boats to suspicious cases of arson. In the nearby towns of Seabrook and Kemah, other Vietnamese fishermen found crosses burning on their front lawns. Eugene Fisher was himself a shrimp fisherman, and he also happened to be a Vietnam veteran who didn't take kindly to the influx of Vietnamese fishermen. Fisher called his friends in the Ku Klux Klan, including Louis Beam, the Grand Dragon of the KKK in Texas, who was also a veteran of the Vietnam War. Fisher and Beam organized rallies together, burning more crosses and calling for the expulsion of the Vietnamese fishermen. "On March 15, a shrimp boat carrying robed, hooded and armed Klansmen startled Sunday afternoon diners as it moved past the windows of a waterfront restaurant, patrolling the harbor."[11] Witnesses claimed that they'd heard the Klansmen aboard the boat threatening Nguyen Van Nam, a man who'd been a colonel in the South Vietnamese Army. Once outside the harbor, a pair of Klansmen fired a small cannon that had been brought aboard the ship while another hacked an effigy, dressed in Asian clothes, from the bow. Within weeks, the Seabrook City Council condemned the Klan, calling them "merchants of hate" and demanding that they leave.

Mr. Nguyen and his fellow Vietnamese fishermen sued the Klan shortly after their "boat ride," and they drew allies from the Southern Poverty Law Center in Birmingham, Alabama, an organization with a long history of fighting against White supremacist groups like the Klan. Amazed that he and their Klan friends had been sued, another Klansman, David Collins, accused the Vietnamese fishermen of being communists, and he said that the Vietnamese were the ones who'd been determined to undermine "American fishermen" all along. Collins, Beam, and Fisher said that they would collaborate with the KKK's paramilitary wing, which called itself the Texas Emergency Reserve, to train American fishermen to defend themselves from these communist Vietnamese. One could have reminded Mr. Collins that, had he actually been a communist, Mr. Nguyen would not have been living in Galveston in 1981.

Nguyen and his fellow plaintiffs did not prevail in their first federal lawsuit against the Klan in 1981, but in the second cause of action, the federal judge ordered Beam and the Klan to desist from paramilitary training, and to refrain from any further intimidation or threat against the Vietnamese fishermen. Moreover, Judge McDonald ordered members of the Klan to pay the Vietnamese fishermen for court costs and lawyers' fees – the final orders suggested that the Klan would continue to pay for violating the terms of the judgment. This case drew widespread attention throughout the United States, and it did suggest an important change in the American criminal justice system: for decades in the late nineteenth and early twentieth centuries, White supremacists *were* the government, they *were* police officers, judges, and prosecutors. And so it was quite something that a federal judge was now protecting shrimp fishermen from Vietnam, and that he had also sent a very large bill to the Ku Klux Klan, and to all of their hooded and unhooded members, for engaging in hateful and intimidating forms of speech.[12]

We note that, by 1985, as race-based violence appeared often in sensational cases such as these, over 40 state legislatures had approved various kinds of "sentencing enhancement" statutes. These rules allowed prosecutors to introduce evidence of racial motive, so that, if the defendant was found guilty of assault or battery or murder, jurors and judges could consider *additional* penalties against such persons if the perpetrators had been motivated by hate or prejudice. In a clear majority of states, legislators were horrified by the accounts of racist violence and threats of violence coming from places like Douglas or Detroit or Galveston, and they were allowing local prosecutors to talk openly about racial motives, racial bias, and race-based crimes. Legal scholars and advocates coined novel phrases to describe such crimes – they were "hate crimes" – and the advocates for legislation against hate crimes said that such acts were worse than simple assault, or battery, or murder. Because hate crimes tore apart civil society, because they reflected a history when some Americans had harmed other Americans with impunity, these rules were necessary, they said, as if the rules could serve collectively as a modest antidote to the decades of unprosecuted racist violence. For their proponents, hate crimes statutes allowed public officials to express an additional level of revulsion for violence motivated by hate.[13] By 1985, in at least 30 states, the legislatures had also approved new rules allowing for civil actions on behalf of victims of racially motivated crimes and torts – in most state jurisdictions, members of White supremacist organizations had to be prepared to pay money damages for intimidating and harming people of color. Since then, civil lawsuits like the ones filed by the Vietnamese fishermen have become more common. Prosecutors and attorneys, moreover, have used these rules in many criminal and civil cases in which the victims were White and the perpetrators were people of color.[14]

At the federal level, Representative John Conyers of Michigan had pushed for a range of new rules designed to give federal prosecutors the same kind of authority. In 1990, for example, Conyers sponsored in Congress the Hate Crimes Statistics Act, a rule that directed the Department of Justice, through the Federal Bureau of Investigation, to keep track of crimes which "manifest prejudice based on race, religion, sexual orientation, or ethnicity." Over time, Congress has expanded the Act to include crimes that were motivated by bias against persons with disabilities (in 1994), or against a victim's "actual or perceived gender, sexual orientation, or gender identity" (in 2009). Moreover, after the Hate Crimes Sentencing Enhancement Act of 1994, sponsored by Representative Chuck Schumer of New York, federal prosecutors could also ask for enhanced penalties for defendants charged with violating a person's civil rights, again in a way similar to sentencing enhancement statutes in the various states. All of these rules suggested that the state and federal governments were less tolerant of overt, violent forms of White supremacy.[15]

And yet, still, violent crimes against immigrants, and then between American citizens of different races, continued to be a recurring problem. In the months after September 11, 2001, after terrorists had caused havoc and mass death, dozens of American citizens targeted persons of Middle Eastern descent, as well as any person who simply appeared to be. Within one week of the terrorist attacks, two young men threw a Molotov cocktail at a convenience store owned by Arab Americans in Somerset, California; another man threatened to bomb a store in Chicago; and still another man set fire to a restaurant in Salt Lake City. On the 15th, a Sikh American man was shot to death outside a gas station in Mesa, Arizona. The gunman in that case continued to drive around and to target anyone who looked "Arab." These kinds of attacks rolled through the end of 2001 and over the next few years. Indeed, in this age of terrorism, whenever Americans have experienced subsequent, smaller-scale, and still horrifying attacks – at Fort Hood in 2009, in San Bernardino in 2015, or in Orlando in 2016 – Arab Americans have had to brace themselves for acts of "revenge." Disturbed and unbalanced people had attacked Americans, any Americans, but then disturbed and unbalanced White men often reacted to these terrorist attacks by harming people who had nothing to do with them.[16]

Knowing of this pattern, Arab Americans sometimes felt the need to announce, in public, that they were not terrorists, and that they, as a community, did not condone acts of terror. But that they did these things every time such instances occurred – that tended to underscore their vulnerability in a nation where others were suspicious of them all. We should note, though, that when troubled White men shot up the local schools or killed innocent people in church, White political and religious leaders never engaged in the same sort of apologizing for White people as a whole. Nor were they pressed to tell all of us, including the people of color harmed by White supremacists or by the mentally deranged, that not all White people were like those domestic terrorists or those other unbalanced murderers who just happened to be White.

Managing Culture and Difference

After 1965, as the nation grew multiracial, and even as the residents of different backgrounds could grow wary and cautious of one another, crimes *within* immigrant communities could also appear shocking. In 1985, for example, a Laotian immigrant man kidnapped a Laotian immigrant woman near Fresno, California, and he drove her to a remote cabin in the Sierra foothills. According to the criminal complaint that she filed against Kong Muoa, he had kidnapped her, then sexually assaulted her, and after a number of days like this, he took her back to her family and announced that they were married. His defense attorneys insisted that their client had no intent to kidnap, falsely imprison, or sexually assault – their client had been performing a ritual not uncommon in the highlands of Laos, where "marriage by capture" involved, in part, the bride's *pretended* unwillingness to engage in the ritual itself, so that she could show her devotion to her own family. Kong Muoa said that he had not expected the young woman to go to the police.

That same year, in Los Angeles, a younger immigrant Japanese mother was spotted near the Santa Monica Pier, walking into the sea with her two small children. Fumiko Kimura's children drowned; she did not. The District Attorney in Los Angeles filed charges for double homicide against her, but her attorneys insisted that she herself had intended to die, for she was despondent that her husband had been unfaithful to her, and that, to restore her honor and to bring shame upon her husband, she was committing a ritual murder-suicide. Her attorneys intimated that, in such circumstances, if the case had happened in Japan, she would likely not be facing any criminal charges. A year later, in Montgomery, Alabama, another defendant claimed that he was performing a similar kind of ritual murder-suicide when he discovered that his wife was cheating on him. Quang Bui had called his wife just before he had murdered his own children, dressing them in nice clothes before slitting their throats. His wife called and sent paramedics to the house, but by then, the children were gone, and Mr. Bui was bleeding from a self-inflicted wound on his neck. He survived. Again, in this criminal case, Mr. Bui's attorneys suggested that his actions would not be prosecuted as triple capital murder in his native Vietnam, where murder-suicides to restore one's honor and "face" were not treated like other crimes.

In 1987, a trial court in New York ruled in yet another case that Dong Lu Chen, who had killed his wife with a hammer, should not be guilty of first-degree murder. His actions were like a "crime of passion," his attorneys said, and he would not be prosecuted in his native China for first-degree murder in these circumstances. His lawyers insisted that the court should consider his "cultural background" as an immigrant, thus unaware of criminal norms in the United States. The court agreed, and the judge said that he was guilty of second-degree manslaughter, and he sentenced Mr. Chen to five years of probation.[17]

Many dozens of critics and scholars were upset by these claims, in New York and elsewhere, and subsequent works formed detailed, extensive criticisms of what was commonly called "the cultural defense." Leading scholars came to describe and to analyze cases where defendants – and sometimes entire immigrant communities – referenced their cultural backgrounds to limit criminal liability, or to defend themselves against claims that they were committing crimes here. Members of immigrant communities often said that these same acts were not criminal, or even uncommon, in their home countries. Again, there were numerous examples: in the 1970s and 1980s, the Los Angeles Unified School District had noted that more than a few children of Korean immigrants reported that their parents had "physically abused them," especially around the time that the schools sent report cards home. When school officials asked a number of parents whether they had, in fact, hit their children for getting bad grades, a few said that they had, because they loved their children and wanted them to do better, just like many other parents would have done and continued to do in Korea.[18]

In the late 1990s, a South Asian landlord in Berkeley, California, was accused of having "bought" young girls from his native village in Velvadam, India, bringing them to the United States, and then "using" them as servants or workers in his businesses and in his home. In the federal case against Lakireddy Bali Reddy, his attorneys suggested that "buying" people, which involved paying the parents for the right to take their children, was not uncommon in that portion of India. Prosecutors replied that slavery was unlawful anywhere in the United States under the 13th Amendment.[19] Other instances and cases have illustrated the same trend. After 2000, prosecutors in several states requested new rules to ban female genital mutilation, or to stop marriages among people who were minors, or to require standard medical treatments for minors, instead of religious rituals or other "unproven remedies" to address epilepsy or mental illness among the children of immigrants. State legislators have revised criminal codes accordingly, and they indicated in public debates that these reforms were necessary in light of the actions and "rituals" brought into the United States by its recent immigrants and refugees.[20]

Feminist scholars and children's advocates also noted a disturbing pattern in many of these cases: the victims were almost all children and women; the perpetrators were more often men; and the courts did not seem to investigate very closely whether these claims about culture were accurate, or whether they should decrease criminal liability at all, even if they were accurate. Immigrants were left victims, as though the courts often left them unprotected only because they were from weird or strange foreign cultures. Critics noted that if Kong Muoa, for example, had taken a White girl into the Sierra foothills over many days, he would have been sent to prison for a long, long time, and the judge and the prosecutor would probably have been far less sympathetic to his claims that he was "marrying" the White woman. Feminist scholars tended to be from the left of the political spectrum, but they shared an anxiety about cases like these with people on the far right.

For right-wing nationalists, a few of whom were still White supremacists, the very strange behavior of these exotic immigrants was the best argument for excluding them in the future. They just weren't acting like Americans, and whenever they did these odd or weird things, they should be punished to the full extent of American law, for they were, in fact, in America. One didn't necessarily have to be a White supremacist to have this position: the prosecutors in the case from Montgomery, Alabama, showed the jury graphic photos of what Quang Bui had done to his own children, in their house, in their bedrooms. Photos of the house itself were familiar, like many other houses in Montgomery, and yet inside, there was blood everywhere, the police officers said, pointing to the photos, and they couldn't stop thinking about the horrible things that Mr. Bui had done. At the end of his trial, the judge and the jury couldn't stop thinking about them either, and they thus sentenced Mr. Bui to die. The case suggested that the cultural defense did not, and should not, always "work."[21]

In many other cases, though, feminist scholars and other advocates had also claimed that the punishments were way too lenient for people referencing a "cultural defense." The young man in Fresno, accused of kidnapping, false imprisonment, and sexual assault, against the woman whom he'd claimed to have made his "wife," served only 120 days in prison, and he was ordered to pay the woman's family $1,000. Fumiko Kimura got one year in prison, plus five years on probation, for having drowned her two children. Dong Lu Chen's lenient sentence for killing his wife with a hammer so upset so many people that legislatures in New York, Michigan, and California referenced his case for tougher, mandatory penalties in cases of domestic violence.

Yet, since the late 1990s, defense attorneys have still presented the cultural backgrounds of their clients, and prosecutors have still responded to these defenses. They have remained major questions in law and society scholarship and in the social sciences generally, and there was no consensus across the country about whether "cultural background" should or should not be admissible. On the one hand, it was unavoidable – within our justice system, criminal liability depended upon "mens rea," the state of mind of the perpetrator, and so if there was evidence that a defendant was acting in reference to a cultural practice or ritual, this may be an important fact for the jury or judge to hear. It spoke directly to his state of mind. However, men killing their wives with hammers, or mothers and aunts cutting the genitals of their daughters – these struck many Americans as barbaric under any circumstances, blowing past any arguments for cultural tolerance.[22]

What was intolerable? In cases that were not domestic or intimate, where the "victims" weren't even people, cultural diversity and tolerance were not easy, nor was it obvious that all Americans should embrace every practice. In Arizona and Missouri, some Mexican immigrants kept 40 or 50 chickens for cockfighting contests, this being somewhat common in portions of Mexico. In 1989, a pair of Cambodian immigrant men in Long Beach were accused of eating a dog. A neighbor had heard strange sounds, and then she smelled cooking. In the 1990s, animal rights activists in San Francisco objected to the turtles, frogs, snakes, and other exotic animals on sale in Chinatown's meat markets, where patrons could point to the frog that they'd wanted, and then a helpful butcher would skin the thing alive and put that bleeding, twitching creature in a plastic bag. Fishmongers shoved chopsticks into live fish, twisted, and then pulled out the guts, before wrapping them in Chinese-language newspapers. San Francisco residents took pride in being some of the most progressive, open-minded people on the planet, and yet watching a live turtle carved from its shell (they can't just pop out, like in some cartoons) can be jarring. People in Chinatown said that the hippies and animal lovers were just squeamish, and hypocritical, too: Americans preferred their meat wrapped in plastic, the killing and the agony having been done elsewhere. They should let the Chinese experience their meat however they wanted. But by 2015, cockfighting was illegal in Arizona and in Missouri. California had banned dog meat. And San Francisco ordinances regulated live animal markets, so that none of the butchering was to be done in plain view of customers or children.[23]

Moved By War, Moving Into Civil Unrest

Some disputes were not subject to regulation, nor were they easy to control at all. After 1965, the participants in and victims of urban violence in the United States came from all over the world, and to a country that has had, since the seventeenth century, every five to ten years, a major, race-based slave revolt, riot, massacre, or other mass social disturbance that claimed the lives of many people, often over several days. These spasms of violence have names: the Stono Rebellion; the Denmark Vesey Conspiracy; Nat Turner's Rebellion; and the Massacre at Wounded Knee. In the Anti-Chinese Hysteria of 1885, Asian immigrants were the objects of violence in at least five different states – White mobs killed them, drove them out, or attacked them without mercy, in spasms of violence that consumed whole towns. In the twentieth century, in Los Angeles in June 1943, police officers and members of the United States military went on a rampage against Mexican, Latino, and then Filipino men and women, in a civil disturbance widely known as the Zoot Suit Riots. The rioting lasted over three weeks, and then spread to similar civil disturbances in Detroit, Philadelphia, and New York, and in smaller cities and towns in California, Arizona, and Texas.[24]

As many scholars have shown, race riots and mass civil disturbances have been a common feature of life in the United States, and they had large-scale political consequences. President Grover Cleveland said, in his first inaugural address in 1885, that "the laws should be rigidly enforced which prohibit the immigration of a servile class to compete with American labor, with no intention of acquiring citizenship, and bringing with them and retaining habits and customs repugnant to our civilization." During his presidency, in light of the on-going violence against the Chinese throughout the United States, he became a staunch exclusionist, his theory being that the very presence of the Chinese seemed to incite violence among White men. Through violence, White mobs were expressing their desire for exclusion, and thus Asian Exclusion became a standard part of American public law until 1965. It was as if White men had said, collectively, that "Asians make us violent," and so other White men, the political elites who wanted their votes, agreed to exclude all Asians for the next eight decades.[25]

In the late 1980s and early 1990s, even before the riots that would consume the city in late April 1992, many residents of Los Angeles felt racial tensions in their daily lives. Newer Latino immigrants felt unease in the city's historically African American neighborhoods. Many African Americans who'd lived in the city since World War II did not understand why or how so many Latinos came to settle in their neighborhoods so quickly. Korean immigrants had moved into the Mid-Wilshire District west of downtown, too, making the place a "Koreatown," to the surprise of many Latinos and African Americans. Korean immigrants purchased liquor stores and smaller convenience stores in South Central Los Angeles, where the departure of mainstream retailers and supermarkets after the Watts riots had left a kind of "retail service vacuum" in that area of the city.[26]

Other economic developments were not promising: defense contractors and manufacturers were closing or moving from Los Angeles, as part of a process that the economists and social scientists had termed "deindustrialization." Companies that had offered manufacturing jobs were closing their factories, and many of them moved abroad. This left fewer families with steady incomes and jobs, while at the same time creating large pockets of poverty along a major corridor connecting downtown Los Angeles with its major ports in Long Beach and San Pedro. South Central, Watts, Inglewood – these areas were suffering economically in the late 1970s. Residents had to pay more for basic necessities, and other public services were deteriorating. According to the sociologists, the people left behind were now members of an "underclass," a concentrated group of poorer residents who could not afford to leave for the affluent suburbs, and so they were stuck in neighborhoods that were falling apart – no jobs, no services.[27]

Mexican and Central American residents were moving into these areas during this same period, because housing near downtown Los Angeles was relatively inexpensive, and because these migrants were fleeing conditions in their home countries that were far worse. Many Mexican migrants had settled in East Los Angeles, but migrants from Mexico, El Salvador, Honduras, Nicaragua, and Guatemala were also settling in areas just west of downtown, in the Pico-Union area, making this neighborhood one of the most densely populated places in Los Angeles. Pico-Union was just south of Koreatown. The residents there were very poor, households were often sharing smaller apartments, and more than a few of the recent migrants were still suffering the lingering effects of having to flee for their lives.

In the late 1970s and early 1980s, El Salvador, Honduras, Nicaragua, and Guatemala were all embroiled in horrifying civil wars between landlords and peasants, between people who had held large tracts of land and the people who had worked that land. In the 1970s, the landlords hired death squads, recruiting young men from among poorer peasant families, and they also supported political leaders who accused the peasants and their organizations of being communists. By then, many peasant organizations had taken weapons and support from countries like Cuba, which was in fact run by a communist government after 1959. Fidel Castro gave moral and material support to the revolutionaries in Central America, funneling guns and aid that he had acquired from the Soviet Union. In response, the United States took the side of the established governments in Central America, which were allied with the major landlords of places like El Salvador and Guatemala. The United States armed them, they armed death squads, and they thus contributed to seasons of misery and death throughout the region.[28]

The Salvadorans and Guatemalans who had arrived in Los Angeles in the first half of the 1980s had seen things that were haunting. They had seen the work of death squads, as well as the American advisers and their weapons in the major cities. They saw these "advisers" directing military campaigns against the communists, and then they saw the communist guerillas themselves, who targeted people that they suspected of supporting the other side. For over a decade, many Central Americans had walked or had taken trains *through* Mexico to escape the terror, and even though gunfire also punctuated life in urban Los Angeles, Pico-Union seemed generally safer to them than Guatemala City or San Salvador.

Adjusting to Los Angeles could be very difficult, however: the Reagan Administration had declared Central Americans "economic migrants," and because many of them had crossed the Southern border without inspection, many of them had no legal status. The American government refused to acknowledge that these persons were refugees. They were fleeing anti-communist, right-wing governments that President Reagan had chosen to support. And so, Central American migrants lived and worked in the shadows of the American economy, in places like Los Angeles, during a period when that economy was already shrinking. In addition, many Central Americans complained that some of their Mexican neighbors were hostile to them, and that the Mexican American children often threatened the Central American kids in the schools and in the neighborhoods. By the end of the 1980s, the Los Angeles Police Department had formed a separate unit to monitor Central American gangs, the Maras, these groups of young men who were challenging African American and Mexican American gangs for the drug trade and for other nefarious activities. One can hardly imagine the heartbreak of many Central American fathers and mothers, these people who had traveled such vast distances to save their children, only to lose them again in Los Angeles.[29]

By the middle of the 1980s, Korean American shopkeepers were common in many areas of the United States, as fruit and vegetable vendors in New York, as small shopkeepers in Chicago, or as liquor and convenience store entrepreneurs in Los Angeles. Their stores were in those very neighborhoods where many thousands of Central Americans were settling. Some Americans theorized that these Koreans were just entrepreneurial, as though they were naturally prone to dry cleaners and liquor stores. Nothing, however, in classical Confucian philosophy, recommended Koreans for dry cleaning or gas stations in dangerous urban environments. A more obvious explanation for this pattern of entrepreneurship was economic, not cultural. Many Koreans had faced "downward mobility": although over half of all Korean immigrant shopkeepers had had college degrees from Korea, they were unable to find professional jobs in the United States that reflected their level of education. This was because American employers didn't know what to make of a Korean college degree, and also because the immigrants themselves had trouble with licensing and certification requirements in their chosen professions. Graduates of Korean medical schools might open medical supply shops when they couldn't get Board certification to practice as doctors, for example, and college graduates in the liberal arts and in the social sciences were often the ones who'd opened the delis, the liquor stores, the gas stations, and the dry cleaners, when the only other options were menial and paid poorly.[30]

Unable to use their college education, and unwilling to toil forever in low-wage jobs, Korean immigrants were trying to recover, through entrepreneurship, at least an income that would propel them into the American middle class. Again, in Korea, shopkeepers had occupied a very low social status before the twentieth century – there was nothing especially honorable about a Korean shopkeeper in traditional Korean society, and yet there were so many Korean shopkeepers in

Los Angeles by the 1980s that they made their way into American art and film. In 1989, Spike Lee featured a Korean American shop-keeping family in a neighborhood in Brooklyn in his film *Do the Right Thing*, which contained within it a larger story of how that neighborhood tore itself apart. In retrospect, that film was like a foretelling, although in the film, the Korean Americans were spared. This proved less true in real life.

In the mid-1980s, small businesses could be especially lethal for Korean immigrant entrepreneurs. In 1984, just in one month, four Korean immigrant shopkeepers had been shot dead during armed robberies and burglaries in Los Angeles. According to the shopkeepers, the perpetrators were predominantly Latino and African Americans. It didn't help that in New York and in Chicago, African American and Latino patrons had accused Korean shopkeepers of being racist and disrespectful, of charging too much for basic necessities, and of following them around the store, as if all of them were potential shop-lifters. Some Korean Americans admitted that there was some truth in these complaints, and that a few Korean shopkeepers behaved in these racist ways, but they also pointed out that the heated rhetoric was likely to make more of them into targets of wanton killing. Beyond all the talk, at times, the relationships between African Americans, Latinos, and Korean Americans seemed inflected with nothing but violence.[31]

In 1989, a man named Rodney King had used an iron bar to club a Korean immigrant shopkeeper in Monterey Park, California. He took about $200, but then he was caught and sentenced to prison. In 1990, Mr. Billy Du, the Korean immigrant owner of the Empire Liquor Store in Los Angeles, had chased away a young Black man who'd ducked into his store during a drive-by shooting. That young man was subsequently murdered that very evening. And on the evening of March 3, 1991, the same Rodney King was himself nearly beaten to death on the freeway in the San Fernando Valley. A bystander caught on videotape the four police officers bludgeoning Mr. King over several agonizing minutes. Rodney King had been driving a Hyundai; one of the officers who'd beaten him was Latino. Robbery, violence, murder, police brutality – all of this was a depressing part of life for many residents in Los Angeles.

Still, some acts of violence were utterly shocking even in a city growing accustomed to shocking and senseless. On the morning of March 16, 1991, Soon Ja Du, Mr. Billy Du's wife, killed Latasha Harlins, a 15-year-old student. Miss Harlins had gone to the Empire Liquor Store before school. She had picked up a bottle of orange juice, $1.79, and she had put this in her backpack. Ms. Du suspected that the young woman was shop-lifting. The two got into a physical altercation, the 41-year-old grabbing the teenager, the teenager then spinning around and punching the older woman in the face. As Miss Harlins was leaving the store, Ms. Du shot Latasha Harlins in the back of the head with a .38 caliber pistol. The police arrived shortly after. They pronounced Miss Harlins dead at the scene, and they also noted that she had been holding two one-dollar bills in her hand when she had been shot dead.

The District Attorney filed criminal charges against Ms. Du. In the terrible 1980s and 1990s, shootings at liquor stores in Los Angeles were quite common, depressingly so, and many Korean shopkeepers were robbed at gun-point, and pistol-whipped and terrified, and shop-lifting was a constant problem. In Korea, military service was mandatory for all young men – they used American guns and machine guns as a standard part of their military training in the South Korean Army, and so was it surprising that so many Korean shopkeepers kept guns, shotguns, and automatic weapons in their stores? But even in these seasons of violence, even in Los Angeles, where some people may not have paid attention to yet another shooting at a nondescript liquor store, Latasha Harlins' death was different. This case was explosive.

Professor Brenda Stevenson had taught in the Department of History at UCLA, and her academic work had been primarily in African American history, especially the history of African American families during slavery. She had also written about African American folklore and story-telling traditions in the eighteenth and nineteenth centuries, and yet like many people who remember those years in Los Angeles, she became so preoccupied with the Latasha Harlins case that she just could not turn away from it. She found herself researching its history – its prehistory – and, two decades later, she published a book about the case that was haunting in its tragic dimensions. Stevenson focused on three women – Latasha Harlins, Soon Ja Du, and then Joyce Karlins, the judge assigned to the criminal case against Ms. Du.[32]

Stevenson described the broader social forces, especially the race and class dimensions, that brought all three women to Los Angeles, and then she gave a detailed account of the trial itself. There, Ms. Du's defense attorneys portrayed her Korean American family as hard-working, pushing toward their American dream, and yet they were besieged, their liquor store surrounded by people and gangs wielding guns and threatening each member. This was why they kept guns at the store, why they were planning to sell the store altogether and move away. The lawyers suggested that Latasha Harlins herself resembled the family's tormentors: Miss Harlins had assaulted Ms. Du; Miss Harlins was tall for her age; and "[she] was possibly as tough as any guy at the same age." The attorneys admitted that Ms. Du's family not only kept the gun near the cash register, but that they had modified the trigger, so that it would fire with little pressure. Ms. Du, they said, meant to scare Miss Harlins, and she did not intend to kill her.

In front of the jury, however, the prosecutors insisted that Ms. Du's actions were reckless, negligent, and without regard for Miss Harlins' life. The prosecutors clearly won their argument in front of the jury: in October 1991, the jury returned a guilty verdict against Ms. Du for voluntary manslaughter, a felony, and they also found that using a gun in the commission of this crime made the killing worse. Pulling a .38 caliber pistol, shooting a young woman dead as she was *leaving* the store – this was an excessive, unreasonable use of force. The jury returned this verdict knowing that the maximum sentence for a defendant under these conditions was 16 years in state prison. Indeed, after the sentencing hearing one month later, the jury recommended precisely this penalty. And yet Judge Karlins set it aside: Ms. Du's "over-reaction" was "understandable." The judge said that Latasha Harlins had been the aggressor during that morning, that Ms. Du had behaved as a normal person would under the circumstances, and that Ms. Du should not serve any time in prison. "Joyce Karlins ordered that Soon Ja Du receive a suspended ten-year term in the state penitentiary; five years' probation; 400 hours of community service; a $500 fine; and the cost of Latasha Harlins' funeral and medical expenses."[33]

Many thousands of people in Los Angeles and elsewhere were shocked by this lenient sentence – community activists sought the removal of Judge Karlins, and they protested outside her home in Manhattan Beach. They could not quite believe what she had said as she was sentencing Ms. Du. They said that this case and her remarks represented yet another instance where the criminal justice system punished no one for the murder of an African American child. The case had an afterlife in art and in music: Tupac Shakur referenced Latasha Harlins several times in his songs. Ice Cube alluded to merchants like Ms. Du as "Oriental one penny countin' motherfuckers." "Juice with the people," said Ice Cube, "pay respect to the black fist or we'll burn your store right down to a crisp." We did not know whether Judge Karlins regretted her decision to set aside the jury's verdict or its sentence, and yet other people in Los Angeles seemed not to mind or to know of her role in a case that many African Americans saw, in art and in music, over and over again, as yet another example of gross injustice. Judge Karlins retired from the bench, she ran for the city council in Manhattan Beach, and she served as its Mayor.[34]

In the end, the Empire Liquor Store did burn down, along with hundreds of other liquor stores and businesses in South Central Los Angeles. This store was consumed two days after another jury in Simi Valley, California, a suburb of Los Angeles, acquitted the four police officers who'd been charged with beating Rodney King. Although other neighborhoods in Atlanta, Chicago, and New York experienced civil disturbances and collective protests after the King verdict, Los Angeles was on fire for about ten days. The Los Angeles Fire Department was overwhelmed by the 7,000 separate fires reported in the city. Over ten days, about 50 people were killed throughout the city, and many others were beaten almost to death. Korean merchants perched themselves on top of their stores, armed with rifles and automatic weapons, and a few were recorded on CNN running down the street, firing their pistols. Entire families looted stores – a dad running with a television, mom with a radio, the children with smaller electronics still in their boxes. President George H. W. Bush deployed troops into the city to handle the chaos, but before there was any semblance of order, about a billion dollars in property had gone up in flames, over 6,500 people had been arrested, and Los Angeles from the air looked like a giant bowl of smog, fire, and ash. Since May 1992, scholars and commentators have struggled with what to call the events following the Rodney King verdicts on April 29, 1992 – an uprising, a race riot, a civil disturbance, or a rebellion. Over two decades later, there was still no consensus.[35]

We did know, though, that this event was unusual in American history in its scale and variety. The race-based patterns from the riots were so obvious. A majority of the people arrested were Latino, and many of them were out of status or undocumented. A majority of the property damage fell upon Korean immigrant and Korean American merchants, many of whom also discovered that their insurance policies would be useless. And African Americans participated in the looting and in the burning, too, but not always in mindless ways. Someone had posted a sign on the burned wreckage of the Empire Liquor Store, for example, one of the first places to be firebombed: "Closed for Murder and the General Disrespect for Black People." As residents and public officials all took stock of what had happened in Los Angeles, they accused one another of causing the riots, of making things worse, of failing to see what was obvious, like the videotape of those four police officers, beating Rodney King. Prominent African American politicians, including Maxine Waters, suggested that Korean merchants not rebuild their stores in South Central, especially not the ones selling liquor. Emergent Korean American politicians, including Jay Kim, proposed deporting all "Mexicans." Governor Pete Wilson of California also identified the failure of the federal government to control immigration as one of the primary reasons why things had gotten so out of hand in Los Angeles.[36]

In 1994 and 1996, immigration rules and the criminal justice system would take a harsher turn, both in the state of California and then throughout the United States. Politicians promised an end to "lawlessness": in the wake of these developments, many wondered whether a multiracial city, or a multiracial country, could survive, and whether racial and ethnic diversity were strengths rather than a set of fissures ready to break apart region and country. For ten days, a major American city – one of the most diverse places in the Northern Hemisphere – had exploded. From the smoldering ruins, one could wonder how any state or government could manage the aftermath. Many scholars and citizens alike wondered whether such a place was, by its very nature, ungovernable.

Immigration, crime, lawlessness – these themes have remained an integral part of the national dialogue in the United States and all over the world over the past 40 years. Many millions of people have been on the move, as societies collapsed in civil strife, and as inequalities between states persisted and perhaps even grew worse. In national political campaigns, leading candidates in Europe, Asia, and the United States have often rejected race-based diversity, immigration, or both, in terms that were both novel and familiar. In 2016, the Republican candidate for President of the United States complained about immigration from Mexico (that was somewhat familiar), but he also referred to Mexican immigrants as "rapists," and he proposed building a "big, beautiful wall" across the Southern border (the characterization and the proposal were both quite novel). He did not win the popular vote, but he did win the Presidency, and in his first address to Congress, Donald Trump challenged those who opposed his harsh immigration rhetoric. He asked them to consider the American victims of immigrants: "What would you say to the American family that loses their jobs, their income, or their loved ones because America refused to uphold its laws and defend its borders?" Later in the same speech, he announced that he had directed the Department of Homeland Security to create a new office to keep track of the "American victims" of immigrants, because "[they] have been ignored by our media and silenced by our special interests."[37]

Throughout the campaign and after this speech, leading scholars of immigration law and policy had replied with a number of facts. According to the Federal Bureau of Investigation, for example, immigrants were more likely to be the victims of crime than to be its perpetrators. The victims of immigrants also tended to be other immigrants. Mexicans in general were not rapists. Moreover, according to the Border Patrol, a great many unlawful immigrants flew over the Southern border rather than crossing by land. And yet here he was, the President of the United States, touching raw nerves about immigration, crime, and lawlessness, and then casting the Americans as the primary victims of these outsiders. In immigration, as well as in other areas of law and policy, he seemed "fact-resistant," and none of this seemed an impediment to winning the Presidency. A few months after the election, when neo-Nazis, Klansmen, and White supremacists marched in Charlottesville, Virginia, the President denounced them, but then he suggested that "very fine people" could nevertheless march among neo-Nazis, Klansmen, and White supremacists to protect "their history" and "their culture." His comments left many to wonder whether the United States government would continue to condemn hate crimes and White supremacists unequivocally, as it mostly had after 1965, or whether that government would be more sympathetic now to those Americans who loved and cherished things like confederate monuments.[38] Even a few of his own supporters winced when the President described these objects as "beautiful," when he lamented their removal. Among Republicans overall, though, his approval ratings did not drop after such episodes.

Ungovernable indeed.

5

COMMON WEALTH

The word "commonwealth" combines two obvious roots, and, through those roots, we envision a community in which people share resources with one another. By definition, a commonwealth implies cooperation: the farmer grows food for himself, but he shares the surplus with someone who raises livestock, or another who makes shoes. Through such exchanges, the farmer also enjoys meat and he wears shoes, too, even though he may have no obvious talent or skill for herding or for shoe-making. All of his fellow citizens benefit also from these mutual forms of exchange. They literally share their skills and talents, so that their efforts form a kind of "common wealth." In addition, in a commonwealth, not all relationships involve simple economic transactions: when a person becomes ill, when someone can no longer work, when another suffers an accident, members of a commonwealth can tend to the sick or to the injured, as well as those fellow members who are temporarily or permanently disabled. Everyone is subject to bouts of poverty, and misfortune – suffering, as the Buddhists say, is but an integral, inescapable part of life, and so belonging to a group of others helps all to bear misfortunes together. Crime, mutual predation, rioting – these were antithetical to any functioning commonwealth.

Who belongs to the community, and how could we avoid those circumstances that make community impossible? From time immemorial, once-closed communities encountered people who were not locals, not members, and they were thus forced to ask these questions anew. The outsiders often came in different forms, across land, in smaller groups, and then sometimes in organized units, armed, sometimes on ships from across an ocean. The most dramatic moments in human history may be about those first contacts: the Persians invaded Greece, the Spanish and the Americans came upon the Chumash, and the Japanese invaded the Korean peninsula. Hundreds of thousands of commonwealths have faced a dizzying array of choices when confronted with outsiders. Should they trade and exchange for mutual benefit? Should they incorporate or welcome the stranger? Should they arm and protect themselves? Should they build a wall? Should they expel the invaders? Would it even be possible to resist the foreigners, if you were, say, the Chumash in nineteenth-century California? The newcomers were so numerous – perhaps also more advanced in their technologies and organization, although maybe not in their morals. Their culture and their sheer numbers were overwhelming.

Whether to resist, to incorporate, to yield – we begin with these thoughts not because they are original or somehow "new" in our political debates, but because, in some deeper and more fundamental way, they stretch back to times we can only imagine now, even as they reappear before us today. These days, many people felt as if their countries had been *invaded*, and not by force, but by immigration. Their feelings of being over-run are recurring themes in politics – they *are* politics, and they bring out the best and worst in people. "Host" is a contronym, a word with two opposite meanings – a host receives guests in a pleasant way, and yet a host can also mean a multitude, perhaps an overwhelming group of others, sometimes armed "hostiles," which is that classic synonym for "enemy." The two meanings of "host" capture the opposite feelings that can follow when we see the outsiders come upon our commonwealths. Shall we be open, or should we defend ourselves? In this context, and against this reality, European artists and scholars sometimes portrayed their commonwealths as leviathans, as gigantic entities organized to confront the Other from a position of strength, often with a sword held in one massive hand, its head the head of the King, the head of state.[1]

The Strains of Commitment

In the modern age, care for the other members of the commonwealth began in the wake of war. Members of every commonwealth have celebrated and revered the people who've sacrificed their lives for the sake of their country, the people who'd carried swords and then fallen in battle. In the United States, for example, when thousands and then millions of people died in the American Civil War, charitable organizations were overwhelmed by the needs of the survivors, the widows and orphans left destitute. As many scholars have shown, by the late nineteenth century, state and federal policy-makers responded to these popular sympathies by building a system of social welfare to tend to the needs of families who'd lost a veteran. When the head of a family had died in war, politicians and public officials felt an even greater moral obligation to assist his family, even if that meant raising taxes among all of their citizens, who were, after all, the beneficiaries of the soldiers' sacrifice. Surviving veterans were at the forefront of efforts to relieve the survivors: had a sword fallen one way instead of another, had a bullet caught me instead of the man next to me, my own family would be the one in need of relief.[2]

Into the early twentieth century, churches, civic organizations, public schools, and other major institutions in American civil society worked with, and drew support from, state agencies to tend to the needs of American veterans and their families. Families who'd lost a son, a husband, a father – they could rely on a network of charities and public offices to offer support, so that their grief would not be compounded by destitution. Philanthropies and civic organizations funded a range of institutions, from non-profit hospitals to scholarships for younger people to attend college. They institutionalized care for the less well-off, and for the benefit of large numbers of people who were considered deserving of support and care. In 1929, when the global markets collapsed, and then hundreds and thousands of people lost their jobs and experienced a humiliating, grinding poverty, President Franklin Roosevelt and other leading politicians grew the federal government to meet yet another vast population of people facing poverty. His administration expanded federal forms of social welfare and public assistance to an unprecedented extent.[3]

There were compelling reasons behind these national efforts. During the Great Depression, many thousands of people moved from one state to another in search of economic opportunities and other forms of relief. Some states responded in hostile ways. For example, legislators in California amended a section of the Welfare and Institution Code in 1933 to say that "every person, firm, or corporation or officer or agent . . . that brings or assists in bringing into the State any indigent person who is not a resident of the State, knowing him to be an indigent person, is guilty of a misdemeanor." The rule was commonly known as the "anti-Okie" law, a rule to discourage the migration of Americans fleeing the Dust Bowl states, including Oklahoma, to California during the horrible years of the Great Depression. "Okies" were impoverished people, the kind of people that we might regard as "economic refugees." State legislators had noted that California companies, including large agricultural producers, were exploiting the Okies and other economic migrants, paying them well below a living wage and thereby taking advantage of their misery. Better that they not come, the state legislators said – best that no one bring them.

But in a unanimous decision for the United States Supreme Court, Justice James Byrnes of South Carolina, a former Secretary of State, said that:

> [No] single State [should] isolate itself from difficulties common to all of them by restraining the transportation of persons and property across its borders. It is frequently the case that a single State might gain a momentary respite from the pressures of events by the simple expedient of shutting its gates to the outside world. But, in the words of Mr. Justice Benjamin Cardozo: "The Constitution was framed under the dominion of a political philosophy less parochial in range. It was framed upon the theory that the people of the several States must sink or swim together, and that, in the long run, prosperity and salvation are in union, and not division."

The Supreme Court thus struck down the California rule against the transportation of "indigent persons."[4]

This important case from California had multiple dimensions, but one of the most obvious was that poorer people in the United States were moving across state boundaries to look for economic opportunities, maybe even just to survive. Many thousands were leaving, and not only by rail, but in their cars, thousands and thousands of cars, from one side of the country to another. States were blocking poorer people, who in turn would seek residency in another state, thus shifting poverty from one place to another without alleviating conditions for the poor. That is, if the California rule had been upheld, then every state would have had incentives to be the least generous, all states would race to a bottom hostile to the poor, and then the poor would become miserable indeed.

For political leaders like President Roosevelt, a nationwide economic depression required national solutions – a federal minimum wage, for example, and federal standards for health and safety in the workplace, and for food and drugs in the marketplace, and for all forms of interstate commerce. American citizens, irrespective of their state residency, should help each other. American companies should refrain from exploiting American citizens, or from hurting them with harmful products. By 1935, Roosevelt had signed the National Labor Relations Act to protect American workers who wished to form and to join labor unions – after decades of street battles and pitched fighting between workers and corporations, the federal government had recognized collective bargaining rights among workers. Under federal protection, throughout the United States, labor unions could now negotiate with companies to wrest a larger share of wealth for workers engaged in nearly all forms of production. Later that same year, Congress approved the Social Security Act, whose purpose was to create a "social safety net" – a minimum income for older Americans, and then aid for needy families with children, and unemployment insurance for those out of work. All of these provisions would be financed through income taxes paid by those who were working. People who had jobs were now paying to support a system that would provide a minimum income for when they retired. They were also paying taxes to help people who were out of work, and to support families who had no other means of support.[5]

Dozens of scholars have written about the development of social welfare policies in the United States, from those massive national efforts after the American Civil War for its veterans to the creation of the Social Security Administration. To make sense of that scholarship, we might turn to John Rawls, the late political theorist, who proposed that all members of a commonwealth often feel "the strains of commitment," those moments when caring for and tending to the needs and demands of fellow citizens might feel like a burden, a strain. In any community, citizens might experience how, when they are forced to go along with collective decisions, this can be challenging, especially when they disagree with those decisions. Moreover, if the community decides to use our resources to care for people that we ourselves don't especially care for, we can feel our commitments strained even further. Citizens may know that a person in need may not be at fault for being in need, and yet their needs might seem persistent, even overwhelming.[6]

Rawls' concept – "the strains of commitment" – has intuitive appeal for anyone who's taken care of other people, whether a spouse, a parent, a child, or anyone who may not be able to care for herself. If I struggle, for example, to tend to my own child when she is hungry or screaming her head off, imagine the strain I might feel when I'm caring for *your* child, assuming that you are unable to care for her yourself. We note that many people feel so strained by their *own* families that they leave; such persons especially may not be of a mind to care for others totally unrelated to them. For citizens who may prefer to be left alone, rules about redistribution have always been a challenge. In 1938, President Roosevelt and Congress agreed to a new federal law that required all employers to pay a minimum wage to all workers. Thousands of companies complained: they felt as though the federal government was now forcing them to pay higher wages in circumstances where many workers had been willing to work for far less.[7]

This tension helps us understand why many American citizens have never liked Social Security, labor unions, federal regulations, or taxes of any kind. They still talk about repealing these systems of "coercive redistribution," as if these systems continue to over-strain income-earning, productive people to help those in need. Many citizens may not mind if some (small) portion of their labor or their wealth is taken to benefit those in need, but if government agencies take too much – if they put too much strain upon one part to support the other – and if complex bureaucracies waste an enormous sum while engaged in redistribution, some citizens will not respond well. In their darker moments, faced with the needs of others, members of a commonwealth can sometimes ask murkier questions: Are the people in need deserving of help? Did they bring their misery upon themselves? If, say, a social program helps drug users and alcoholics, might a taxpayer be justified in feeling as though the drug users and alcoholics were unworthy of help? Moreover, if some simply wish to be unencumbered – unbothered by the needs of others, no matter how grave – should they have the right to be left alone? Should "freedom" include the freedom not to care? These moral and political questions were only partly settled in legislation during the New Deal, and they have remained unsettled ever since.[8]

In addition, legislators in the United States had long injected social welfare policies with racism – African American veterans of the Civil War received considerably less support than their White peers. During the New Deal, to draw political support from Southern legislators, President Roosevelt allowed changes in many rules that let the states address the needs of poorer White citizens, while neglecting African Americans altogether. Indeed, White majorities have never much cared for the needs of racial minorities, and public assistance programs ran in many states as though all African Americans or people of color were the "unworthy poor." Immigrants of any color were never welcomed to public assistance – in his scholarly work about the "lost century" of American immigration law before the Chinese Exclusion Act, the legal historian Gerald Neuman has pointed to numerous state and federal rules designed to discourage poorer migrants, or to demand their removal for being a "public charge." Immigrants, like people of color, were expected to support themselves, and if you were, say, Chinese *and* poor in the late nineteenth and early twentieth centuries, American citizenship wasn't going to be possible, and poverty itself could be the grounds for deportation.[9]

This topic itself remains most unsettling because, in many modern states, in the twentieth century, some governments had been the opposite of caring. They were instead brutal, murderous. In Europe, in Nazi Germany, the fascist state proposed in the 1930s that there were some people living "a life unworthy of life." German children born with disabilities, younger Germans with incurable mental and psychological problems, Germans who were chronically ill, and the very old – many prominent Nazis said that such people should be put out of their misery, so that they would not burden their families or the great German state. Nazis produced illustrated graphs showing how some people burdened the others. They even developed a vocabulary to talk about such people – they were *Untermensch*, or "subhuman," people who could not contribute to their own care, let alone to the wealth of their communities or of their state. *Untermensch* implied that some people were not fully people.[10]

The Nazis knew that, in the United States, Americans were calling such people "imbeciles," "feeble-minded," and "infirm," and several states had sterilized mentally and physically disabled people, including a disproportionate number of racial minorities. Eugenicists, people who were promoting "good genes," supported policies that encouraged "normal," healthy people to have children, while preventing the "infirm" from doing the same, under the theory that some people simply shouldn't reproduce. Their defects were in their genes. In cases like *Buck* v. *Bell*, in 1927, the distinguished justice Oliver Wendell Holmes upheld the right of state officials to sterilize a "feeble-minded" young woman. Other states continued similar policies – before the end of World War II, health officials and physicians had sterilized about 60,000 Americans in public and private hospitals.[11]

The Nazi state went further. Its officials worked with German medical professionals to develop complex ways for killing many disabled and hospitalized people at once, whether by giving overdoses of narcotics, or by using mobile gas vans. This happened in stages: staff members who gave fatal doses of narcotics killed many people, but then they were haunted by having killed so many. Administrators then turned to lower-level staff members to perform the killings: they attached hoses from the exhaust pipes of vans and trucks to the insides of their passenger compartments. Driving around for several minutes, they used these vehicles to kill dozens of people in a single day. In the 1930s, at the height of their power, German officials were learning how to kill large groups of people by killing their own citizens, and the most vulnerable among them. Jewish people, homosexuals, and communists – they were *Untermensch*, too, the Nazis said. They should be deported or killed. As we know, the Nazis *did* commit mass murder through horrifying forms of industrialized killing unprecedented in any modern state. They were so concerned with the mental health of their own, their *Übermensch*, that they designed systems in which the prisoners killed other prisoners, hundreds at a time, day after day. And still, when they were captured, the most unrepentant Nazis insisted that the victims were not really people at all, and that they did all of this killing legally, to further a greater German Reich free from human forms of pollution. It was as though, by then, they had become so accustomed to dehumanizing others that they could not recognize the extent to which they had dehumanized themselves. They seemed wholly unable to put themselves in their victims' position, or to comprehend what they had done from another point of view.[12]

Primary Goods and the Impulse Toward Exclusion

The United States military was still segregated when World War II began, and so White Americans, African Americans, and even Asian Americans, many drawn from the Japanese American internment camps, fought in segregated units. Military leaders had long argued for the necessity of segregation: they did not expect White soldiers to risk their lives for Black soldiers, and they indicated that, in most instances, Black units should not be armed, lest they turn against their White peers or officers. They said that "Negroes" should serve as cooks or aides. Yet as the war dragged on, as casualties mounted in almost every unit in Europe and in the South Pacific, mixed-race units became more common, and, to the surprise of some officers, they performed as well as any other. Pressed into horrible circumstances, soldiers of every race sacrificed and died for each other. Almost to everyone's surprise, when the war was over, the most decorated unit of the Army had been a Japanese American combat team, whose members showed a bravery and courage that moved even the most ardent White supremacists.

Harry Truman may have been a member of the Klan earlier in his life, but he made a point of inviting as many international and domestic journalists as possible when he publicly acknowledged the bravery of the 442nd in July 1946. When Truman learned that the managers of a segregated cemetery in California had refused to allow the burials of Japanese American veterans killed in war, he sent General Joseph Stilwell to take medals to the families of the deceased, and to do it in a way that would humiliate the people who'd insulted them so. Truman also authorized the State Department to take prominent people of color on "good will" tours, both with him and separately, to Asia, Africa, and South America, to answer those communist charges that the Americans were racists. President Truman issued an executive order in July 1948 to desegregate the United States Armed Forces, and, throughout his Administration, he insisted that the Department of Veterans Affairs treat all American veterans – no matter what their race or ethnicity – with respect and provide them all with equal access to its services.[13]

By 1960, all Americans knew that if a young veteran came back as an injured soldier, he could rely on federal and state forms of support. Other veterans enjoyed new benefits, too, including access to a higher education financed by the federal government. Government support for a broad range of programs benefitted veterans, but then many more people became beneficiaries, too. If a hard-working factory worker lost his job, he faced considerably less risk of losing his family or his dignity in 1960. Labor unions were bargaining collectively by 1950, so that average workers in unionized jobs were much more likely to have health insurance, retirement savings, paid vacations, and pensions. More families could afford their own homes, to pay for a college education, and to imagine a life for their children much better than the hardships many of them had known in those years before the war. People of color also participated in the economy and in society to a much greater extent than before, in civil service as well as in many other sectors. Having paid taxes, and thus contributing to public services, they were much less willing to tolerate racist policies that limited their lives or the lives of their children.[14]

Several hundred thousand people from Mexico had migrated through the Bracero Program, and then thousands of others migrated outside of the Program, too, thereby changing the demographic composition of the American

Southwest. In the postwar years, as the economy grew, the federal government would continue bringing foreign workers from Mexico and making them "available" to growers in California, Arizona, or Texas. By 1950, though, many Americans had turned against the Bracero Program, and they lobbied hard for the federal government to stop recruiting Mexican laborers. State politicians and even some prominent agricultural growers said that too many Mexican nationals had come, both legally and illegally. Mexican immigrants had committed crimes, they said, and these immigrants were straining social service agencies. As we've noted before, a few prominent Mexican Americans turned against the braceros, including Hector Garcia of Texas and Cesar Chavez of California. Garcia was a physician and civic leader in Texas, he was himself a veteran of World War II, and he was among the founders of the American GI Forum, an influential civil rights group among Mexican Americans. Cesar Chavez had served in the United States Navy, and he too was becoming one of the most influential political figures on the West Coast.

Civil rights leaders like Garcia and Chavez pressed federal officials to end the Bracero Program, or at least to control the labor migrants outside the lawful boundaries of that program. They asked the federal government to remove unlawful Mexican immigrants throughout the Southwest. In time, General Joseph Swing, the new head of the Immigration and Naturalization Service in 1954, turned to talking about the Mexican workers themselves as if they constituted a foreign "host," an overwhelming number of outsiders that threatened the quality of life for American citizens. Swing was charged with implementing Operation Wetback, a large-scale plan to remove illegal Mexican migrants from the United States. Working with state and local governments, federal agents removed over 1.3 million persons over eight years.

The very name of this operation reflected its bigoted character. Federal officials were so zealous in targeting "wetbacks" that they did not seem to care about abusing Mexican nationals or even deporting several thousand American citizens of Mexican ancestry. Operation Wetback had several consequences: the federal government would take a much more formal role in policing the Southern border, and federal officials developed new ways to exclude and to remove unauthorized migrants. These officials learned that although they could deter and remove thousands of unlawful immigrants at the Southern border, many others would bypass immigration enforcement to work and to live in the United States. Deporting someone once didn't always work. Some Border Patrol agents took to shaving the heads of people who'd been deported once, while others took fingerprints and photographs. Many agents abused the migrants, or "punished" them by releasing them into remote areas so that the migrants would suffer.[15]

From a longer perspective, the experience proved dehumanizing to everyone, and it also proved the popularity of an idea against the difficulty of realizing it: public officials and American citizens believed that economic opportunities, in the form of jobs, should be reserved for members of the American commonwealth, for citizens and for lawful residents expressly invited to participate. When they perceived a shortage of labor, more than enough jobs for everyone, then they were open to importing more people to satisfy that need. When they could no longer control the thousands of people coming, however, they tried to close the border, as if to protect against a host, as if to preserve economic opportunities that might go to "wetbacks" instead of American citizens. American citizens then took to denigrating the immigrants, the very people that they'd sought – they were dangerous now, criminals, impoverished, and a drain on American society. Even more disturbing, in response to federal policy, more Americans took to thinking of persons of Mexican ancestry as aliens, outsiders, "illegals," and unworthy of belonging. Constantly repeating the word "wetback" suggested that wetbacks were not quite people, and so when local, state, and federal officials spoke through this new vocabulary, they dehumanized the very people they now sought to exclude.[16]

Before the Immigration Act of 1965, Congress had tried many times to exclude poorer immigrants. In a revision of the immigration law in 1950, Congress reiterated a rule against poorer migrants, variations of which had been in effect since the Chinese Exclusion Act of 1882. In the latest federal version in 1950, Congress reaffirmed that immigration officials could deny admission to anyone likely to be a "public charge." The revised statute suggested that if someone appeared of this category, that immigrant could request an affidavit of support from an American citizen or lawful permanent resident, usually the person sponsoring the immigrant's visa to the United States. This affidavit stated, in part, that the sponsor was "ready and willing to deposit a bond, if necessary, to guarantee that such person will not become a public charge during his or her stay in the United States." As they were petitioning for immigrants, sponsors signed other affidavits that read in similar ways, without reference to a bond: "I am ready to and willing to support the above named [person] in the United States, and I guarantee that he will not become a public charge." Before 1965, state agencies were suing sponsors to recover the costs of public assistance provided to the purported beneficiaries of these affidavits. And within the Immigration Act of 1965 itself, Congress said that "any alien likely at any time to become a public charge" should be inadmissible, and any alien who becomes a public charge within five years of his admission was subject to deportation.[17]

But, throughout the 1950s and 1960s, cases involving indigent immigrants were making their way through the state court systems, in Michigan, New York, and California, and in each instance, the state courts were unwilling to interpret the affidavits as legally binding contracts. In almost all of these cases, the state agencies argued that they often had no choice but to offer services to immigrants who could not pay for them. In the California case, for example, a man named Aguirre had been admitted to the United States in 1960, he had worked for four years as an agricultural laborer, and then he himself sponsored his wife and three children to live with him in San Diego. By 1964, however, he had had tuberculosis, and he and his family had received treatment at a public hospital. "State law [required] the County of San Diego to furnish hospitalization to an indigent person," and "while Aguirre was in the hospital he was unable to pay anything for the services rendered him." Lawyers for the County of San Diego sued Anatalio Viloria to recover the costs associated with treating Mr. Aguirre, as he was the sponsor who'd agreed in 1960 that Mr. Aguirre would not become a "public charge." As this case moved from a trial court to the appellate courts, President Johnson signed the Immigration Act of 1965, which, on its face, allowed for the deportation of people like Mr. Aguirre, and perhaps his whole family, too.

Yet, after reviewing the federal statutes and other state court precedents, the appellate court in California agreed with the state Supreme Courts in Michigan and in New York – the affidavits of the kind that Viloria had filed for Aguirre were primarily for immigration purposes. These affidavits may have created a moral obligation between Viloria and Aguirre, but they were not legally binding promises of financial support. The affidavits were too general and thus unlike conventional contracts; they were designed to provide evidence and reassurance to immigration officials; and because the immigrant beneficiary himself did not sign or agree to anything, his own responsibilities and obligations were vague. The appellate court in California underscored that last point: under the affidavit, "[the alien] is not obligated to do anything which would prevent his becoming a public charge," "[he] may neglect his health to the extent he contracts a disabling disease ... and in a variety of other ways may so conduct himself that he will become a public charge." In other words, it wasn't Mr. Viloria's fault that Mr. Aguirre had had tuberculosis. Thus, neither Mr. Aguirre nor the County of San Diego could recover from Mr. Viloria the cost of Mr. Aguirre's illness. This case from 1969 reaffirmed the idea that immigrant sponsors could not be held financially liable when their immigrant beneficiaries became indigent.[18]

And yet, because the various states had implemented federal public assistance programs in different ways, some states were more generous than others, and so, in several states, the legislatures again attempted to limit the number of poorer immigrants eligible for state and federal forms of relief. All of these efforts unfolded around the same period that Congress was debating the Immigration Act of 1965. In Arizona in 1962, and in Pennsylvania in 1968, for example, new state rules prohibited anyone from collecting public benefits unless they were American citizens or had fifteen years of residency in the United States. In *Graham* v. *Richardson* (1971), the United States Supreme Court dealt with cases in which immigrant plaintiffs had complained that state agencies had denied them various forms of public assistance. The Court ruled such restrictions unconstitutional under the Equal Protection Clause of the Fourteenth Amendment: "the citizenship bar to the receipt of general assistance in Pennsylvania discourages continued residence in Pennsylvania of indigent resident aliens, and causes such needy persons to remove to other States which will meet their needs." Speaking for a unanimous Court, Justice Harry Blackmun said immigrants were similar to racial minorities, that the states should refrain from discriminating against them solely based on their immigration status. Blackmun suggested that allowing states to do so would only create incentives for the states to shuffle away to other states as many indigent noncitizens as possible. Critics of the ruling complained, though, that in the states, poorer legal residents continued to strain social service systems that simply were not designed to care for immigrants.[19]

Sanctuary Movements, Sanctuary Cities

In the 1970s, the needs of strangers could appear totally daunting. From so many places, millions of people were leaving their countries, from regions torn apart by war and civil turmoil. Several thousand sought admission to the United States every month. Some were victims of the Cold War: in Cuba, communist revolutionaries had seized the island in 1959, and many thousands fled over the next two decades; and in Southeast Asia, by 1970, communist insurgencies and communist governments were gaining the upper hand in Laos, Cambodia, and Vietnam, despite years of American military involvement intended to deter the spread of communism. In Eastern Europe, people in the Soviet Union and others in countries dominated by the Soviet Union turned to the Americans for asylum, too. And still other displaced persons were leaving countries because of popular revolutions. In 1979, for example, the Shah of Iran fled his country in the face of an Islamic revolt that shook the entire Middle East. Hundreds of thousands of his supporters fled with the Shah, and many had asked for asylum in the United States precisely because the Americans had supported the Shah against the ayatollahs who had driven him away. Thousands of other refugees from Eastern Europe, the Americas, the Middle East, and Southeast Asia, also wanted to come to the United States as well, and their numbers reached millions of persons by 1980.[20]

Federal officials knew, however, that refugee admissions were unpopular in the United States: resettling large numbers of people was expensive, and in many jurisdictions, American citizens were less than thrilled by the sudden arrival of foreigners, no matter how destitute or sympathetic, and even though they had been former allies of the United States. In the late 1970s, Senator Edward Kennedy of Massachusetts sponsored new legislation that would help executive officials sort through the millions of people displaced by war or revolution: under the Refugee Act of 1980, signed by President Jimmy Carter, Congress redefined the term "refugee" to fit standards established through the United Nations after World War II. A "refugee" was a person with a "well-founded fear of persecution" based on his "race, religion, nationality, political opinion, or membership in a particular social group." Executive officials could admit up to 50,000 refugees per year, although the President did have the power to declare an emergency and admit more, after consulting with members of Congress. On the one hand, the Refugee Act appeared generous – the cap on refugees had been 17,400 persons per year before the new rule – and yet, on the other hand, the Act was passed when about 2 million people were fleeing from just Vietnam, Laos, and Cambodia, three countries that had had deep military ties to the United States. By limiting refugee admissions to those with a well-founded fear of persecution, the Americans signaled that they would take only a very small fraction of displaced persons. If a prospective refugee could not establish by "clear and convincing evidence" that they would be subject to persecution, the American officials did not have to resettle that person in the United States. The Refugee Act of 1980 almost ensured that the United States would turn away many thousands more than it would receive.[21]

At the heart of this policy was a kind of "compassion fatigue," a phrase repeated by Senator Alan Simpson of Wyoming, a Republican who, like many other Americans, said that too many impoverished people were coming to the United States. All of this felt overwhelming. Senator Simpson had served on a special committee on immigration during President Carter's term, but he was the leading member of yet another committee on immigration formed by President Ronald Reagan in the early 1980s. In that committee, Senator Simpson proposed reforms to limit the number of poorer persons admitted to the United States: perhaps the Southern border ought to be strengthened to deter patterns of illegal crossings that had become common during the Bracero Program. Perhaps immigrant sponsors should be held financially responsible for their immigrant beneficiaries, especially if they were family members. Perhaps Congress should limit or restrict family-based immigration altogether. Perhaps, to make sure that employers hired only American citizens or lawful residents, there ought to be fines and other sanctions levied against employers who gave jobs to people who shouldn't be in the country. And maybe there should be a national, counterfeit-proof identification card, so that government officials and private employers could know who was or wasn't legally in the United States. Patricia Harris, the Secretary of Health, Education, and Welfare under President Carter, cautioned against these proposals, especially that last one: in a speech, she reminded her audience that the Nazis had issued national identification cards, too, using complex new rules to determine who was or wasn't a German citizen, and then spelling out their rights accordingly. In Nazi Germany, a national identification card had been the first step toward cutting people off from public employment or public benefits. Senator Simpson and many other influential legislators still believed, though, that these were good ideas, and that the United States had the right to protect itself against the arrival of too many poor migrants.[22]

In the presidential primaries of 1979 and 1980, the candidates discussed at length topics related to immigration in ways that hadn't dominated the last few election cycles. Members of the media and his Republican critics had asked President Jimmy Carter what he might do with the thousands of Southeast Asian refugees still coming to the United States, after American forces left Vietnam in 1975. They also berated him about Iran, for not being able to see how a group of ayatollahs there could topple an American ally even as they were taking Americans as hostages. Gas prices jumped as supplies of oil stopped in light of the chaos in the Middle East – Americans were thrust back into gas rationing and long lines at fueling stations, sights not seen since World War II. Iranians were seeking asylum in the United States. During that presidential campaign, Ronald Reagan promised to stand up to communists and to ayatollahs everywhere, and to restore American prestige abroad in the wake of Vietnam and Iran.

In 1981, President Reagan pointed to Cuba and to its support of communist insurgencies in Central America as important foreign policy problems. In many border states, public officials and private citizens noticed that more people crossing the Southern border were, indeed, not Mexican, but rather Central American. They were from Honduras, Guatemala, and El Salvador; they were desperately poor; and they had stories that told of unspeakable violence in their countries. Indeed, in March 1980, in the same month that Jimmy Carter had signed the Refugee Act, the Archbishop of San Salvador, Oscar Romero, was shot to death after delivering his sermon during Mass, in a brazen attack that stunned the entire region. Over 200,000 people attended his funeral in late March, many of them convinced that the ruling government – a target of Romero's fierce sermons – was behind the murder. At least another 30 people died during the funeral itself, when guns and bombs scattered the crowds. Events such as these convinced many people in El Salvador that their future there would be hopeless, and, just like people from Honduras or Guatemala, the migrants from El Salvador felt that the new American President was more sympathetic to the right-wing governments than to their victims. They considered Romero's death and Reagan's election as telling signs that their civil wars would last for many years.[23]

For many Americans who encountered Central American migrants for the first time, however, it seemed obvious that these people were "refugees" under the standard definition articulated in the Refugee Act of 1980. But after winning the presidency, Ronald Reagan had sent aid and support to the ruling governments in El Salvador and in Guatemala to fight communist rebels supported by Cuba, the Soviet Union, and then Nicaragua, whose government by 1980 was also allied with those established communist states. The Reagan Administration was reluctant to define Central American migrants as "refugees" because this would suggest that they were fleeing governments that the President's own Administration had supported. Indeed, when they spoke about their horrors, Central American refugees had described government soldiers and death squads using American weapons, as well as planes and helicopters with American markings.[24]

Even when Central Americans described fleeing communist rebels, members of the Reagan Administration said that their stories supported pleas for more aid to the right-wing governments in Guatemala or El Salvador, to suppress the communists and make these places safe again for migrants who *should be returned* to these countries. President Reagan insisted that Central Americans who'd crossed the Southern border were "economic migrants," not refugees under the Act of 1980. Political context mattered a great deal: throughout most of 1980, when Fidel Castro helped to coordinate the mass exodus of Cubans to Florida, President Carter and his presidential opponent, Ronald Reagan, were more than willing to admit these persons as "refugees," for they were fleeing Cuba and from Castro, a man that many Americans considered a brutal *communist* dictator. People fleeing from communist governments were thus much more likely to be identified as "refugees."[25]

Alarmed by these responses, leading religious leaders in Arizona and in California were opposed to sending back their newest and most vulnerable congregants. The Archbishop of Los Angeles, Roger Mahony, the Presbyterian minister John Fife of Tucson, and James Corbett, a Quaker, also in Tucson, spoke publicly about the need to help Central American migrants. They appealed to fellow congregations in other parts of the country, and they ran a "sanctuary movement" through which church members would shuttle and house Central Americans. Many parishioners were surprised by their own participation in these efforts: Kathleen Kelly was a stay-at-home mom, a Republican, and not an overtly political person. She was a bird watcher. But, by the mid-1980s, Ms. Kelly was using her binoculars to spot Central American migrants across the border in Arizona, so that she and her colleagues could deliver water and offer aid. These migrants would then be able to move far north, to receive assistance from Jewish, Baptist, Unitarian, Lutheran, and Roman Catholic congregations in Chicago, Philadelphia, New York, and other major cities.

Federal immigration authorities regarded these activities as illegal, as an unlawful harboring of people who had no right to be in the United States. Federal immigration agents attempted to locate, detain, and remove as many migrants as possible, and government agents paid informants to collect evidence against key leaders of the sanctuary movement. The informants pretended to be members of the church, willing to help the migrants; they taped conversations and they otherwise collected evidence against about a dozen key people, including senior clergymen and three nuns. Federal prosecutors moved against church congregations in South Texas and in Tucson, Arizona, under the theory that criminal convictions would put a stop to such coordinated violations of the immigration law. At the federal trial in Tucson, James Corbett, John Fife, Kathleen Kelly, and five others were indicted and then convicted of "shielding, harboring, and transporting illegal aliens" in May 1986.[26]

The federal agents, the paid informants, and the trials, however, did little to deter the movement – in fact, many more parishioners and congregants insisted that they would continue to violate the law, to follow instead biblical precepts to "welcome the stranger." They said that the federal government's actions would be seen as shameful in the fullness of time. Even the trial judge thought it utterly distasteful that federal agents had put paid informants within American churches, as though these were criminal organizations. The trial judge and then an appellate court upheld the convictions, but the courts refused to send any of the nuns or clergymen to federal penitentiaries. They got house arrest, or their sentences were suspended. Throughout the trial and well after, the convicted clergymen and nuns lobbied for support in several cities. This was how, in several local jurisdictions in the mid-1980s – including Los Angeles, Seattle, Chicago, St. Paul, and New York City – city councils passed resolutions supportive of the sanctuary movement – in 1985, its Board of Supervisors declared that San Francisco would be a "City of Refuge": "The Mayor is urged to affirm that City Departments shall not discriminate against Salvadoran and Guatemalan refugees because of immigration status, and shall not jeopardize the safety and welfare of law-abiding refugees by acting in a way that may cause their deportation." The Board of Supervisors set aside public funds to support resettlement for these people, even if the federal government continued to say that they were "economic migrants" and "illegal immigrants," not "refugees."[27]

"A Bipartisan Effort ..."

In 1986, when President Reagan signed the Immigration Reform and Control Act, sponsored by Senator Alan Simpson, the Republican from Wyoming, and

Representative Romano Mazzoli, the Democrat from Kentucky, he hailed the law as a major bipartisan reform, perhaps the most significant revision of the immigration law since the Immigration Act of 1965. The Immigration Reform and Control Act contained many important provisions, debated widely in both chambers of Congress. In many ways, though, Senator Alan Simpson had been its key architect: the law required nearly all employers to check the immigration status of all of their employees; and employers who knowingly hired undocumented or unlawful workers could be fined and otherwise punished. The fines ranged from $250 per worker for first-time offenses, to $10,000 for employers who repeatedly and willfully violated the law. The idea was, to paraphrase Senator Simpson, to cut off the possibility that illegal immigrants could find work in the United States. Without legal access to employment, which was the chief reason why immigrants came unlawfully, these migrants would not come at all, or so was the law's promise. Senator Edward Kennedy opposed this part of the bill because he felt these employer sanctions might result in discrimination against Hispanic Americans. Assuming that they looked "illegal," employers would avoid hiring Latinos.[28]

The law also did something remarkable, a result of a strange combination of self-interest and mercy. The Immigration Reform and Control Act provided for a pathway to legalization for undocumented persons who'd been in the United States since before 1982. By paying a fine and any back taxes, and by admitting that they'd crossed unlawfully, while having done nothing *else* unlawfully, undocumented persons could file for legal status. This policy did represent some self-interest: President Reagan knew that many of his long-time supporters were agricultural growers in California and throughout the Southwest – they demanded that he sign nothing that might cut off their labor force. The growers had become dependent upon migratory laborers, many of whom were indeed out of status. Operation Wetback had removed hundreds of thousands of people in the 1950s, but they and others had come back, and the jobs in the fields were still there for them. The federal employer sanctions would hurt this unlawful but persistent work force, and the new law might also cause these laborers to leave the fields altogether, with tremendous negative consequences for agri-businesses and farms in states like California. Finding no other way to support employer sanctions without eliminating that labor supply, President Reagan's Administration proposed a legalization of 1 – perhaps 2 – million people who had been out of status. Thus, these workers would remain available to work, and no one would have to bear the trouble of removing them. Senator Phil Gramm of Texas denounced this provision as "outrageous," as an amnesty for people who'd broken the law to come to the United States. Against such objections, Congress passed the bill.[29]

What was the alternative, and what might mass removal look like in the 1980s? Headed into the last two years of his final term, President Reagan thought the very possibility repellant – drawing from his experience as Governor of California, Reagan said that most agricultural workers, illegal or legal, were decent people, not criminals or a threat to Americans. Having criticized communist governments for many crimes, including the mass deportation of ethnic minorities and political dissidents, Reagan was reluctant to use his own federal government to find and remove tens of thousands of people. Some of his fellow Republicans demanded more enforcement, perhaps a fence all along the Southern border, but Reagan considered the idea of a fence between Mexico and the United States just as impractical: "Rather than talking about putting up a fence, why don't we work out some recognition of our mutual problems?" Immigrants from Mexico were "Americans by choice," like immigrants from anywhere else. Although his critics said that he did not apply this logic consistently – say, to migrants from Central America – President Reagan knew, nevertheless, that more than a few thousand Central Americans would benefit from the legalization provisions of the Act of 1986. As a perceptive politician, he also insisted that having federal prosecutors continue to go after people like Reverend Fife and Kathleen Kelly or the Archbishop of Los Angeles was not going to be a winning electoral strategy. Most congregations in the United States did not join the sanctuary movement, and many influential religious leaders had condemned violations of the immigration law, but President Reagan did not pursue mass deportation as part of the immigration bill he'd wanted to pass.

When he signed the bill, President Reagan was quite pleased, even jubilant, that this bill had made it far enough for him to sign at all. "It truly has been a bipartisan effort," he said, and "future generations of Americans will be thankful for our efforts to humanely regain control of our borders." President Reagan emphasized the humanity of the new law: "The legalization provisions in this act will go far to improve the lives of a class of individuals who now must hide in the shadows, without access to many of the benefits of a free and open society. Very soon many of these men and women will be able to step into the sunlight and, ultimately, if they choose, they may become American citizens." He also insisted that the rule reaffirmed the idea that economic opportunities in the United States should be reserved for American citizens and lawful residents: "[the new law] will remove the incentive for illegal immigration by eliminating the job opportunities which draw illegal aliens here." Altogether, by folding in persons who were once unlawful, and by discouraging subsequent unlawful migrations through a new set of federal laws that governed American companies and American citizens, President Reagan suggested that the law preserved the very idea of a commonwealth. The United States was to be enlarged only by an "orderly," "secure system of immigration," and from now on, American companies would only give work to people eligible for it. The law promised a controlled labor market, it promised mercy and forgiveness, order and security.[30]

When President Reagan left office in 1989, however, professional scholars and politicians agreed on a number of trends: illegal immigration wasn't going to decline; many employers didn't especially fear getting fined or sanctioned for hiring unlawful migrants; and about 3 million people (not 1 or 2) were passing into lawful status under the Act of 1986. Moreover, of those 3 million, perhaps a majority of those folks weren't going to be voting for Republicans, in places where thousands of new voters could switch an entire state from red to blue, from Republican to Democrat. A decade after the Act of 1986, many Republicans were prone to thinking of Ronald Reagan as a great President, perhaps the greatest President – except for this bill he'd signed in that year.[31] In 1965, President Johnson had said that his immigration law was not revolutionary, but then it really was; in 1986, President Reagan said that his bill was quite novel and revolutionary, but then it really wasn't. Reagan's talk of shadow and sunlight, illegal becoming legal – very few members of his party would ever talk that way again, nor would they lobby for rules that acknowledged, on some level, that many undocumented immigrants were part of the American commonwealth. Some found unforgivable that Reagan had legalized so many illegal immigrants who were now free to vote for the other party. In the decades after his presidency, they supported other immigration rules that would take far darker turns in the wake of what many considered the law's failure.

6

THE PRIVILEGED CLASSES

Two years into his own presidency, George H. W. Bush signed the Immigration Act of 1990, the most important immigration law after the Immigration Reform and Control Act of 1986. The new rule was much tougher than the previous one. Major provisions of the law in 1990 mandated more enforcement: the law authorized the Immigration and Naturalization Service to hire many more Border Patrol agents; these agents were to be trained to use deadly force; and they could arrest and detain anyone whom they suspected of being in the United States unlawfully. The law also eliminated judicial relief in cases where an immigrant was deported based on a criminal conviction – that is, even when an immigrant's deportation might harm American citizens or other lawful residents, a judge could no longer grant relief if the immigrant had a criminal record. Congress barred permanently from the United States any immigrant with a serious criminal conviction. In his statements about the new law, President Bush said that the enforcement provisions were in part an extension of the "war on drugs." He noted how his immediate predecessor had targeted drug trafficking, and this necessarily involved greater policing of the nation's borders. By shifting the immigration law toward enforcement, however, the Immigration Act of 1990 expanded overall the number of people who could be deported, and it accelerated a trend that would turn the Border Patrol into a much larger arm of the federal government.[1]

The Act of 1990 had at least four other innovative provisions: first, a "diversity visa," originally set at 55,000 per year, through which migrants from low-sending countries could come to America, provided that they had a high school degree and two years of work experience. Immigrants from major sending countries – the Philippines, South Korea, and Mexico – were ineligible for diversity visas, and early advertisements for the visa featured people who looked pretty darn European. Second, Congress approved a provision to create a "temporary protected status" (TPS) visa for anyone whom the President had considered temporarily unable to return home because of armed conflict, natural disasters, or some other compelling reason. Third, Congress and the President agreed to adjust into lawful permanent residency the spouses and unmarried children of immigrants who'd legalized under the Act of 1986. At least 200,000 additional family members became lawful permanent residents under that rule, although, by 1990, many critics complained that far too many people had already legalized under the Act of 1986. Finally, the Immigration Act of 1990 removed references to homosexuality as a ground for exclusion – in the Act of 1965, such persons were "afflicted with . . . sexual deviation," but a Democratic Congress and a Republican President agreed to strike that provision, against the objections of many religious conservatives.[2]

Of these four provisions, the TPS program would have the deepest repercussions on the largest number of people, simply because refugee crises grew worse during the 1990s. President Bush indicated that he would use TPS visas for Central Americans, some of whom had been turned down for refugee status, but he also had to turn his attention to other burgeoning new problems. In 1989, the Chinese communist government had sent in tanks and troops into Tiananmen Square in Beijing to quash students and other activists who'd been demanding reforms. To embarrass the Chinese government, and to provide refuge to Chinese nationals who wished not to return to the People's Republic of China, President Bush indicated that his Administration would be open to their asylum claims in light of this incident.

Closer to home, in the Caribbean, the government of Haiti was also in the midst of significant upheavals. For decades, the Duvalier family, first François and then Jean-Claude, ran the country with a small group of landed allies. Several thousand Haitians fled for the United States every year after 1970, although both President Carter and President Reagan had classified almost all Haitians as "economic migrants," not refugees. In 1990, a former Roman Catholic priest, Jean-Bertrand Aristide, gained significant political support among poorer Haitians in a presidential campaign overseen by many prominent international observers, including former President Carter. Aristide won the election in 1991, but Haiti was wracked with political violence, an unrelenting violence that would, in the following year, produce one of the most significant and desperate mass migrations in the western Atlantic. Thus, even as he was signing the Immigration Act of 1990, President Bush was uncertain how exactly he would use the humanitarian provisions of the new law.

The Economic Superpower

In Congress, the chief proponent of the Immigration Act of 1990 had been Senator Edward Kennedy of Massachusetts. He had supported the enforcement and removal provisions in part because he wanted the President's support to accomplish other objectives – namely, the major revisions in family- and employment-based immigration. Senator Kennedy got much of what he had wanted: the Immigration Act of 1990 allowed for a greater number of immigrants to come under family reunification preferences, but he re-ordered those preferences to favor the immigration of immediate family members. The Republican Senator Alan Simpson and other influential members of Congress supported this change, the theory being that all people were more likely to take financial responsibility for immediate family than for their extended kin. The preferences for siblings remained, but both President and Congress agreed to study the issue further, perhaps to eliminate that preference in another law.

In the employment provisions, Senator Kennedy had proposed revising to five major categories, all referencing skills, college degrees, and even wealth. Under the fifth employment preference, for example, anyone willing to invest $1 million dollars could be eligible for a permanent residency visa, provided that such an investment could result in the employment of ten or more American citizens. If the immigrant invested in a "targeted employment area," a region of relatively high unemployment, $500,000 would be enough. Lawful immigration under all of the employment categories would increase dramatically under the new law: the number of employment-based visas would rise from about 54,000 to 140,000 per year.

In addition, the Immigration Act of 1990 created a new category of temporary visas for skilled workers – companies in the United States could petition for a skilled foreign worker who could stay for three years, and then renew for an additional three years. The company had to prove first that it had attempted to hire an American citizen or a lawful permanent resident; the foreign worker had to have the same qualifications for the job as if she were an American citizen; and the company had to agree to pay her the "prevailing wage" for this position. Senator Kennedy accepted the recommendations of a group of scholars to limit to 65,000 the number of visas per year under this H-1B visa program, which was a new variant of the H visas that had been used primarily for seasonal, temporary agricultural workers. Over time, some critics referred to workers under the H-1B visa as "high-tech braceros," and yet few braceros in agriculture ever earned more than $60,000 per year writing software at a tech company in California, as some H-1B workers were doing by the mid-1990s. This proved to be a much more important new pathway to the United States.[3]

For Senator Kennedy and for other legislators, the H-1B was itself a kind of compromise. The American economy was changing dramatically: low-skilled and unskilled manufacturing jobs were declining, as major industries like auto manufacturing and steel production weakened. Foreign manufacturers and producers were entering an international market, and automation was changing the nature of production itself. As early as 1961, for example, engineers at the General Motors plants had built welding machines on the assembly lines, and they were quite terrible. But 20 years later, they were much better, controlled by more complex computers, and thus these robots were welding all day and all night with few, if any, errors. By 1985, automakers were investing billions of dollars into robots. They needed highly skilled engineers to perfect and to service these sophisticated machines, but the robots themselves did not support families, nor did they need health insurance or paid vacations. Auto makers laid off thousands of people, and the American Steel Belt – a gigantic manufacturing region stretching from the Great Lakes into the Virginias – was becoming the Rust Belt.

The United States was "deindustrializing," the economists said, but it was more accurate to say that the major industries were changing, away from low-skilled human labor to technology-intensive forms of production. As American companies embraced these changes to production, they had lobbied hard to increase the number of scientists, engineers, and other highly skilled workers who could make and design and improve industries along those lines. In addition, as the American economy lost high-wage unskilled jobs, these jobs did not entirely disappear – they went abroad. In other countries, people worked for much less than in the United States. Many American companies knew this, of course, and they established manufacturing plants in places where labor costs were far lower than in California or New York. Thus, what was a high-wage, unskilled job in the United States could become a low-wage unskilled job in Mexico or in Taiwan. International transportation networks – perfected over the postwar period – provided the critical links that tied together places like Mexico, Taiwan, and the United States.[4]

Advances in transportation facilitated these trends. In the mid-1950s, an enterprising American entrepreneur, Malcom McLean, proposed a novel way of shipping and distributing goods across vast distances. McLean's new business, the Pan-Atlantic Steamship Company, focused on standardized shipping containers – huge metal boxes of exactly the same size, which could then be loaded with goods and shipped by trains, flatbed trucks, and ships – very large ships. His company's containers were stackable, lockable, and weatherproof. McLean's company became SeaLand, but, by 1980, companies based in South Korea, Japan, France, Denmark, and Singapore were also building shipping containers and container ships, all of them getting much bigger. In 1972, the International Convention for Safe Containers sounded like a boring multinational agreement – and it was – but these conventions standardized container vessels even further, and they clarified how governments should update their ports, their roads, and otherwise improve the basic infrastructure to facilitate international trade. In 1956, sending a ton of cargo across the Pacific Ocean cost about $6, but by 2010, that same ton went for less than 20 cents. Thus, even factoring in these transportation costs, it's no wonder that manufacturers in the United States had already moved so many unskilled jobs abroad by 1990, and that foreign companies were also making goods for an American retail market.[5]

Clearly, in the late 1980s, relatively high-paying unskilled jobs were leaving the United States, companies were automating and computerizing operations, and thus they were in need of more highly skilled, technologically proficient workers. But having nearly tripled the number of employment-based preferences, from 54,000 to 140,000, President Bush, Senator Kennedy, and other members of Congress were reluctant to increase permanent residency visas any further, because the influx of new foreign workers might hurt the employment opportunities for highly skilled Americans. Many scholars and politicians said that the United States should re-train its own workers rather than simply migrating foreign workers. As a compromise, although the law allowed for many more highly skilled workers, it would also stimulate foreign investment to reshape American manufacturing, and the H-1B would offer a new kind of flexibility for skilled foreign workers as well. If 140,000 permanent residency visas were insufficient, companies could draw upon 65,000 additional temporary visas. This was how, in 1990, the United States moved toward a new immigration rule through which over 200,000 highly skilled workers were going to come legally to the United States, every year.[6]

Many skilled people had had reasons to leave for the United States, long before these rules. By the end of World War II, most of the world was in ruins, except for the United States. In the immediate postwar world, this huge advantage would explain how the American economy grew out of the Great Depression into the wealthiest ever in the history of the world. For the next two decades, as the United States government had helped to rebuild the infrastructure of several European and Asian nations, American companies had no serious industrial competition from abroad. At the major research universities, where the Americans had developed and perfected radar, sonar, and other novel forms of communication during the war, scholars turned many military applications into commercial technologies. American companies mass-produced televisions and radios. With the federal government's support, American scientists and engineers also tinkered with better and more efficient ways to produce everything – cars, tanks, airplanes, food, clothes, houses, everything. Many unskilled American workers were laboring in coal mines and in steel mills, but even these worksites were changing during and after the war, again because of technological developments that reduced the need for workers. Ever more sophisticated equipment could tell where best to dig for coal or how best to handle molten steel. Instead of digging into a mountain for coal, giant machines could take an entire mountain apart, and then recover the coal with far fewer people.[7]

People who could design, build, repair, and run machines were much more valuable in this kind of economy, here and everywhere. In the postwar world, as the states and the federal government made massive investments in higher education, the United States was also helping to rebuild colleges and universities in Europe and in Asia, to strengthen and to reaffirm political alliances. Through the universities, scholars and entrepreneurs could forge lasting economic relationships, often through the exchanges of scholars interested in American science and technology. In 1949, for example, leading politicians and administrators in the Philippines had asked the United States government for aid to rebuild the University of the Philippines, and over the next decade, with American support, the University expanded to accommodate thousands of students across six new campuses. In Taiwan, the most prestigious university had been Taihoku Imperial University, organized and controlled by the Japanese Imperial Government, just like the Keijo Imperial University in Seoul, Korea. After the war, Taihoku became the National Taiwan University, Keijo became the Seoul National University, and American money and support proved vital for both institutions. In time, by 1970, both universities grew into the leading research universities in each of these countries. Taiwanese and South Korean students have been coming to the United States ever since, often returning to their home countries to serve as leading professors and educational leaders in Asia.[8]

Within Japan itself, the United States supported the reconstruction of several major universities, and American foreign policy had other important consequences. Under the terms of the peace, and according to its new postwar constitution, the Japanese government would no longer have offensive military capabilities, and so Japanese universities – which had been instrumental in developing Zero fighters and Japanese aircraft carriers – turned to basic research for other things. It was amazing what a nation could do, when it *didn't* have to spend billions of dollars for defense. Japanese companies revolutionized consumer electronics and fuel-efficient cars. There were unforeseeable consequences resulting from such inventions: for all of the twentieth century, Japan had to import nearly all of its petroleum, and so people in Japan had paid about three or four times more for gasoline than drivers in the United States. Japanese auto makers felt that they had to build fuel-efficient engines. But when the oil crisis gripped the world in the 1970s, Japanese cars became popular everywhere, thus challenging American dominance in that market. American and then Japanese shipping companies brought those Japanese cars to the United States in those container vessels, stacked one on top of the other, hundreds of cars on a single ship.

Leading American auto makers – Ford, Chrysler, General Motors – had assisted Japanese auto makers in the postwar period, but now the Japanese companies looked as though they might eclipse the Americans. Some auto-workers in the United States felt an existential threat in light of these events, and they railed against "Jap cars," "Japs," and other people whom they thought just looked Japanese, like Vincent Chin. Spates of anti-Asian violence in and around Detroit, the center of auto manufacturing in the United States, did not mean, though, that the two countries themselves were going to declare war, for, after decades of economic, political, and institutional collaboration, they were more joined than ever. In fact, this had been a classic example of "soft power," of the Americans drawing their allies into the American sphere by offering access to their most influential and prestigious institutions. By 1980, Japanese companies had used that knowledge and access to out-perform their American counterparts. Throughout this period, the United States maintained a constant military presence in the Philippines, South Korea, and Japan, and in the South China Sea, but American educators and professors and industrialists were in many ways just as influential and transformative in Asian economies and societies.[9]

Political Chaos and Skilled Migration from Asia

To this day, however, many Americans might miss how important and significant the research universities have been since World War II – how much they've transformed from regional and even parochial institutions to national and international ones. Their relationship to similar institutions in Europe and in Asia was unmistakable. Yale and Harvard looked a lot like Oxford and Cambridge. Michigan and Wisconsin looked a lot like Yale and Harvard, too. Berkeley and Stanford resembled Yale and Harvard, as well. Yonsei University in South Korea had gothic buildings with ivy all over them, while Korea University had built an entrance that looked so similar to the drive into Stanford that one could mistake the approach to one campus for the other. Consider their colors and you'll see what I mean. None of this was an accident: people homesick for Oxford and Cambridge had established Yale and Harvard, the Yalies helped to establish the reputations of the University of Michigan and the University of California, and then key professors and graduates from Yale and Berkeley helped to support places like the University of the Philippines and Yonsei University.[10]

At the major research universities in Asia, one can still *see* the projection of American institutions that transformed these regions, even though most Americans might be unaware of that history. They might consider how these transformations were transforming their own regions. Promising students from Yonsei, Seoul National, and Korea University were coming to Harvard and Michigan and UCLA in those postwar years, a migratory flow that has continued into this century. South Korean students were among the most numerous foreign students on elite university campuses in the United States, but they were just the most recent within a much longer history of migration. Students from the Philippines and Taiwan had also been arriving in large numbers, and, after 1990, students from India and China would outnumber everyone.

By 1970, after the United States had liberalized its immigration rules to allow for the migration of skilled workers through the employment-based preferences, skilled workers from Asia were coming in significant numbers through two obvious pathways. First, college graduates were finding higher-paying jobs in the United States, and they were immigrating with their families. Unlike Asian immigrants in the late nineteenth or early twentieth centuries, most of whom left their family members in their home countries, these migrants were coming to settle permanently with their families. Second, many college graduates were continuing advanced studies in the United States, but instead of returning home to South Korea or to the Philippines, they petitioned to adjust their status into permanent residency as well. Through this second pathway, for example, the engineering student from Yonsei University might pursue his doctorate in Chicago, and then this highly educated person might choose to stay for opportunities in the United States rather than return home. Imagine hundreds of similar stories. Already, after 1965, such highly skilled immigrants from Asia were changing the United States.

There were other obvious reasons for staying here: economic and work opportunities were much richer and more varied in California than in South Korea in the 1970s, and salaries were generally higher. Housing and public infrastructure were much more developed here than there; the public schools were good, if one could imagine having children, or if one already had them; and politics would have appeared more stable in California than in South Korea. South Korea sat below North Korea, and north of there was communist China; in addition, in the 1970s, when a military dictator dominated South Korean politics, the repressive regime there was becoming repulsive even to the middle-class professionals who benefitted most from its economic reforms. Immigration from South Korea averaged around 40,000 persons per year, every year from 1970 through 1990. This was because people who arrived under professional categories or as students then petitioned for family reunification for their extended kin, including siblings, parents, and in-laws. The immigration scholars called this phenomenon "chain migration," a process that started with maybe one immigrant, and then ended – or never ended – with 20 or 30 people related to that one person.[11]

From Taiwan and from the Philippines, educated and highly skilled people also immigrated to the United States in numbers that were unprecedented in American history. Engineers and physicists, doctors and nurses, these immigrants were, collectively, the most highly educated group of immigrants ever, and, like the people from South Korea, they were leaving circumstances in their home countries that were frightening. The United States had directed billions of dollars of aid to Taiwan, and it recognized the Republic of China on that island as the only legitimate government of China. Yet, for nearly two decades, the Republic of China had also been a dictatorship ruled under martial law. In 1979, when the United States normalized relations with the communists in the People's Republic of China, the government in Taiwan grew even more repressive, more anxious, and it jailed political opponents even as it clamped down on the mainstream press. In the early 1980s, police officers and security officials tied to the ruling Kuomintang had detained and assaulted their political opponents, they shut down major periodicals, and they labeled many efforts for political reform as communist agitation. Through National Taiwan University, many thousands of bright young people settled in the United States to flee the political chaos of that island.

In the Philippines, during this same period, the political climate was also paranoid and violent. Ferdinand Marcos was a long-time ally of the United States, he was an avowed anti-communist, and he was also prone to calling his opponents communists and communist sympathizers, even as his own supporters amassed fortunes through their political connections. In the early 1970s, communists in the southern Philippine islands *did* attack the country, drawing support from many poorer Filipinos who saw the Marcos regime as hopelessly corrupt and mired in a "crony capitalism." His critics said that President Marcos would direct government money to those who supported him, but he would do little or nothing for anyone else. In response to growing instability and violence, President Marcos declared martial law in 1972, he retained strict controls over the press, and he supported the creation of a security state that tortured and murdered opposition leaders. But, by 1983, when he ordered the assassination of Senator Benigno Aquino, Ferdinand Marcos was the leader of a nation whose middle class all seemed to be leaving. By 1985, political violence in the Philippines – inflicted by the communist insurgents and by police and security forces – claimed thousands of lives each year with no obvious end in sight. Again, through the University of the Philippines and through other institutions of higher education, educated Filipinos were migrating, both for better opportunities and for a life without political chaos.[12]

Over time, tens of thousands of immigrants came from South Korea, Taiwan, and the Philippines in the decades after the Immigration Act of 1965, and they arrived in the United States precisely because of the alliances between the United States and each of these countries. The United States had supported political leaders in East Asia who were not paragons of democratic virtue, but, as we've noted before, they had one thing in common: Park Chung-hee of South Korea, Ferdinand Marcos of the Philippines, and Chiang Kai-shek of the Republic of China were staunchly anti-communists. Park and Marcos supported the American war against the communists in Vietnam; Chiang Kai-shek swore never to allow a communist government in Taiwan. For those reasons alone, the United States government was willing to look beyond the dictatorial tendencies that were obvious in many of the regimes in Asia. For people living in these countries, however, the United States was both an enabler of dictators and an escape from dictatorship – by taking a college degree in one of the universities rebuilt with American support, educated Asians could leave for America. Once they had established themselves there, they could, in time, bring over other loved ones, all of them thus escaping countries whose very pathologies were tied to the United States.

Not everyone stayed in the United States, of course. The first President of South Korea, Syngman Rhee, had finished college at Harvard, then graduate school at Princeton. Lee Teng-hui, the former President of the Republic of China, took his graduate degrees from Iowa State and Cornell. In the Philippines, President Fidel Ramos was a graduate of the United States Military Academy at West Point, while one of his successors, President Gloria Macapagal-Arroyo, did her graduate work at Georgetown, in the Walsh School of Foreign Service. In addition to these heads of state, hundreds of public officials, educators, artists, and many other social, economic, and political elites in South Korea, Taiwan, and the Philippines had come through the colleges and universities of the United States in the decades after World War II.

Indeed, by 1980, heading to the United States for school or for work was a common option among the highly educated and well-connected in Asia. This migration and remigration was forming a kind of "brain circulation" of people across the Pacific. This pattern remains on-going: Xi Mingze is the daughter of Xi Jinping, the man who became President of China in 2013. Xi Mingze took her Harvard undergraduate degrees in psychology and English in 2014, although this achievement wasn't widely celebrated in the People's Republic of China. She had enrolled under a pseudonym while she was a student at Harvard, and, as far as we know, her parents didn't attend her graduation ceremonies. She was just one among hundreds of thousands of Chinese students studying in the United States at the elite colleges and universities after 1990.[13]

China and India

Since 1990, a much greater fraction of students and highly skilled workers have come from China and from India. Economic and development policies in both countries can help us see why: in the 1970s and 1980s, even the communists became dissatisfied with communism. In China, the Great Leap Forward was only officially a great leap forward – in reality, it was a disaster that contributed to the Great Chinese Famine, when as many as 15–30 million people may have died from 1958 to 1962. When his critics sought to re-establish market mechanisms in industry and in agriculture in the wake of the famine, Chairman Mao Tse-tung fought to control his party and his Revolution. Leading historians of China have shown that Mao's Great Proletarian Cultural Revolution may have made economic and social conditions even worse for a majority of Chinese people, so much so that by 1976, the year of Mao's death, most senior members of the party had planned for a Chinese Communist Party that would no longer support Mao's economic policies, let alone his devastating political tactics. Deng Xiaoping advocated "socialism with Chinese characteristics": the Chinese communist government would still regulate and plan economic development, but there would be private ownership and market competition again, and protections for foreign investors willing to do business in China. It's not hyperbole to say that everyone around the world still feels the reverberations of these monumental changes in China after 1980.[14]

The Chinese Communist Party allowed individual initiative for collective ends in other areas of Chinese society. Deng Xiaoping supported reinstatement of the Gao Kao, the national higher education entrance exams, and his government also made massive investments in higher education that were unprecedented. Higher education was the central pillar that would support Deng's Four Modernizations, in agriculture, industry, science and technology, and national defense. Expenditures for higher education thus grew from several million dollars per year to billions of dollars per year by 1990, and in recent decades, they were exceeding hundreds of billions of dollars per year. Fundamental reforms in higher education pushed institutions to combine teaching and research missions, as was similar to elite universities in Europe and in the United States, and Chinese scholars at Peking, Tsinghua, or Fudan were some of the best scholars in the world by any objective criteria. Many of these scholars were coming back to China from abroad. Like their colleagues in the United States and in Europe, they were coming up with inventions and discoveries that had obvious industrial, market-based applications.[15]

In 1970, there were fewer than 500 institutions for higher education in China, but by 2010, there were over 2,000. In 1970, fewer than 100,000 students were enrolled in colleges and universities; by 2010, there were at least 6 million. And instead of allowing not very bright children of high government officials to be admitted to, say, Peking University, as might have been common in the 1970s, the Gao Kao has developed into a grueling, two-day gauntlet that 10 million young people in China were enduring every year after 2005. A high score on the Gao Kao could mean a coveted spot at one of the 40 leading universities in China, and, for students of modest means, this could mean an entirely different life compared to their parents or grandparents. Also, a growing middle class in China after 1990 could also envision studying abroad, for as foreign investors were coming to China in larger numbers, so too were younger Chinese students now leaving for foreign countries to continue their education.[16]

In India, following independence in 1949, the citizens of the largest democracy in the world had elected governments that had five-year plans and central economic agencies similar to the ones in the communist world. Although more conservative political parties had attempted to move the economy in more capitalist directions since the 1960s – by advocating fewer regulations and greater competition among firms – Indian economic policy was dominated by state monopolies and by protectionist policies. Generous state subsidies were popular with agricultural producers and trade unions, but they also propped up farms and companies that were inefficient and uncompetitive in an increasingly global market. This proved unsustainable. India had to borrow money to prop up inefficient industries, including its own public sector.

When the debts became overwhelming in the early 1990s, Prime Minister Narasimha Rao promised basic, structural changes to the economy as part of a bailout agreement with the International Monetary Fund. Thereafter, India agreed to eliminate the License Raj, the elaborate government system designed to control licenses for all private firms in India. The government would gradually eliminate tariffs on foreign goods, and it would privatize state monopolies. As in China, the Indian government would provide basic protections for foreign investors, thus stimulating capital investments from abroad. This turn toward market-based reforms stimulated the entire economy of the second most populous country in the world. By 2000, when economic growth in India was second only to that of China, the central and regional governments in India also turned to policies to strengthen higher education to solidify and further these gains.[17]

Many government officials had been skeptical of public investments in higher education, if only because such a high fraction of college graduates kept leaving India. Indeed, before 1949 and in the two decades after, graduates from the best universities in India – Panjab University, the University of Delhi, and the University of Calcutta – often migrated to the British colonial world, to Singapore, to South Africa, or to the United Kingdom. After independence, the Indian government passed laws to support a new set of institutions, and, of these, the Institutes of Technology Act of 1961 was the most significant. Under this law, the central and regional governments would create and support an autonomous set of institutions, the Indian Institutes of Technology, in about two dozen locations throughout the country, including in major cities like Delhi, Bombay, Chennai, and Hyderabad. Legislators and educational leaders hoped that the system would produce world-class scientists and engineers who would stimulate economic development in India in a post-industrial, global economy. Their founders drew their inspirations not so much from the British system, but from specific American research universities that focused heavily on science and technology research and education, including the California Institute of Technology and the Massachusetts Institute of Technology. Like the students at Caltech and MIT, the students at the Indian Institutes of Technology were going to focus on science and technology, not classical Sanskrit or Indian history during the colonial period.

Graduates from the IITs did go abroad to study in Europe and in the United States, but, just as in South Korea, many of them came back to India to serve as leading faculty members and administrators. In 2016, for example, the Director of the IIT in Delhi was V. Ramgopal Rao, who did his graduate work in Munich and his postdoc at UCLA. Uday Desai, the Director of the IIT in Hyderabad, had completed his undergraduate degree at the IIT in Kanpur, and he had finished his graduate work at SUNY Buffalo and Johns Hopkins. Bhaskar Ramamurthi, the Director of the IIT in Madras, was once an undergraduate there, although he finished his graduate degrees from UC Santa Barbara. Leaving from an IIT after a bachelor's degree to complete graduate education in a European or in an American university was becoming a much more common pathway for scholars in India. With the establishment of endowed professorships, and then the expansion of the IIT system after 2000, the Indian government was relying on a transnational circulation of scholars from India to the West, and then back to India, to develop its premier system of public higher education.[18]

And yet, by any measure, India's system of higher education was not producing sufficient numbers of graduates to meet the demands of its growing economy. Since 2000, 17 new IIT campuses have been established, but, in 2015, all of the IITs enrolled fewer than 35,000 undergraduates. By comparison, about 30,000 students were completing undergraduate degrees in computer science and engineering programs just on the campuses of the University of California. Of course, the UC system enrolled more than 180,000 other students, studying everything from English literature to sociology, subjects that the central Indian government did not prioritize. A student in India faced fewer opportunities, all concentrated in just a handful of academic fields, within a much more competitive environment. Many stories illustrated this problem: the 2009 Nobel Laureate in Chemistry was Venkatraman Ramakrishnan – he had completed his Ph.D. at UC San Diego and he did his postdoc at Yale, but when he was a younger man, he didn't score high enough on the national university entrance exams to secure a spot at one of the IITs. His Nobel Prize may have been somewhat reassuring to the thousands of students who also didn't get a spot in an IIT, but the story revealed an underlying problem. Many thousands (hundreds of thousands?) of students in India were not getting the opportunities to pursue college or graduate degrees, and although the pathways to higher education had expanded tremendously over such a short period of time, the impact of those changes would still take far more time. In 2015, the IITs had about 170,000 alumni; the University of California had 1.7 million.[19]

Still, a small fraction of a huge number yields a significant, large number, and when a significant fraction of that large number migrates to the United States, it's hard not to notice. By 2000, there were 1.3 billion people living in the People's Republic of China, and there were nearly as many people on the Indian subcontinent. A relatively small number of young people in these huge countries were getting an elite higher education by 2000, but because so many of these young people were then coming to the United States to pursue educational opportunities here, their presence has been significant and obvious. In 2005, approximately 80,000 students from India and 65,000 students from China were enrolled at private and public institutions of higher education in the United States. By 2015, there were about 170,000 students from India, 330,000 from China. These two countries – India and China – sent more than half of all international students to study in the United States. They surpassed all other sending countries from Asia combined, including Japan, Taiwan, South Korea, and the Philippines. And, as both India and China continue to increase their investments in higher education, and as a growing middle class in both countries makes similar investments in its children, this pattern will probably remain robust for the foreseeable future.[20]

Ethnic Entrepreneurship and the Model Minority Myth

As early as 1950, in the mainstream American press, Asian Americans and Asian immigrants appeared as a "model minority," a racial group that had experienced White supremacy and racism, and yet was emerging as a discernible middle class. This was a "myth," many said in reply – Chinese Americans were overwhelmingly laboring in working-class jobs, having faced years of structural discrimination in the labor markets, and Japanese Americans had yet to recover from wartime internment. Compared to national averages, a much higher fraction of elderly Chinese and Japanese Americans faced poverty in old age in 1960. Several prominent historians have argued that the "model minority myth," as it pertained to Asians, was mostly a product of the Cold War, of American foreign policy efforts to court Asians into an American sphere, rather than see Asian countries drift into the communist Chinese or Soviet Russian world. As we've seen, Congress and President Johnson had supported the Immigration Act of 1965 to stress how anyone could be an American now, even those people who'd been subject to Chinese Exclusion or Japanese American internment not one generation ago. After the Act of 1965, though, as many thousands of highly skilled Asian immigrant professionals migrated to start a new life in the United States, scholars and journalists were again talking about persons of Asian ancestry as model minorities. These immigrants were establishing their careers, raising families, and living middle- and upper-middle-class lives by the 1980s.[21]

A middle-class life seemed possible even for Asian immigrants who'd come under family reunification visas or as refugees. Vietnamese refugees in the 1970s experienced some of the most harrowing conditions of the twentieth century – even when they could flee Vietnam by land or by boat, they often fell prey to pirates in the South China Sea, or they languished in refugee camps in Thailand, the Philippines, or Hong Kong. Before and after the Refugee Act of 1980, the American government resettled Vietnamese migrants through churches throughout the United States, so that they might not burden any single region or state. Extended families were often cast across vast distances, and many Vietnamese families were missing a mother, father, or one or more children during the passage out. The clear majority of these families relied on various forms of public assistance in the first few years of settlement. And yet, in time, many Vietnamese families migrated again, this time *within* the United States, to places like Westminster, California, or to the Gulf Coast near Houston and Galveston, or Fairfax and Falls Church in Virginia.

Many thousands of Vietnamese refugees started small businesses by pooling together community and family resources. In ethnic enclaves, they formed essentially their own "commonwealths," places where fluency in English was not as necessary, or where a handful of professionals could advise others about business licenses and permitting rules. Vietnamese refugees had nothing when they came to the United States, and yet, because many of them had allied with the Americans against the communists, and because they ran the government and economy of South Vietnam, these migrants were more likely to know how to run a business and how to finance an enterprise. More than a few knew how to send the kids to a good public school, maybe by buying that least expensive house in that one neighborhood with the best public school. Without question, Vietnamese refugees after 1980 did suffer poverty, trauma, and dislocation – like Laotians and Cambodian immigrants, many Vietnamese people, especially elderly refugees, never opened businesses or lived free of public assistance. But, after 1985, a significant number of Vietnamese refugees ran supermarkets, grocery stores, bakeries, auto repair shops, and beauty salons, including nail salons. Even though they had started life in the United States as janitors or cooks, some of the children of Vietnamese refugees were becoming engineers, prominent lawyers, and college professors.[22]

For Asian immigrants who'd arrived under family reunification provisions, upward mobility also seemed to be the primary point of migrating to the United States. In 1970, there were perhaps 40,000 persons of Korean ancestry in the United States, but by 1980, there were almost 300,000. In another ten years, that figure doubled. At first, many South Koreans had worked in low-wage industries – as household servants or in garment factories or as restaurant staff – but then, by 1975, South Korean immigrants were starting small businesses at a much higher rate than the national average. The Korean American grocery store in New York, the Korean American liquor store in South Central Los Angeles, my mother-in-law's deli in Berkeley, California, and my late mother's dry cleaner in Oakland – these were just a few examples of an unusual trend among immigrants of Korean descent. The trend was unusual for a variety of reasons: running a small business was not the apex of a neo-Confucian world view, Korean immigrants had no special training or background for entrepreneurship, and operating a liquor store or gas station in a poorer neighborhood could be unimaginably stressful.

Many scholars have studied this trend precisely because it's so unusual, and many of these studies have noted the crushing hours and the unrelenting pressures of small business entrepreneurship. However, this move away from low-wage work into shop-keeping did provide a crucial pathway for many more Korean Americans to experience a middle-class life – a house that they owned, the kids in school and in college, and thoughts of a more comfortable retirement. In 1992, when Korean Americans lost over $500 million in the days of rioting and chaos in Los Angeles, many of those dreams went up in flames, and members of that immigrant generation suffered deeply. Korean Americans who saw their shops burn and their family members killed were never going to be the same again. Still, after 1992, although Korean immigrant entrepreneurship changed and dispersed, it certainly didn't disappear – Korean American entrepreneurs set up in places like Dallas, northern Virginia, suburban New York, and Atlanta. Through ethnic churches and extended family networks, Korean immigrants were still opening businesses and pursuing economic opportunities in ways that were distinctive in American immigration history, and at a rate that was quite pronounced for most of the 1990s.[23]

The Immigration Act of 1990 had a profound impact on migratory flows from South Korea and from other Asian countries. Since 1990, a smaller fraction of immigrants has been coming for family reunification, and a growing fraction for employment as skilled workers. The EB-5 never drew the flood of foreign investment that some had envisioned, but South Koreans did take advantage of the visa from its very early years, and South Korean venture capitalists and transnational businesses moved many of their operations to southern California after 1990. South Koreans were much more likely to apply for an EB-5 than almost anyone else, and they also applied for the new L visa for intracompany transfers, for those people who might leave the Samsung division in Seoul to work at the Samsung division in Austin or in Los Angeles. To a great extent, Koreatown in Los Angeles was rebuilt with transnational capital and repopulated with skilled transnational labor – the Wilshire Bank, Assi Supermarkets, the Koreatown Galleria, and many other highly capitalized businesses and places would not have been possible without the basic changes to immigration law after 1990.[24]

Investments from abroad enhanced the value of existing properties, especially in commercial real estate, and some Korean Americans who were nowhere near the riots also did well. Dr. David Lee was 17 when he came to the United States with his parents in 1971, and he got his medical degree from Northwestern University and a degree in public health from UCLA, and he had a medical practice in West Los Angeles. He began investing in commercial real estate after 1992, almost as though it were a hobby. His properties increased in value, and then his company expanded its holdings after the earthquake in Northridge in 1994. In the early years, his analysts had invested in commercial spaces that to them seemed undervalued, mostly on the outskirts of downtown. In 2002, they bought their first property near the city center for $6 million. More followed. They did very well. The company benefited from the boom in commercial property values, at least through 2008. By 2015, Jamison Properties had holdings worth about $3 billion, and Dr. Lee was a major philanthropist in Los Angeles who was still investing in commercial properties in the city. In manner and demeanor, Dr. Lee was the opposite of the flashier tycoons on the East Coast – he didn't put his own name on every building, even when he gave $1 million to the UCLA School of Dentistry; nor was he seeking publicity for being one of the most affluent men in Southern California. He did not star in reality television shows. His children did help with the family business, but most people didn't know that his family was among the richest in the state.[25]

Overall, the rate of immigration among Koreans has declined – nearly 40,000 persons of Korean ancestry used to settle in the United States every year in the late 1970s and 1980s, but in recent years, they've been less than 20,000 per year. But ever since 1990, of those who arrived, more Korean immigrants were professionals, they were more likely to work for the American subsidiaries of Korean companies, and they, too, were experiencing a middle-class and upper-middle-class life. Before 1965, elite South Korean families used to drop off their children at the stuffier East Coast boarding schools – places like Groton, Choate, or Deerfield; nowadays, a much wider range of South Korean families have sent their children to the United States, and not just for the best private schools everywhere, but for the best public schools, too. In California, nearly all of the elementary and secondary schools marked as "distinguished" by academic performance have significant Asian student populations, and they all have at least a few families who've migrated and settled near those schools precisely because they've been marked as "distinguished."[26]

Over the last quarter-century, in these ways, immigration rules – even the targeted refugee resettlement policies of the Refugee Act of 1980 – have given a new dimension to an older "model minority myth," except, this time, many trends did suggest that aspects of the myth were in fact true. They were not true because Asians had superior cultural values or better genetics, but rather because American immigration law and policy had selected and drawn to the United States a completely unrepresentative sample of Asians. The Asian migrants after 1965 and 1990 were a unique group – refugees who had formed an elite class in their home countries, aspiring students and professionals who were fleeing dictatorships, and then their equally aspiring family members who came here for a better life. They all appeared to press their children to want more, especially when the parents were stuck minding delis or dry-cleaning clothes all day. "I have no choice but to do this," they might say to their children, "but you should do more than this." By 1980 and 1990, Asian immigrant families were sending their nerdiest children to elite colleges and universities at a rate that had no precedent in American history. The college administrators developed a bureaucratic term to describe these kids – they were "over-represented" minorities, meaning that they were less than 4 percent of the United States, but over 20 percent of the students at Stanford or at Harvard, and over a third of all students at the University of California. These younger, highly educated people were becoming professionals and members of the privileged classes.[27]

The Knowledge Class and the American Ethnoburb

It's not just that professional Asian immigrants and Asian immigrant entrepreneurs worked in core sectors of the American economy – their numbers were so significant that, should they decide to live amongst each other, they could form distinct ethnic communities notable for their size and economic activity. Sociologists and urban studies scholars developed a new term to describe these communities, "ethnoburbs," which were places defined by vibrant commercial activity, ethnic control of local politics, and social networks where an ethnic identity was an asset, not a liability. In the late 1920s and 1930s, Monterey Park, California, in the San Gabriel Valley northeast of Los Angeles, was one of the centers for Ku Klux Klan activities in Southern California. Alhambra and Monterey Park had hosted several Klan groups, and San Marino was a town where nearly every property had a racially restrictive covenant. In the mid-1970s, when Chinese Americans and other Asian professionals started moving into Monterey Park, some older White residents responded in ways that might seem "Klanish." They demanded, for example, that the City Council do something about all of the Asian-language signs all over the new businesses in the city, and they did not like how the new residents were requesting permits for granny units and in-law re-models.[28]

Local politics took on uncomfortable racial overtones, and to an extent that the Chinese residents responded by taking the United States citizenship test, and then voting in those local elections. As newer residents elected Chinese Americans to the City Council, one and then another, and still another, those older White residents saw that the times they were a-changing, and so they left – some might say "fled" – and yet, unlike in other instances of White flight, property values and the local schools and the local tax base did not collapse. They went up. Even more Asian professionals moved in. Valley Boulevard, one of the central thoroughfares that connects Monterey Park to its equally Asian ethnoburbs, became a unique, Asian and American commercial experience.

In the late 1990s, the "ethnoburb" was still a new term, and places like Monterey Park were exceptional. But as the Immigration Act of 1990 brought more professionals from Asia to the United States, and as new rules accelerated the trend, the story of Monterey Park appeared like a sign of things to come, rather than the one-off exception. Again, basic changes in the immigration law explained why: that H-1B visa created in the Act of 1990 was becoming popular among high-technology companies, particularly in the growing information technology sector. In the mid-1990s, executives from influential companies like Microsoft and Oracle complained that they had too many job openings, and not enough American citizens to fill them. The 140,000 visas for the employment-based categories in the Act of 1990 were simply insufficient, they said – some even suggested that perhaps there should be no limit on the number of highly skilled workers coming under employment-based visas. The demand for highly skilled workers in the information technology industries was so robust, they said, that Congress should allow whatever the market could bear. Critics of the H-1B visas replied that foreign workers were already depressing wages in this industry, and that a major increase in permanent employment-based visas would be a big mistake. This debate dragged on in Congressional hearings for most of the mid-1990s.

In 1998 and 2000, President Bill Clinton requested that Congress approve two rules to increase dramatically the number of H-1B visas, from 65,000 per year, as was stipulated in the Immigration Act of 1990, to an average of 110,000 per year from 1998 to 2001. In 2000, when the number of H-1B applications exceeded 200,000, Congress agreed to increase the ceilings again, to 195,000 for at least two years. President George W. Bush did not renew these higher ceilings, but, over time, the total number of H-1B visas per year hovered around 85,000 per year, as Congress approved exemptions for people who'd earned graduate degrees in the United States, for example, or exemptions for applicants working at American colleges and universities. Congress changed the rules for the H-1B as well: H-1B workers were no longer tied to the companies that sponsored them; they could apply for other jobs, and for permanent residency status; and they could remain in the United States as long as their applications for permanent residency were current. These tweaks reflected the fact that H-1B workers were different – they were highly educated, they knew how to lobby Congress, and they themselves had helped to develop the technologies that made social networking and on-line activism possible. They thus leveraged their skills to help make their immigration status less constraining and more flexible.

Despite these changes in the visa – up-and-down caps, exemptions, and political shifts in the popularity of the program – one thing remained constant: a clear majority of H-1B workers were from Asia, from countries like India, China, and South Korea. Under the H-1B program, even the migrants coming from, say, Canada, sometimes had Asian ancestry, and so this one single program brought many more highly skilled Asian migrants to the United States into a growing, core sector of the American economy in the late twentieth and early twenty-first centuries. Moreover, even though the H-1B was this "temporary" visa, more than half of all persons who were admitted under the H-1B eventually adjusted status to a permanent employment-based visa. Within five years, they could apply for citizenship. Many of them were not going back.[29]

In California, Asian immigrant professionals moved to cities like Monterey Park and Cupertino, Cerritos and Mountain View. Asian immigrants in the Chicago region were drawn to the University of Chicago, Northwestern, and the University of Illinois. In North Carolina, they lived within the Research Triangle – Duke University, the University of North Carolina, and North Carolina State. And in Massachusetts, they settled around Route 128, which formed a circle around Boston. Several hundred major technology companies, including Sun Microsystems and Wang Laboratories, were based around this highway, this "Magic Semicircle," where the supernerds from Harvard and MIT had been cashing in on the latest scientific inventions. Route 128 symbolized the "Massachusetts Miracle," a renaissance in the economy following a horrid period of deindustrialization and high unemployment. Indeed, throughout the United States, around the major research universities, and around any place that had a significant concentration of high-technology firms, Asian immigrants were making entire regions look like ethnoburbs.[30]

For the highly skilled and the wealthy – for people who had engineering degrees or computer science skills, or maybe just half a million dollars to invest in the United States – getting a job, gaining permanent residency, and living in the United States was not really that difficult. Indeed, American immigration rules made this much easier than ever before, starting with the Immigration Act of 1952, then reaffirmed in the Immigration Act of 1965. Congress greatly expanded these pathways for people with skills and wealth in the Immigration Act of 1990, and subsequent rules brought even more skilled workers. In another book, my older brother and I had argued that these rules were "engineering a model minority," in the sense that so many migrants coming under these visas were from Asia, and Asian immigrants and Asian Americans were thus, in a strange twist, *becoming* an affluent racial minority under these rules. My brother was right to spot that argument.

Yet, in a more profound way, what we might have also been seeing is the fact that, for a certain class of persons, we were already living in a borderless world. People who were highly educated, people who had vast wealth – they did not have to worry about fences or walls or cuts to public assistance or deindustrialization. People who could design or engineer robots, who had the skills to write software, or who had the wealth to invest in such enterprises could come and go across international boundaries more freely than ever before. Political scientists and philosophers discussed, throughout the last three decades, whether we should have "open borders" in the advanced industrialized world. For a subsection of the world's population, we already *had* open borders, as governments gave even greater freedom to skilled workers and wealthy people to live and work where they wished, through expansive rules like the ones in 1990, 1998, and 2000.[31]

Most people throughout the world did not have a college education or software program skills or a medical degree or $1 million – in fact, less than 1 percent of the world's population had access to an elite college education at the turn of the century. In 2000, Indian and Chinese educational institutions still fell far behind American colleges and universities, despite heavy investments in the previous decade. But because India and China were such huge countries, educating one-tenth of 1 percent in each country could still yield very large numbers. (Just try the math.)

These large figures could dwarf significant changes that these same immigration rules had been yielding in other important communities. For instance, after 1965 and 1990, a significant number of highly skilled people have migrated from African countries and from the Caribbean. The highly educated from Kenya, Ghana, and South Africa, and college graduates from Haiti and from Jamaica, came to the United States even before the Immigration Act of 1965, under programs to encourage students from everywhere to study at the American universities. These highly educated immigrants were, by 2000, disproportionately middle-class and upwardly mobile, and then their children were more likely to be highly educated than native-born African Americans. In addition, refugees from Africa, especially from eastern African nations like Eritrea, Somalia, and Ethiopia, also added new complexities to existing African American communities. And those "diversity visas" created by Congress in 1990, the ones with official advertisements featuring European-looking people who were invited to come to America, proved popular with people in many African nations as well. Altogether, these immigrants represented a major new migration of African and Afro-Caribbean persons to the United States in the late twentieth century. Indeed, at many of the major universities, students and faculty members of African ancestry were often African and Afro-Caribbean immigrants: these were people who had to pass into American citizenship rather than being born into it. They and their children were also members of the privileged classes, of a "knowledge class," of a group of people for whom international boundaries were not hard barriers.[32]

However, because Asian countries had made more investments overall at the major Asian universities, they were just bigger, perhaps vast and massive by comparison to what was available for young people in Ghana, Kenya, or Jamaica. This was why so many more Asian professionals and skilled workers were circulating around the world by 2000 and 2010. The *scale* of migration varied greatly: hundreds and thousands of people were coming from African countries every year, but tens and then hundreds of thousands of people from Asia were coming over that same period, year after year. Barack Obama was the son of a highly educated Kenyan immigrant, and yet, for every Barack Obama, Sr., there were just a lot more highly educated Asian immigrants, all of them having kids like Nikki Haley and Bobby Jindal. In time – maybe sooner than many Americans might expect – one of those nerdy kids born of Asian immigrant parents could very well win the nation's highest office.

We should at least pause for a moment to remark on the status and position of Asian Americans and Asian immigrants in light of these immigration trends. In 1882, Congress had insisted that Asian persons should not come at all to the United States, and over the next seven decades, local, state, and federal government rules restricted their economic opportunities, segregated them relentlessly, and otherwise made American citizenship impossible. Nowadays, though, more people from Asia come to live and to work in the United States than ever before, all legally, in industries where starting salaries are about twice the household income for average Americans. In the aggregate, persons of Asian ancestry were better educated, better paid, living longer, and amassing more wealth than other Americans – many scholars even suggested that newer immigrants fared better than more established Asian Americans in the third or fourth generation, as if assimilation into American life was rolling persons of Asian ancestry into a lower mean rather than keeping them higher than average. For scholars who specialized primarily in late nineteenth- and early twentieth-century United States legal history (like me), the trends remained mind-blowing. I think that they leave open the distinct possibility that the primary beneficiaries of the American Civil Rights Movement were Asian immigrants and their descendants. Moreover, Asian immigrants left not just because of changes in policies made in the United States, but also because so many Asian countries had used their leverage with the Americans to invest in the very people who then *became* Asian immigrants in the United States. The United States also supported governments in Asia that made staying in Asia an unattractive option for people who'd had options. Skilled immigrants, too, were "moved by war," civil strife, and political chaos.[33] Immigration policies here, and then investments in higher education there, in addition to the stresses of living under dictators – they made highly skilled migrations from Asia possible and likely, and without all of these factors working together, we wouldn't be seeing so many Asian professionals in Massachusetts or in North Carolina or in California. To my knowledge, no one in 1965 had predicted any of this.

7

OUT OF STATUS

Illegal Migrations as a Recurring Problem

Even as the world opened to the privileged, it was quite a different place for the very poor, the displaced, and the less educated and unskilled, especially if they were coming to the United States without permission. Hostility toward undocumented migrants was nothing new: during and after the Bracero Program, as many Americans discussed "illegal aliens," they often spoke of Mexican immigrants as though they were not really people. Willard Kelly, an official with the Border Patrol, described illegal immigrants collectively as the "greatest peacetime invasion ever complacently suffered by any country." Federal and state officials intimated in these statements a criticism about the American government itself: that government was failing, that it wasn't doing nearly enough in the face of the threat. After 1965, and certainly after 1986, more state and federal officials, politicians, and commentators were speaking along these same lines, to the point where illegal immigration became one of the most dominant themes in American immigration law and society, yet again.

Illegal immigration and illegal migration were not new problems. Indeed, before we discuss the period after 1965, we should take a step back to note that, although the dimensions of illegal immigration may indeed be new, Americans have always had, in one way or another, to confront people who were out of place. Most people might miss how fugitive slaves were migrating unlawfully whenever they left their masters without permission, but fugitive slaves were out of place, "out of status." There were so many of them that many states and the federal government legislated against their migration in every decade before the Civil War. By 1850, the problem had grown so much – with so many White American citizens harboring and helping fugitive slaves – that the federal government attempted to punish state and local officials for refusing to detain and return runaway slaves.

The Fugitive Slave Act of 1850 took a hard line against any state official who did not help to apprehend and to return runaway slaves. In the Midwestern and Far West states, White supremacists passed numerous rules to ban the settlement of all African Americans, free or slave. Thus, from the perspective of American citizens in, say, Illinois or Oregon, persons of African descent were illegal migrants, too, simply because the state legislatures did not envision African American citizenship north of slavery.

After the Civil War, race-based migration restrictions were still common and popular: shortly after the Gold Rush in 1849, California's legislature had passed a Foreign Miners' Tax, and, over the next two decades, the state passed numerous rules to limit and discourage the migration of Chinese immigrants. When California became the center of an anti-Chinese movement, White working-class labor unions were at the forefront of laws and policies directed against the Chinese, and the nationalist, economic logic of their arguments was inescapable. The labor unions said that wealthier Americans could "use" Chinese workers, but that this would harm White Americans and European immigrants, who would then experience "degrading" labor conditions. People in the state saw the same Chinese immigrants in profoundly different ways: for example, when Leland Stanford employed Chinese workers for the Central Pacific Railroad, and when they constructed their portion of the transcontinental railroad on time and under budget, Stanford proclaimed that Chinese laborers would be critical for other infrastructure and economic projects in the new state. He proposed no immigration restrictions against Chinese immigrants whatsoever.

Labor unions complained vehemently, and then violently, that Stanford had paid his Chinese workers much less than he had paid Irish workers (this was true), and that this kind of behavior, over many thousands of employers and labor contracts, would render White working-class men impoverished, unemployed, and degraded to the condition of "wage slaves." Forced to compete with Chinese men, White men said that they would never earn enough income to live a dignified life, to support a family, or to acquire property of their own. Rather than behaving as though Chinese immigrants might also want decent lives, families, and property, White working-class men insisted instead that the Chinese were racially inferior, unfit for citizenship, and thus should be subject to exclusion. As White citizens could vote and the Chinese could not, White working-class voters got what they had wanted, against the objections of wealthier White men and their corporations. When Congress approved the bar against Chinese labor immigration in the Chinese Exclusion Act of 1882, this represented a major victory for White labor unions, and for that racist idea that economic opportunities – in the form of jobs or property – should be reserved for Whites only, within a broader economic system that promoted White citizenship.

Runaway slaves and Chinese migrants were "illegal" for different reasons, and under conditions that were quite different from one another, and yet their experiences suggest recurring themes that are useful for understanding our own contemporary problems. In the eyes of White political majorities, neither African Americans nor Asian Americans were fit for American citizenship.

Notions of White supremacy drove federal and state restrictions throughout the late nineteenth century. State jurisdictions attempted to block the arrival of non-White persons – they represented, in many places, indigestible elements that tended to pit White people against one another. And even when exclusion proved less than completely successful, White majorities continued to disable and to disenfranchise people of color by reference to race, migration status, or both. Instead of thinking of "illegal aliens" as a new problem, then, as some scholars have claimed, we might best consider how they fit into a much longer history of illegal persons in American law and society, if only to appreciate how history might not repeat, and yet it did seem to rhyme.[1]

"Braceros," "Illegals"

Illegal immigrants from Mexico most probably crossed the Southern border just as President Johnson was signing the Immigration Act of 1965. In a peculiar way, the rule itself made those persons "illegal," as migrants who'd crossed the Southern border hadn't been regarded as "immigrants" in the classic sense. After all, from 1942 through 1965, the United States government itself had encouraged and stimulated the migration of Mexican nationals, and federal officials did little or nothing to stop migrants who'd come outside the boundaries of the Bracero Program. After 1910, many Mexican nationals fled north in the wake of the Mexican Revolution, and the American government didn't "admit" them as refugees, but rather did little or nothing to stop this migration. Even after large-scale enforcement actions like Operation Wetback in 1954, migrations back and forth were common, there were no fences or walls, and living for a time on one side of the border and then the other was rather routine. The border would not be militarized for another two decades.

In that time, hundreds and then thousands of migrants crossed the border, and for a range of reasons. Most often, they crossed to find work: the United States enjoyed a rate of economic development in the postwar years that far outpaced Mexico, and so American workers were, on average, earning considerably more than their Mexican peers, even in comparable forms of low-wage work. Well into 1960, growers in California paid more than most employers in almost any other form of low-wage work in Mexico, thus providing the largest pull for workers from south to north. In 1952, when Congress passed a comprehensive immigration law, representatives from Texas included what became a "Texas proviso" – in general, no one should "harbor" or assist illegal immigrants, according to the rules in 1952, but offering them a job would not be considered "harboring" under that proviso. Growers and their political supporters did not want to be punished for offering work, and so many thousands of growers continued to do so to people coming and going across the Southern border.

In the Immigration Act of 1965, President Johnson promised that Mexico would be like any other country – there would be an annual quota, and there would be preferences for skilled workers and for family reunification. His Administration promised an end to uncontrolled migration across the Southern border. The Immigration Act of 1952 had created an H-2 visa for temporary unskilled workers, and members of the Johnson Administration insisted that growers apply for this visa to hire agricultural workers legally in the Southwest. But because the Immigration Act of 1965 did not eliminate the Texas proviso, growers had very little incentive to hire workers legally when so many illegal workers were available. They did not require any government paperwork, and so neither the growers nor the Mexican immigrants had any real incentives to follow the law. Because Mexican immigrants continued to find work, they continued to come well after the Act of 1965.

Moreover, as we have discussed in previous chapters, jobs were not the only reasons for steady migrations across the Southern border – political turmoil in Central America drove thousands of people, from several countries, through Mexico and into the United States after 1965 as well. Peasant guerrillas and government forces had traded low-level violence ever since the Cuban Revolution in 1959, but their battles exploded into intense civil wars in El Salvador and in Guatemala, and these dragged on from the late 1970s into the early 1990s. The violence spilled across the borders into Honduras and Costa Rica, and Mexico itself had a significant "illegal" population for most of that period. As we saw, even when American congregations offered "sanctuary" to people whose stories were so horrifying, the American federal government defined the vast majority of these migrants as "illegal" under prevailing American immigration laws. And we should also note that, although the "sanctuary movement" did expand to include many more congregations and local jurisdictions throughout the United States, most American churches and jurisdictions did not offer shelter or help to Central American migrants. A few religious leaders agreed with the federal government that to do so would be to break the law. Thus, almost immediately after the Act of 1965, Americans were divided again about large groups of people who were "out of place."[2]

Americans could not agree about who was or wasn't an "illegal immigrant" or an "economic migrant" or a "refugee," or whether such persons should have access to jobs or to asylum, or whether they should all be removed back to their home countries as quickly as possible. It wasn't just Central Americans: in 1991, a military coup toppled the fledgling government of Jean-Bertrand Aristide, the newly elected President of Haiti. In the ensuing crisis, thousands of people fled the country, crossing over into the Dominican Republic, or boarding ships of various sizes and conditions to try for the United States. In the decade between 1980 and 1990, the United States Coast Guard had intercepted about 25,000 Haitians at sea, and it had returned many of them back to Haiti. But in 1991 and 1992, at the height of the latest refugee crisis, the Coast Guard intercepted over 40,000 migrants from Haiti, and President Bush authorized the use of Guantanamo Bay Naval Station, on the southeastern tip of Cuba, to house and to detain these migrants. The Coast Guard spotted many hundreds of bodies off the coast of Florida during those terrible months.[3]

And further north, in the summer of 1993, a cargo vessel ran aground off the shore of Long Island, New York, with about 300 Chinese migrants aboard; 10 people drowned as they tried to swim ashore. Over the next four years, as many of these migrants requested asylum in the United States, members of our own government could not agree whether these Chinese migrants were "refugees" fleeing from communism, victims of human trafficking, or just plain illegal immigrants. Over land and over sea, thousands of migrants were risking their lives and enduring horrors to come to the United States, and Americans could not agree about what to do with all of them.[4]

In the late 1960s, Mexican Americans were also among the confused Americans who did not know how best to address this problem. On the one hand, Cesar Chavez and other prominent labor leaders knew that braceros and undocumented agricultural workers were living and working in deplorable conditions, and that they would benefit the most from joining labor unions and gaining collective bargaining rights. On the other hand, however, some growers had become so dependent upon undocumented workers that they had little incentive to bother with legal residents or American citizens at all. In time, Chavez came to believe that *all* foreign workers had to go in order for those who had legal residency or American citizenship to have a chance to bargain collectively against the growers. If foreign workers remained available for agricultural growers, the United Farm Workers (UFW) said, then the union would never have sufficient leverage to improve wages and working conditions for people who had an indisputable right to work. Thus, Chavez was among those who'd pressed President Johnson to limit migration from Mexico.[5]

The UFW also lobbied for tougher rules in the states. In the years after 1965, California and nine other states passed rules that punished employers for hiring undocumented immigrant workers. Governor Ronald Reagan signed a California statute in 1971 that provided for sanctions against employers who "knowingly employ an alien who is not entitled to lawful residence in the United States if such employment would have an adverse effect on lawful resident workers." Through the United Farm Workers, Cesar Chavez promoted an "Illegal Campaign," through which they urged their own members to report when employers were hiring undocumented workers. The growers sued, and an appellate court in California agreed that, because this was an immigration regulation, and because Congress and the federal government had "occupied the field," the state rule was invalid. The California appellate court noted that, in 1952, Congress had exempted growers from sanctions of this kind when they hired foreign workers.

On appeal, the United States Supreme Court reversed that decision. Justice William Brennan said that the California rule was a reasonable exercise of the state's power to regulate labor markets in the state. The Supreme Court's decision in *De Canas* v. *Bica* in 1976 upheld regulations against undocumented workers in several other states, despite the Texas proviso. This precedent also added support for that federal version of the rule in 1986, when President Ronald Reagan signed the Immigration Reform and Control Act. But, by 1986, Cesar Chavez was also supporting the humanitarian provisions of the Act – indeed, many of his own closest allies within the UFW were out of status, and they indicated clearly that they wished to remain in the United States and to work with their colleagues to improve conditions in the fields. For many members of the UFW, the legalization provisions were deeply personal, touching their families and closest friends. Having been in the struggle so long, Chavez and other union leaders pushed to legalize the very people that his own organization had once sought to remove. Some members of the UFW opposed employer sanctions as well, the theory being that these provisions might lead to discrimination against anyone who might look "illegal." If all of this sounded contradictory and odd, it was because immigration issues had tended to pull many people in different, opposing directions.[6]

For example, in 1975, in what was a somewhat obscure provision of a bill about a completely different topic, the Texas legislature and governor had approved a rule that allowed school districts to charge $1,000 in tuition per child, every year, to any family who could not prove that they were in the United States legally. This provision did not stir a great floor debate, nor was it especially controversial in Texas, where many local school officials had been complaining about the costs of educating children who spoke Spanish as their first language, and whose dress and manner suggested that they weren't American citizens. In Tyler, Texas, a town that was over 100 miles away from the southern border, the Superintendent applied the rule and sent notices to parents in English and in Spanish, telling them that the district was now going to charge tuition accordingly. Several families simply moved out of the district, while other parents consulted with lawyers to prepare a case against the rule. Attorneys for the state contacted their federal immigration enforcement colleagues, and they considered deporting the plaintiffs, under the theory that they were suing precisely because they were illegally in the United States. A federal judge blocked those actions so that the case could proceed. Already, this was becoming an important and very strange case, one that implicated public finance, public education, state power, and the American Constitution. During the case itself, the Superintendent James Plyler, the object of the lawsuit, wasn't sure that he wanted to win, as a "victory" would lead to many more children unable to attend school. Decades later, he said that he was glad he'd lost.[7]

"Fundamental Conceptions of Justice …"

Many scholars of the immigration law have been captivated by *Plyler* v. *Doe* (1982), that landmark case from Texas. In *Plyler*, decided seven years after Texas had passed the rule, Justice Brennan and four of his colleagues on the United States Supreme Court struck it down, primarily because they agreed that the children in this case were not responsible for their unlawful status. That is, they were in Texas unlawfully, but this was because their parents brought them there – their parents were the ones morally responsible for the family's unlawful status, and yet to cut off access to public education was unfair to their children. The Justices cited other cases where the federal courts had rejected policies that harmed children based on the actions of their parents. Such rules often appeared as unjust: "Even if the State found it expedient to control the conduct of adults by acting against their children, legislation directing the onus of a parent's misconduct against his children does not comport with fundamental conceptions of justice." In response to this legal analysis, many scholars (including me) have been quite taken with this case, with the unwillingness of the Court to uphold state policies that discriminate against children for a status that they did not control. I think *Plyler* appears in every book I've written, including now this one.⁸

Philosophically, the case raised interesting questions because *no one* controls the circumstances of their birth. Also, if it was true that disabling children for the actions of their parents was unjust, then it might also be true that privileging children who just happened to have wealthy citizen parents might be problematic in similar ways. How many such spoiled and rotten children have each of us encountered? They appeared all the more annoying because we knew, intuitively, even though they did not, that they did not deserve any of the advantages that they'd received – they *happened* to have been born into a family and into a set of circumstances that made their lives more comfortable. The retired Senator from Nevada, Harry Reid, once said this of the businessman Donald Trump: "He was born on third base, but he acts like he hit a triple." The observation was funny because we generally preferred people who were born on third base to acknowledge that they had significant advantages. People thus incapable of acknowledging their privileged position might strike us as lacking in self-awareness, as perhaps too self-absorbed or narcissistic, even ridiculous.

Analyses of privilege can lead us to consider the other side of the underlying problems with status-based inequalities: they tend to disable some *and* advantage others based on characteristics that members of *neither group* can control. In race-based inequalities, for example, it wasn't just that people of color suffered legal disabilities, it's also that White folks enjoyed a privileged position with respect to people of color in ways that were undeserving. Neither people of color nor the White folks "deserved" these disabilities or privileges: people of color did not deserve to suffer loss of opportunities or access to resources based on a racial identity that they did not control. And White folks also didn't deserve to enjoy those same opportunities or access based on an identity that they, too, did not control. Really, what was the sense of having handed a White child, born the same hour as an African American child, a full set of constitutional rights as well as robust economic opportunities, while denying the same to that other kid? Gender-based discriminations have the same problematic quality: it seems odd to confer so many more advantages to a child just because he is born male rather than female. Again, it isn't simply that gender-based discriminations harm women – the other related moral problem is that they advantage men, for no other reason than that they are men. Nowadays, in liberal democracies, citizens have rejected sex-based discriminations not just because they denigrated women, but also because they elevated men for no good reason.⁹

In the context of immigration, scholars drew from these analyses to suggest that immigration status might be as troublesome and indefensible as race- or gender-based discriminations. Some people were born in more stable, prosperous countries – they acquired citizenship in those countries through circumstances of birth, really by doing nothing other than being born within the territory or to parents who were already citizens. Discriminations against non-citizens in those countries were thus problematic in both directions: they disabled people who weren't fortunate enough to be born into membership; and they also conferred advantages upon citizens who themselves didn't do anything to deserve their citizenship. To paraphrase the arguments of several leading scholars, immigration status – especially the acquisition of birthright citizenship – thus appeared similar to a "feudal privilege," like winning a "birthright lottery" if you happened to have been born into a wealthier country. This remained a status acquired through birth for the clear majority of citizens, but it certainly wasn't based on merit or any other kind of purposeful action.[10]

Since the mid-1990s, opponents of illegal immigration have tended to agree that birthright citizenship was arbitrary and unfair, but they often made such arguments to revoke or to limit birthright citizenship for children born to undocumented parents. At least one parent should be legally present in the United States for a child to have American citizenship at birth, they said, and automatically giving this citizenship to anyone – simply because they were born here – was irrational and unjust. In 2015, Senator Lindsey Graham of South Carolina, Senator Ted Cruz of Texas, and a number of other Republican candidates for president, including Ben Carson, Chris Christie, Marco Rubio, Jeb Bush, and Donald Trump, all questioned the birthright citizenship clause of the 14th Amendment. They railed against "anchor babies," and each insisted that they were tougher than the others on this issue, to the point of promising that they would either amend the Constitution or overturn standing precedents to deny "automatic citizenship" to the children of parents who had no legal status in the United States. Their arguments, though, missed the underlying moral problems associated with giving *anyone* a legal status based on the circumstances of birth – it's not as though Ted Cruz or Marco Rubio "deserved" their American citizenship any more than the children whose citizenship they would deny. If it was unfair and irrational to give those kids American citizenship, then how was it any more fair or rational to have given it to Ted or to Marco? Donald Trump had seemed especially obsessed with the circumstances of Barack Obama's birth, but, like the other Republicans, he never discussed how he himself didn't quite deserve his own American citizenship. All of their talk was more politics, not philosophy. Indeed, this debate among the Republicans was more telling in other ways, as it perhaps reflected a deep anxiety about how the children of undocumented parents might *actually* vote, if and when they started voting.[11]

If the system of nation-states was roughly equal – if being born into one state was no better or worse than being born into some other state – then assigning citizenship status through an ascriptive system may not pose serious moral problems, nor would the status itself appear as unjust. Between the advanced industrialized states, this kind of rough equality might exist already – the citizens of Germany and the citizens of France nowadays haven't complained about the injustice of being born to the right or to the left of the Rhine. South Koreans weren't rushing to be Japanese, and Japanese folks weren't moving en masse to Korea. Yet between states that were unequal or profoundly unequal, due to a wide range of complex factors, the boundary itself can still represent significant differences in status and in opportunities.

The Rio Grande was a river that marked that kind of boundary, and so much so that being born on the one side could represent a huge advantage compared to children born on the opposite side. The Supreme Court Justices in *Plyler* behaved as though they knew of this reality – that public institutions in Texas were better than the ones in Nuevo Leon or in Coahuila. They treated the possibility of removing or forcing away the children of undocumented aliens as something likely to cause them real harm. In the decision itself, the Court suggested harm in the other direction as well: the federal government may never get around to deporting these children or their parents, and thus, left on this side, these children might form an uneducated underclass of non-citizens, perhaps growing dangerous and threatening for not having been folded into American society. Instead of offering an education, perhaps using the education itself to make them more American, the rule in Texas was in the long run irrational, according to the Court's majority. Either way, the rule was too mean to people who were too innocent, or not mean enough to eliminate the foreseeable problems arising from the rule. The dissenters agreed in part that the Texas rule was probably not the most rational or the most empathetic piece of legislation, and yet they insisted that the state was within its rights to pass the rule. Public education was not a constitutional right, nor was it obvious that local taxpayers should have to shoulder the burden of financing the education of people who had no right to be in the United States at all. Five Justices composed the majority in *Plyler*, four dissented. The nine Justices filed five opinions in the case. Their disagreements foreshadowed further divisions about this most divisive issue across all Americans.

Many people were thinking about *Plyler*. Through the legalization provisions of the Immigration Reform and Control Act in 1986, President Reagan and members of Congress did seek to bring people "out of the shadows," while deterring others from coming into the United States. Many of the "Does," the families who were the protagonists in *Plyler*, benefitted from the Act of 1986, and President Reagan alluded to them when he signed the bill into law. But legalization proved only partly successful, and, as we've noted, even though President Bush further expanded the number of family members who could benefit from the Act of 1986, the overall number of people who were unlawfully residing in the United States grew over the next decade, and then doubled again in another ten years. By 1992, at least 2.5 million people had adjusted into lawful permanent residency, but as many others were now out of status. A few scholars and politicians blamed the policy of legalization itself: prospective unlawful migrants might think that if the federal government could adjust so many people once, perhaps it would do so again. Many Republicans thus swore never to support another "amnesty."[12]

Republicans like Pat Buchanan, a former speechwriter for President Nixon, and one of the leading rivals for the Republican presidential nomination in 1992, said that Ronald Reagan's own support for the legalization provisions was a big mistake for the country and for his party. As a conservative commentator, Buchanan had also cautioned against the Immigration Act of 1990, because it greatly increased legal migration, enlarged those pathways for legalization and adjustment, and did nothing to stop the migration of poorer non-Europeans. Non-Europeans were a problem, Buchanan said, during a moment when other conservatives were reconciling themselves to multicultural and multiracial realities. Indeed, other national politicians spoke in a more "dog-whistle" language about race – their closet White supremacist supporters might know, for example, that when Ronald Reagan talked about "welfare queens," he meant

African American women living large on public assistance. Buchanan was more direct than Ronald Reagan, and, as he was approaching the presidential primaries in 1992, he said many things bluntly: multiculturalism (like homosexuality) was bad, the United States should remain a Christian nation (Muslims should be discouraged), and Mexican immigrants had too many children (as well as nefarious plots to reincorporate the Southwest back into Mexico). He said that mass immigration was a threat to the character of the United States, and that the race-neutral principles of the Immigration Act of 1965 were all wrong. He provided this illustration in one of his speeches: if the federal government had a choice between admitting, say, Zulus or British immigrants in a state like Virginia, it seemed obvious to Buchanan that the federal government should pick the British (even though they'd once been the mortal enemies of Virginians).[13]

Progressive critics and politicians said that people like Pat Buchanan were degenerate, regressive racists. But these criticisms arose at an unfortunate time, when places like Los Angeles or New York, where thousands of immigrants had adjusted, were mired in race-based conflicts and interethnic tensions. Combined with further, widespread joblessness, all of this seemed headed toward various kinds of urban catastrophes. In 1992, the year of the Los Angeles riots, the national unemployment rate was 7.5 percent, Los Angeles County recorded over 2,000 homicides – as did New York City – and many politicians insisted that these trends required much harsher measures, especially in the criminal justice system. Pat Buchanan challenged President George H. W. Bush from the right wing of the Republican Party, and new candidates, including the Governor of Arkansas, Bill Clinton, challenged the President from the Democratic side.

President Bush did reclaim the Republican nomination, but in a badly weakened position. H. Ross Perot, a businessman from Texas, ran as an independent in 1992, having only declared his candidacy earlier that year. He drew over 18 percent of the popular vote in that November election, the highest fraction of any third-party candidate since George Wallace in 1968. Ross Perot and Pat Buchanan were both adversaries and allies – they acknowledged that they were competing for the same voters, the ones who didn't like Washington DC, Democrats of any kind, moderate Republicans, immigrants, or multilateral trade agreements, such as the North America Free Trade Agreement (NAFTA). Both men said that, although NAFTA was supposed to reduce tariffs and other barriers to trade between Canada, Mexico, and the United States, it would hurt American workers in the long run, and it would do nothing to control immigration from Mexico to the United States. In 1992 and in 1996, Ross Perot's presidential campaigns very probably helped Bill Clinton by splitting Republican constituencies – Clinton won the presidency in both elections with less than half of the popular vote. He signed NAFTA. Ross Perot and Pat Buchanan remained active in national politics throughout the 1990s, although the men split to support new political parties. Ross Perot formed and ran for President under the Reform Party in 1996. Pat Buchanan was an important affiliate of a new political party in 2002, one that was calling itself America First.[14]

"Officers Shall Not Initiate Police Action ..."

By any measure, urban crime rates rose to horrible levels in the early 1990s, and they caused many law enforcement officials to wonder how the nation might deal with rioting, drug use, chronic joblessness, or gang violence. Nothing was getting better: many observers noted that members of organized gangs of every hue and variety were turning neighborhoods into places that were like war zones, fighting and killing each other primarily over the trade in illicit drugs. In some places, the drug trade seemed to be the only remaining economic activity. Long-term trends in criminal justice were looking very bad: in 1970, the state and federal prison systems held fewer than 500,000 people, but by 1980, prison populations were growing at an alarming pace, so that, a decade later, more than 1 million people were incarcerated in the state and federal prisons. This did not include people who were on probation, or people in local jails and county facilities, whose numbers would have added even more evidence of a trend toward mass incarceration. Many scholars have since argued that by criminalizing non-violent drug offenses, President Reagan's "war on drugs" added significantly to the rate of incarceration, as did mandatory sentences and new rules for people convicted of multiple offenses. Whatever the reason – for a great many reasons – people in the United States were much more likely to be under the supervision of the criminal justice system than in any other advanced industrialized country. All of this was expensive: each inmate in a state prison cost a small fortune to house and to supervise, and because many states built more prisons to house a growing number of inmates, state legislatures devoted a greater share of the state budgets to crime and to punishment. Nowhere was this trend more obvious than in California.[15]

When he was a United States Senator from California in 1986, Pete Wilson had supported the Immigration Reform and Control Act, calling it "a much needed step in the right direction." On the floor of the Senate, Wilson had been pessimistic about the employer sanctions within the law, as they might "reduce illegal immigration at most by only 20 percent to 30 percent," but he still supported the bill's legalization provisions, as he agreed with President Reagan that agricultural workers were essential to the economies of the Southwestern states. In 1990, when Governor George Deukmejian chose not to seek a third term, Pete Wilson defeated the Democrat Dianne Feinstein to become the state's chief executive, but during a rather tough patch in California history.

Governor Wilson inherited a budget crisis: the Cold War was coming to an end (the Americans had won, the Soviet Union would cease to exist by the end of 1991), but federal spending on national defense had already been falling sharply, with disproportionate consequences on California's defense contractors. In addition, other light manufacturing and heavy industries in the Bay Area, Los Angeles, and San Diego continued to shed jobs, following a longer pattern of deindustrialization, while the state's agricultural sector suffered through its fifth year of drought, plus a hard winter in 1991 that left many of the state's largest farms with nothing to harvest. The state's recession seemed multi-directional, and some said it was biblical in scope; leading economists described the state's problems as "fairly spectacular." Governor Wilson asked the legislature to raise taxes, which was something that he'd promised not to do during his campaign. Indeed, when he was still in the Senate, Wilson had voted against President Bush's tax bill in 1990, arguing that Bush was less of a Republican for even having proposed a tax increase at all.[16]

By 1991, though, nearly everyone in California was paying more. The Governor and the legislature approved an increase to the state sales tax and to car registration and licensing fees. They also taxed novel things, like newspaper subscriptions and "snacks," which occasionally led to absurd arguments about what was or wasn't a "snack." Some joked that the tax on newspapers was the Governor's response to bad press. Other increases were more serious: the state's recession resulted in such severe funding cuts that students were paying upwards of 40 percent more in tuition at the University of California. All of these fees and taxes and tuition hikes made Governor Wilson rather unpopular among large segments of the California electorate. To complicate his life further, Governor Wilson had also inherited an on-going drug war based in Los Angeles, one that was spreading beyond the county, involving dozens of criminal organizations. The street gangs in Los Angeles were as diverse as the rest of the city – they were Mexican, Salvadoran, Korean, Chinese, African American, and plain White. Then, just a year into his term, Los Angeles imploded during the riots of April and May 1992, and President Bush had to send the California National Guard to quell the chaos.[17]

Among the historians who specialize in immigration history, one recurring truism has been that hard economic times also spawn harsh immigration rules: people who might have been open to immigrants and to immigration become, in hard times, far less sympathetic, perhaps devolving into a hostility that, in the fullness of time, they themselves found surprising, even regrettable. For most of his political life, Pete Wilson did not express an aversion to immigrants: as the Mayor of San Diego and as Senator from California, Wilson knew that many of his political allies – like many of Ronald Reagan's supporters – were agricultural growers allergic to government regulations, including labor regulations that might endanger their work force. Pete Wilson wasn't going around embracing Cesar Chavez or singing protest songs with farm workers, but he also didn't propose mass deportations, nor did he talk of undocumented workers as persistent threats to the state of California.[18]

Like Ronald Reagan, Wilson considered them primarily as agricultural laborers who worked hard, took jobs that American citizens didn't want any more, and thus kept vegetable and fruit prices low for consumers in California and elsewhere. Especially elsewhere: California growers sold most of their produce and commodities outside the state. Citizens of the state could not consume several metric tons of almonds or thousands of tons of peaches. These were canned, processed, frozen, refrigerated, and preserved, and then sent on trains and planes to places all over the world. Wilson was not prone to talking about people who had no lawful status as though they were an existential threat to the republic, when in fact they were vital to this sector of the state's economy. But then he did. Right around the time of the Los Angeles riots, when his administration faced its worst days and when he had to consider the very real prospect that he would be a one-term Governor, Pete Wilson led his state and then the nation into a much harsher period of "immigration reform," directed first at illegal immigrants, and then at immigrants in general.[19]

Governor Wilson's sharpest turn on immigration occurred during and after the riots themselves, when he learned that the National Guard, the Los Angeles Police Department, and the Los Angeles County Sheriff's Department had apprehended hundreds of people who had no lawful status in the United States. Since 1979, during the sanctuary movement, the Los Angeles City Council had ordered officers for the Los Angeles Police Department not to act as an extension of the federal immigration enforcement services: "Officers shall not initiate police action with the objective of discovering the alien status of a person," and "officers shall not arrest nor book persons for violation of . . . the United States Immigration code." By 1992, although many police officers knew that this Special Order 40 was designed to protect people who may have been eligible for refugee status, at least in the eyes of the City Council, officers with the LAPD and other law enforcement officials were wary of following the order during the riots. Many of the people that they'd arrested had no driver's licenses or other official forms of identification. Indeed, hundreds of such persons were in their custody in late April and May 1992, for criminal mischief, for arson, for taking diapers and baby formula and food from stores left abandoned to rioters and looters. Key field officers decided to contact federal immigration officials to have them pick up those people, if just to free up space in the city jails and county prisons. Before May 4, local officials had remanded over 1,200 people, and over the next few weeks, their federal colleagues put nearly all of them into deportation proceedings.[20]

Governor Wilson had known vaguely about Special Order 40, and he also knew that the Pico-Union district of Los Angeles was one of the most densely populated places in the state, with a higher concentration of residents per square mile than any other part of California. Many thousands of poorer migrants from El Salvador lived there. When Governor Wilson had heard about the looting and the arrests in that neighborhood, he demanded to know why so many people without lawful status were in Los Angeles, and then why they should remain at all in the United States. Governor Wilson also demanded that the Los Angeles City Council and other local governments *cooperate* with, rather than ignore, federal immigration enforcement efforts, and deport as many "illegal aliens" as possible. His political opponents, including Dianne Feinstein and Kathleen Brown, said that Governor Wilson was finding an expedient scapegoat in the wake of his own shortcomings. But as the elections for United States Senate and for Governor of California were approaching in 1994, Wilson grew more strident in his position against illegal immigrants.[21]

Governor Wilson threw his support behind a state-wide ballot measure introduced by Republican Assemblyman Dick Mountjoy. This measure became Proposition 187, and it represented a complete turn against illegal immigration and illegal immigrants. The first section stipulated that all state law enforcement officials should cooperate with federal authorities to identify and to detain persons who were out of status. They "must investigate" immigration status when making arrests, if they believed that the suspect was an illegal immigrant.

If a state public official suspected that an illegal immigrant had applied for a public benefit or public service, including any form of public assistance, those officials were required to report such persons to federal authorities. And students who could not prove legal residency in the state of California were not to be admitted into the state's public schools. Public school districts would have two years to check everyone's status to make sure that no such students were enrolled. In these direct ways, Proposition 187 meant to undo Special Order 40, and to challenge the California appellate case in *Viloria*, and the United States Supreme Court opinion in *Plyler*. California state officials were to find and to facilitate the removal of all persons who were out of status, and the "illegals" would be entitled to nothing.[22]

Governor Wilson had approval ratings that were terrible in 1992, and his chief opponent for the governorship, Kathleen Brown, had had many advantages. She was the daughter of Pat Brown, one of the most popular Governors in California history, and she was the youngest sister of Jerry Brown, Pat's son and a former Governor of the state for two terms. Kathleen was to be the first woman to hold the governorship of California. She could not have had a more stellar political pedigree, as well as extensive experience in the private and public sectors. She had held executive positions at Goldman Sachs and at the Bank of America, plus three years as the State Treasurer of California. In the summer of 1993, many political experts thought that she would beat Governor Wilson by a wide margin. She tried for a unifying theme, and she opposed Proposition 187, saying that the measure was too extreme and divisive. Hundreds of thousands of people also opposed Proposition 187 – in the months and weeks leading up to that November election, they demonstrated in marches and in political rallies that were some of the largest in the state's history. His critics called Governor Wilson a hypocrite – after all, he had supported the Immigration Reform and Control Act in 1986, even though, more recently, the newspapers said that he had been violating the same law by hiring people on his household staff who were out of status. But Kathleen Brown, as well as both candidates for the United States Senate seat in California, Diane Feinstein and Michael Huffington, also had similar "nanny problems." Every major political candidate in California had hired an undocumented worker, even though they swore up and down the state that each one of them would do something about illegal immigration.

In November 1994, Governor Pete Wilson won re-election, having defeated the woman who had been leading for most of the race. That result was less stunning than this one: Proposition 187 had passed by a wide margin, with nearly 60 percent of votes cast coming out in favor of the rule. A majority of Californians, it seemed, were eager to cast aside local policies, state-wide precedents, and United States Supreme Court precedents – they had approved a new immigration measure that was, to paraphrase one moderate Republican, "the epitome of meanness." For people who were out of status in California, and for others who did not think of such people as criminals or existential threats, the results of that election were shocking, maybe unbelievable. Voters in California had rejected a highly qualified and well-recognized woman with a familiar last name, and, instead, they chose a man whose most obvious shift in politics came at the expense of people who couldn't vote against him. He had promised to do whatever he could to remove some of the poorest and most marginal people in California. Thousands of people had marched against the rule, but political observers pointed out later that many of those marchers were probably immigrants, and then perhaps many of them had no lawful status. They were *participating* in politics, but they were legally disenfranchised, and they were now in a much more precarious state than before.[23]

Entitled to Nothing

The election had consequences for other people, too. After the riots in 1992, a Korean American businessman from a city east of Los Angeles had declared his candidacy for the United States House of Representatives. A graduate of the University of Southern California, Chang Joon Kim had had some experience in city government as the Mayor of Diamond Bar, but he had not been active in state-wide politics, let alone the federal government. He ran in a brand new Congressional district, in an area that had not been the target of rioting or looting, but close enough to see and to smell the smoke of the fires that had consumed Los Angeles. Mr. Kim went by Jay Kim when he sought and got the Republican nomination for the 41st Congressional race, and in the summer of 1992, he made several trips to Koreatown, west of downtown Los Angeles, to meet with business leaders and Korean American entrepreneurs who'd been shaken by the riots. He promised them that if they supported his candidacy, he would sponsor new rules to punish anyone for this kind of lawlessness, and to deport anyone convicted of a crime and who wasn't an American citizen.[24]

Although he was a political novice, and dismissed as such in mainstream circles, Jay Kim drew large, angry audiences of Korean Americans wherever he spoke. He said that he could bring them justice, maybe vengeance. As an engineer and as a businessman with a lucrative and successful company, Kim said that he found immigrants who'd relied on public assistance rather revolting – they should be thrown off social welfare, he said, and they should work hard like Korean immigrants. To older Korean Americans, Jay Kim seemed like *their* representative, even though most of them didn't live in his district. To anyone who understood Korean, however, his slurs and racist comments against Latinos and African Americans were as blunt as they were obvious. No one would mistake him for a bleeding-heart liberal. Jay Kim won the Congressional seat in 1992, he had received a great deal of financial support from Korean Americans throughout Los Angeles in that campaign, and he became thus the first Korean American ever to sit in the United States Congress.

When he came to Washington DC in 1993, Jay Kim met and befriended the House Minority Whip, Newt Gingrich of Georgia, a man widely rumored to be in line for Speaker of the House should Democrats ever lose control of that chamber. Gingrich was hopeful in that regard: he knew that Bill Clinton won the 1992 presidential election by a plurality vote, that Clinton was embroiled in sex scandals before and during his early presidency, and that he had flip-flopped on tough issues, including immigration policy. During the campaign, Clinton had suggested that President George H. W. Bush did not like persons of African descent, for why else would he use military resources to interdict Haitian refugees at sea, and to imprison them on Guantanamo Bay, instead of offering them refuge from yet another right-wing regime in Haiti? Clinton promised to reverse that policy. But then he didn't. Having criticized his predecessor relentlessly, he kept those policies in place once he was in office. Clinton was no more likely to release Chinese detainees who were also seeking asylum – in the case from Long Island, for example, the Clinton Administration approved of detention in federal facilities while the Chinese migrants pursued their asylum claims. Clinton tended to alienate the left wing of his own party – he signed the North American Free Trade Agreement, which had been opposed by mainstream labor unions, and his major health care reform went down in a stinging defeat in 1994, after two years of debate, further demoralizing members of his own party.[25]

In 1994, in that same election when voters approved Proposition 187 in California, Newt Gingrich engineered the single biggest election victory for Republicans in the United States Congress since World War II. It was a "revolution": the Republicans gained 54 seats in the House, 8 in the Senate. They controlled Congress for the first time since 1952. Senator Bob Dole became the Majority Leader in the Senate, and Newt Gingrich was now the Speaker of the House, broadly lauded among the Republicans for engineering a national strategy that brought them new power in Washington DC, as well as in many key state governorships. Gingrich had promised a "Contract With America," elements of which included basic reforms to reduce the size of the federal government, including its public assistance programs, while also calling for a greater role for the federal government in the criminal justice system. The Contract made no explicit mention of immigration or immigrants, but Jay Kim of California was re-elected in 1994, too, and he was incensed to learn that the federal courts had blocked Proposition 187 despite its broad support. To his most powerful friends in Congress, who happened now to be members of the majority party, he insisted that his own victory, Governor Wilson's victory, and the success of Proposition 187 all suggested that Congress should revisit immigration law before the next election.[26]

In early 1995, Representative Jay Kim sponsored two distinct rules: H.R. 484 would prohibit aliens not lawfully in the United States from any federally funded public assistance programs; and H.R. 637 would limit public assistance programs to aliens permanently and *lawfully* in the United States. These bills mirrored and then went well beyond Proposition 187, which had dealt with illegal immigrants. Kim had proposed doing away with all forms of public assistance to lawful immigrants, saying that no new immigrants should be eligible for these programs until *after* they had paid their taxes. Other members of the party agreed: his colleague in the House, Lamar Smith of Texas, had introduced a bill to require prospective American sponsors of immigrants to show that they themselves were not living below the poverty line, and that they would be financially responsible for all of their immigrant beneficiaries. Before 1994, his bill did not survive, but in 1995, Representative Bill Young of Florida revived the basic ideas in Smith's bill. Congress was now considering rules to cut off all new immigrants from public assistance, and to limit family reunification to only those lawful permanent residents and American citizens who were themselves not living below the federal poverty line.

In addition, to fulfill those promises for a tougher criminal justice system, Young's bill also provided for a much greater military presence along the Southern border, as well as reforms in deportation policy to facilitate deportation for anyone convicted of a crime. Any criminal conviction for which the penalty could be one year could trigger "removal"; people facing removal on the grounds of a criminal conviction would not be entitled to judicial review; and the rule was to be retroactive, so that anyone with a conviction in the past could still be removed under the new rule. Moreover, persons who resided unlawfully in the United States for certain periods of time would be subjected to new penalties: if you were living unlawfully in the United States for more than 180 days but less than 1 year, you were barred for 3 years from coming back to the United States; and if you were living unlawfully here for more than 1 year, you would be barred for at least 10 years. The rule was designed to deter persons who were "falling out of status," people who'd arrived under student or business or tourist visas, but who had then stuck around long after those visas had expired. In the Senate during that same year, Bob Dole sponsored yet another bill whose primary purpose was to fight terrorism, but the bill also expanded the criminal grounds for deportations even further – anyone with an "aggravated felony" conviction, which included drug trafficking convictions, could be barred permanently from the United States.[27]

These new rules laid the basis for "crimmigration," a term coined by the immigration scholars to define the stark overlaps in immigration and in criminal justice that were now becoming a part of American law in 1996. Bill Clinton was upset that, during his presidency, the Democrats had lost Congress, and so, as he was fighting for a second term, he decided to cooperate with an emboldened Republican Congress. He signed Bob Dole's bill into law in April 1996, then a massive welfare reform law that included elements of Kim's bills in August 1996, and, finally, Young's bill in September 1996. During his re-election campaign, Clinton had pledged to "end welfare as we know it," and although he complained that the provisions cutting off all new immigrants from public assistance went too far, he signed that bill anyway. Under the welfare law, all immigrants – including those admitted as lawful permanent residents – would be ineligible for public assistance for 10 years or until after they had passed into American citizenship.[28]

Together, the Anti-Terrorism and Effective Death Penalty Act, the Illegal Immigration Reform and Immigrant Responsibility Act, and the Personal Responsibility and Work Opportunity Reconciliation Act all indicated a sharp turn against immigrants – one might see these rules as ambitious federal efforts to reduce the costs of immigrants and immigration, in redistributive public assistance programs, and especially in the criminal justice system. By removing a broad range of persons who'd been convicted of crimes, the new rules suggested that the states and the federal government would probably spend less on incarceration. Bill Clinton won re-election in a three-way race against Bob Dole and Ross Perot, but he still did not get a majority of the popular vote in 1996. Clinton was perplexed by this result: he thought that by moving to the center of

American politics, he would build a lasting middle coalition for the Democratic Party. For example, in September 1996, Clinton had signed the Defense of Marriage Act, a rule that allowed the states to reject same-sex marriages, thinking that this would help him and his party toward a rapprochement with religious conservatives. It tended to alienate his base: some Democrats joked that there were three conservatives running for President in 1996. Clamping down on immigrants and courting religious conservatives did not help him either. Instead of that rapprochement, Clinton got impeachment in the House in 1998, when it turned out that he *did* have sex with "that woman," a 22-year-old Monica Lewinsky, somewhere near the Oval Office. All that moving toward the center had yielded very little.[29]

In profound ways, these immigration laws that President Clinton had signed in 1996 were harsher, federal versions of Proposition 187, far to the right of center. One federal court had blocked the state referendum three days after the voters had approved it, and another federal court declared its provisions unconstitutional in 1997. But by then, a new Congress and the President had given federal and state governments broad new powers to exclude poorer immigrants, to cut them off from public assistance programs, and to remove a much wider group of immigrants who'd been convicted of crimes. Clinton worked with Congress to restore some public benefits to long-time residents after he'd won his election, but other aspects of these laws worked as they were intended. Without question, deportations became much more common – in the 1980s, deportations numbered around 30–40,000 persons per year. At the end of the Clinton Administration, over 100,000 persons were being "removed" every year. Indeed, to avoid some of the procedural protections that had developed around "deportation," Congress used a new word, "removal," in the laws of 1996, and then Congress made "removal" far easier than ever before. Every state was now remanding to federal officers those immigrants who'd had a criminal conviction, and the federal government was removing at a clip. On the eve of Barack Obama's presidency, the United States was removing over 300,000 persons per year. In 1992, Jay Kim had spoken of mass deportations as though they were a kind of revenge against "bad immigrants," banished forever from America, and then, 10 and 20 years later, that stark vision had become a reality.[30]

In other respects, the new rules in 1996 seemed to be working: by law, poorer lawful permanent residents and American citizens could no longer sponsor family members, and yet those who had met the income thresholds were still applying for family reunification visas. Compared to the period before 1996, though, they were petitioning much more often for members of immediate families, and not as much for extended kin. Scholars surmised one obvious reason: sponsors were much more willing to be tied financially to immediate family members than to extended kin. The rule thus seemed to be working. Moreover, in this decade and in the decades after, so many people here were living apart from their families that laborers in the United States were sending, collectively, enormous sums of money to family members abroad. This trend arose in part because, even when a sponsor requested a valid family reunification visa, actual reunification could take a while – persons requesting family reunification from Mexico or from the Philippines, for example, had to wait in long queues created by the immigration law itself. In 1992, about a million people in Mexico had applied for a family reunification visa, but Congress was only giving several thousand a year to residents in Mexico, using the preference categories in the Immigration Act of 1990. This meant that if a person applied for a family reunification visa from Mexico in 1992, she wouldn't get that visa for another nine or ten years. Members of Congress knew of these backlogs, but by 1994, with Republicans in control, they indicated clearly that they would not increase family reunification visas even for countries with very long wait times. By 2010, family members here were sending their relatives about $20 billion every year just to Mexico, and remittances to the Philippines, China, and India were all showing massive upward turns.[31]

The family reunification queues tended to grow worse over time: in 2000, for instance, if a person from the Philippines had applied for a family reunification visa, she wouldn't get this until 2013 at the earliest. Again, if Congress was interested in controlling and limiting family reunification, under the theory that immigrants coming through family reunification tended to be poorer and less educated than persons coming under employment preferences, the law seemed to be working. Congress' own inaction seemed to be working, even if it was only by slowing (perhaps deterring?) family reunifications by a decade or longer. Throughout the period, and quite on purpose, leaders in Congress chose not to adjust lengthy family reunification queues long after they had proposed those rules to make family reunification harder in 1996. But were these rules really working?

Maybe not. Between 1996 and 2006, the population of people who had no lawful immigration status in the United States went up, from about 5 million persons in 1996 to over 10 million persons by 2006. After the terror attacks on September 11, 2001, the federal government paid renewed attention to immigration and to illegal immigration, and the new Department of Homeland Security collected a variety of reports and data from several different scholars and agencies to reach similar conclusions – people who were out of status were more numerous now than ever before. How was this possible? After the Immigration Reform and Control Act of 1986, the Immigration Act of 1990, and the set of rules in 1996, illegal immigration should have been under control. Under law, illegal immigrants should not have been able to work, they were committing a federal crime just by being here, they were more easily removed than ever before, and public assistance was completely off the table. New *legal* immigrants were ineligible for any form of public assistance. After 1996, there were new fences and physical barriers, too. Why, then, were illegal immigrants still here? Disagreements around that very question drove a kind of paralysis in federal immigration law and policy over the next two decades, a period when comprehensive immigration bills failed and presidents were issuing executive orders in one direction or another. In the absence of comprehensive reform at the federal level, the states and local governments pursued widely divergent pathways over two long decades of frustration.

8

LOCAL, STATE, AND FEDERAL

In the last twenty years, since the immigration reforms in 1996, jurisdictions throughout the United States have taken radically different positions on immigration and immigrants. Some local jurisdictions have defined unlawful immigrants as a "public nuisance," and they've ordered local police departments to identify and to detain such persons. Some local governments have required private parties, including landlords, to check for immigration status prior to offering any services. Other local jurisdictions have moved in the opposite direction – they've directed their local police officers not to ask or to tell federal authorities anything about the immigration status of their residents. In some states, young people who have no lawful immigration status may matriculate at the public colleges and universities, perhaps even draw state aid for their higher education; in other states, this is outlawed; and still in other states, such young people can go to some public colleges and universities and not others. The state of Georgia segregated them away from its best public institutions.

At the federal level, based on the occupant of the White House, political leaders have said that immigrants – including the ones who have no legal status – were "assets," de facto members of their communities, and beloved members of families that ought to remain together: "They are Americans in their heart, in their minds, in every single way but one: on paper." But then the most recent President has also described them as "rapists" and "bad hombres," or "radical Islamic terrorists," who should be excluded, detained, removed, or killed as soon as possible – at least until they could prove that they were not bad hombres or terrorists. Sure, some were good people, he has said, but he would much prefer a wall. Scholars in the immigration law have coined a new term, "immigration federalism," to describe and to conceptualize this tangle of immigration rules at the local, state, and federal level, and this chapter will explain these tangles in greater detail, and yet the broader point might be to show just how sharply Americans have disagreed about immigrants and immigration in recent years.[1]

On the one hand, these disagreements were new, and they have had many novel dimensions, one being that they are national in scope. In 1965, for example, local jurisdictions in Pennsylvania or in Utah didn't feel the need to say anything about immigrants or immigration; nowadays, there are hundreds of jurisdictions that have passed an ordinance or a zoning rule or a policing regulation with immigrants in mind – so many that the professional scholars have had a hard time keeping up with all of them. The legislatures of the interior states, like Kansas or Nebraska, very rarely said anything about immigration in the period before 1965, but every state now – no matter how land-locked or rural – either supported or contradicted federal policies about immigration, and some supported *and* contradicted those policies, depending on the circumstances. For example, in Kansas, people who cannot prove lawful immigration status cannot get a driver's license, and yet younger college students who did not have lawful status could matriculate at the state universities and pay in-state tuition, just like any other state resident. An undocumented 19-year-old can be a Jayhawk at the University of Kansas, and she would pay as much as any other resident Jayhawk, but she wouldn't be able to get a valid driver's license. After college, it wasn't clear that she could legally work in Kansas, for new state rules required all employers to verify immigration status using a federal database, and so she would not appear as an eligible worker in any jurisdiction.[2]

Many people will look at these rules and say that they make no sense, that they're internally inconsistent. They are. Like many other students of immigration law and policy, I have had a hard time keeping up with the wide range of state and local regulations governing immigration and immigrants, and I've also long given up any hope of consistency or rationality across all of those local and state rules. Even as this book is published, this chapter will very probably become out-of-date, as local and state and federal rules have evolved so fast, and the rules passed and repealed so often, that they are all quite unpredictable. As a student of American history, though, I'm inclined to think that the United States has been in these circumstances before, in another century, when Americans disagreed profoundly about the legality and morality of slavery, and so much so that they tore themselves apart. They also passed local and state regulations that were contradictory and inconsistent, both humanitarian *and* racist in a single legislative session. After 1850, for example, the President of the United States, Millard Fillmore, insisted that all American citizens should comply with rules allowing slave holders to recover their property. In Oberlin, though, a college town in Ohio, the residents indicated very publicly that they would do no such thing. Once again, our own cacophonous, contradictory, and inconsistent responses to our own "illegal people" appeared to arise from the fundamental differences in the ways we *see* the strangers among us.

"Educating Kids," "Coddling Criminals"

As of this writing, *Plyler* v. *Doe* (1982) remained "good law," in that it was still unconstitutional to deny undocumented children access to public schools or to charge their families tuition. When they approved Proposition 187, many voters in California had hoped to challenge and to overturn *Plyler*, but subsequent federal court decisions rather supported the precedent, and the United States Supreme Court chose not to hear cases that challenged the essence of the original ruling in *Plyler*. When Gray Davis became Governor of California in 1999, he decided not to press the state's case at all – Proposition 187 was never enforced in California. But top officials knew that state agencies and the state courts had been divided about the extent of *Plyler*: should the principle apply beyond the public schools – say, into the state's public colleges and universities?

In 1984, in response to a request from the Chancellor of the California State University system to clarify this issue, the California Attorney General John Van de Kamp said that *Plyler* should not apply to higher education. He wasn't suggesting that professors and administrators turn over applicants or students within the public university systems, but, at the very least, he said that all of the colleges and universities should be able to charge out-of-state tuition for anyone who couldn't prove legal residency in the United States, no matter how long they'd actually lived in California. At the California State Universities, tuition for an in-state resident was about $1,000 per year in 1984, and at the University of California campuses, it was about $2,000. For students who were not in-state residents, CSU was about $6,000 per year, and UC was about $7,000. Van de Kamp said that all students who could not prove legal status in the United States should be charged the higher tuition.[3]

Later that year, undocumented students at the University of California at Berkeley sued to challenge Van de Kamp's instructions. The trial court in Alameda County was sympathetic to their arguments: many of these students had been living in California well before college; they had attended California public high schools; and they were otherwise indistinguishable from other residents of California. As in *Plyler*, they said that their immigration status was not their fault. Relying on an interpretation of the state constitution, the judge overturned Van de Kamp's instructions, and then suggested in his order that all public colleges and universities should adopt "residency" policies uniformly to determine who should or shouldn't pay out-of-state tuition. Based on this ruling, public colleges and universities in California were admitting and charging many students who were out of status as in-state residents, as long as they had attended public schools in California.

An employee at the University of California, Los Angeles, objected to this policy shortly thereafter, and he was "invited to resign" for his opposition to it. He did resign, but then he sued, and in his lawsuit, he asked the California trial court to force the University of California to comply with the original policy outlined by Attorney General Van de Kamp in 1984. In 1990, a California appellate court agreed with David Bradford that undocumented students were precluded from receiving in-state tuition benefits, and in another case in 1995, yet another appellate court said that this ruling should apply to all of the state's public colleges and universities. Thus, the policy shifted yet again, and undocumented students were now to be charged the higher, out-of-state tuition.[4]

A year later, Representative Christopher Cox supported a garbled provision in the Illegal Immigration Reform and Immigrant Responsibility Act that said, in part, that an alien "not lawfully present in the United States" cannot be eligible for "any postsecondary education benefit." The provision was confusing, as it suggested that the States could offer such benefits if it didn't refer to "state residency," but Cox himself told fellow members of Congress at the time that this provision would render illegal aliens ineligible for in-state tuition at public colleges and universities. After Bill Clinton signed this bill, in-state tuition benefits seemed no longer possible for students who were out of status in *any* state, and so in states like New York, the largest public university system stopped offering in-state tuition benefits to students who were out of status, even though they had attended New York public schools.[5]

In California, Democrats in the State Assembly were upset by the appellate decisions in 1990 and in 1995, not to mention the new federal immigration law in 1996. They proposed state rules to circumvent the federal rule, including a frontal attack against it in a proposed state law in 1999 that gave public colleges and universities the right to treat undocumented students as "residents" for tuition purposes. Governor Gray Davis was a fellow Democrat, but he vetoed the bill in 2000, citing the 1996 rule. Marco Firebaugh, a member of the State Assembly, persisted, and he was surprised by the support he received from a broad coalition of students enrolled in the state's public universities, including nearly all of the UC campuses, as well as students in the CSU system. Many young people conveyed heart-wrenching stories about wanting to attend college, but being completely unable to afford the much higher out-of-state tuition. As he listened, Firebaugh was also paying attention to political developments in Illinois and in Texas: a broad coalition of politicians and educational leaders in these states had also said that charging out-of-state tuition to relatively poorer immigrant students and their families was simply unjust. The United States Senator from Illinois, Dick Durbin, persuaded his Republican colleague from Utah, Orrin Hatch, to co-sponsor a rule that might undo provisions of the 1996 rule, at least as it pertained to young people who had been brought unlawfully to the United States before they were 16 years old.[6]

Many legislators in Texas, including the Governor Rick Perry and his fellow Republicans in the state legislature Fred Hill and Elvira Reyna, were also moved by individual stories of students who, through no fault of their own, had no legal status, but were otherwise excellent candidates for the University of Texas or Texas A&M. The Texas legislature had passed that infamous rule in 1975 – the same one overturned in *Plyler* – but in 2001, by a near-unanimous majority, Texas became the first state to offer in-state tuition benefits to undocumented students. Governor Perry lauded the new rule, saying that it would expand educational opportunities for the benefit of all Texans. The Texas rule had required students who were out of status to file for legal status "as soon as legally permitted," but anyone who had attended a high school in Texas for at least three years and then graduated was now eligible for in-state tuition.

In California, state legislators and the Governor studied this turn of events, even as young people who were out of status took a more activist role in their own cause. Many insisted that they had had no idea that they were even out of status until they had applied for a driver's license or for college – for them, illegal status was a strange condition, as they'd felt so "American" in most other respects, having grown up and attended schools in the United States with no thought to immigration status. Moreover, many said that the rule was just unfair: contrary to what many people may have thought, their mothers and fathers did pay federal and state income taxes, and everyone paid sales taxes, and they also paid property taxes indirectly, too, when they rented or leased property – that is, their landlords would never be able to make their California property tax payments unless their immigrant tenants had paid rent. In these and many other ways, immigrants – even the unlawful ones – otherwise supported the state's institutions, just like any other state resident, and many of them had been doing so for years. Taxes and death were unavoidable for everyone. Thus, through the existing policy in California, the state was now depriving them of a critical benefit that they themselves had long financed.[7]

In 2000, Marco Firebaugh had introduced in the State Assembly a new bill, AB 540, that decoupled "residency" from the in-state tuition benefits, just like the rule in Texas. Under this bill, anyone who had attended high school in California for three years, and then graduated from a California high school, would be eligible for in-state tuition. Again, by not referencing "residency" at all, Firebaugh's proposed rule seemed to circumvent Congress' law of 1996, as in-state tuition benefits were no longer contingent upon "residency." Governor Davis acknowledged that the intention of this bill was essentially the same as the one he'd just vetoed in 2000, and yet he signed AB 540 into law in 2001, making California the second state since 1996 to restore in-state tuition benefits for students who were out of status. And so, this state that had passed Proposition 187 was moving in an opposite direction, and there was no question that the stakes were even higher in California: Texas had an estimated 700,000 undocumented persons when HB 1403 was approved in 2001; in California that year, there were as many as 2 million people who were out of status.[8]

Many young people were emboldened by these victories, by their own participation in these changes. The social scientists who'd studied this group of young people reported that the very experience of engaging in politics had removed a stigma long associated with being out of status. Many people who learned that they were "illegal" had felt ashamed – they had grown distant from their parents, whom many blamed for their unlawful status, or they had felt despondent about their future, as though all the doors were closing. And yet in Texas and in California, student activists had cultivated powerful allies, and they had won major legislative victories even though they had lobbied from a marginal position. Many found the experience exhilarating, and others described the changes in state rules as occasions for renewed hope, perhaps for full legal status, not just for an in-state tuition benefit. Under other federal rules, undocumented students were ineligible for state and federal financial aid, and so unless they could move permanently out of this disabling status, it would follow them well into and after college, if they could finance college.[9]

Not having access to financial aid, state or federal, remained a formidable barrier for many undocumented students. In addition, did it make sense to extend the *Plyler* principle through higher education while still retaining legal barriers against employment? What could an undocumented student do professionally, even after receiving a college degree? The immigration rules in 1986 barred them from working legally in the United States; the rules in 1996 cut off all public assistance for *lawful* immigrants. When the Senators Dick Durbin of Illinois and Orrin Hatch of Utah sponsored what would become known as the DREAM Act in 2001, they said that their rule would attempt to resolve these tangles, to help adjust at least those worthy young people who were suffering a disabling legal status that had this odd, permanent quality to it. It would follow them through college, into a career, maybe forever. Against arguments that this was another "amnesty," Senators Durbin and Hatch said that only people who had been brought to the United States as minors would benefit from this proposed federal law. They also had to prove good moral character, and they at least had to finish high school – these beneficiaries were earning legal status, not having it handed to them.

This bill failed in the Congress, however, as did similar bills over the next few years, including versions that added as beneficiaries young people who'd been honorably discharged from military service. One version was approved in the House, but then died in the Senate, even though both Presidents George W. Bush and Barack Obama spoke in favor of the many versions of the DREAM Act. Components of the DREAM Act were folded into much larger comprehensive immigration reform bills that President Bush had also supported before 2008, but any talk of amnesty or adjustment or legalization proved fatal to these efforts, just as they did after President Obama took office.[10]

In the midst of this impasse, the states legislated their own rules governing access to public colleges and universities. By 2008, state governments in Washington, Oklahoma, New Mexico, Kansas, Nebraska, and Illinois had passed laws similar to HB 1403 in Texas and AB 540 in California. Other states rejected access for anyone who was out of status: by 2012, Virginia, Arizona, Alabama, and South Carolina all prohibited persons who could not prove legal status in the United States from attending their public colleges and universities. These states were responding, in part, to a California Supreme Court case that upheld AB 540 in 2010, as well as to the United States Supreme Court's decision not to hear an appeal from that case. The United States Supreme Court appeared unwilling to revisit *Plyler*, and the Court did not seem to believe that the state tuition rules in California and elsewhere necessarily conflicted with existing federal laws.[11]

Bitter fights over these rules have continued. Some states approved in-state tuition for students who were out of status, but then eliminated it, while others did the opposite – Wisconsin approved in 2009, then eliminated in 2011, while Colorado eliminated in 2008, then allowed in 2013. In each of these states, opponents spoke about one another in very harsh terms, either as the lawless abettors of unlawful people, or as the heartless nativists (maybe racists?) willing to target innocent people. The states were torn internally: in Kansas, that state's own Secretary of State, Kris Kobach, supported a lawsuit against the Kansas rule allowing for in-state tuition benefits for undocumented students. When the lawsuit failed, Kobach continued to support numerous legislative efforts to repeal the Kansas rule, as did many other state politicians in their own respective states. Kobach helped to draft rules denying such in-state tuition benefits for states like South Carolina, Alabama, and Arizona.

Across the country, the states divided. In 2011, Georgia passed a unique rule that allowed students who were out of status to attend the public colleges and universities, *except for* the top five public institutions, including Georgia Tech and Georgia State. Critics said that this was a new kind of segregation, not by race, but by immigration status. In one way, the Georgia rule treated all students who were out of status in the same way – no matter where they went, they had to pay out-of-state tuition. That same year, however, Governor Jerry Brown of California signed into law a bill that offered state financial aid to undocumented students enrolled in the state's public colleges and universities, the first law of its kind in the United States. The rule made national headlines, and several legislators in other states said that they saw California now as the new model for this area of public law. Other states disagreed: when legislators in South Carolina and in Alabama passed rules prohibiting undocumented students from attending any of the public colleges and universities in those states, they denounced the new rule in California.[12]

Working and Living

Legislators in several states complained that the constant political and material support for undocumented persons – even the ones who were somehow "innocent" – was probably doing nothing to reduce the population of people who were out of status, nor was it going to deter people who might consider migrating unlawfully. Just as Governor Pete Wilson had claimed in 1994, the Governor of Arizona, Jan Brewer, and the Governor of Alabama, Robert Bentley, each described the federal government's effort to control immigration as a "failure" overall, forcing them to support state rules to deter illegal immigrants. By 2010, they noted that many local jurisdictions and some states were talking about illegal immigrants as a kind of "nuisance," a population whose conditions led to exploitation, low wages, and a lower quality of life for all residents. Governor Brewer complained that the state's criminal justice system was breaking under the weight of so many unlawful immigrants already in that state, while the Governor of Alabama promoted harsher rules to deter them from ever settling there. He conceded that some businesses were employing people who were probably out of status, but the point of federal and state rules should be to make life harder for such persons, so that they would leave rather than stay.[13]

Indeed, by 2010, federal law and federal court precedents were increasingly unsympathetic to undocumented persons, even those who'd been victims of unscrupulous or predatory American businesses. For example, in 2002, in a United States Supreme Court case that came from Southern California, the Court ruled that undocumented workers did not have the right to bargain collectively, nor could they recover against an employer who caused their deportation rather than allowing them to join a labor union, as might have been their right under existing federal labor laws. Chief Justice William Rehnquist said that, under the Immigration Reform and Control Act in 1986, undocumented persons were not allowed to work at all – they were only working at the plant in Southern California after having offered false documents to verify a legal status that they did not actually have. Jose Castro, one of the undocumented workers in this case, had used a false birth certificate when he had been hired. Because Congress meant to prevent undocumented persons from working at all, Rehnquist said, these workers should not reasonably expect federal labor laws to protect them while they were working and living here unlawfully. Moreover, knowing that they would be thus unprotected, Justice Rehnquist insisted, fewer of them would come to the United States. The opinion assumed that reasonable people would never put themselves in such a vulnerable position – working in a dangerous plastics factory when they weren't supposed to – and so this kind of labor policy would work in conjunction with immigration restrictions approved in 1986 and then strengthened after to stop people from working unlawfully.

Justice Stephen Breyer dissented, and he suggested that this logic was all wrong: precisely because the Court was leaving such workers unprotected in the labor law, employers would have *greater* incentive to use them at work, knowing in advance that they could deport and remove and exploit these workers with relative impunity. The argument that reasonable people would avoid heinous working conditions was also probably wrong, Breyer suggested. Indeed, social scientists and journalists had exposed horrifying working conditions in the last two decades, and a lot of the cases had involved undocumented immigrants, or immigrants trafficked into the United States in terrible circumstances. In dairy farms in New York, slaughterhouses in the Midwest, or chicken farms in the South, many immigrants did work that was dangerous, and most probably in settings that violated state and federal safety rules, and yet just telling them not to work and to leave, as they would be unprotected in the federal law, wasn't going to change anything. In California, agricultural and construction industries were becoming more dangerous, as growers and firms bothered *less* with health and safety regulations, knowing that their immigrant workers were not in the best position to complain about dangerous pesticides or unsafe conditions.[14]

Some instances of exploitation were just horrifying on a different level. In 1995, for example, law enforcement officials had raided an apartment complex in El Monte, California, and there they found over 70 migrant workers who'd been kept in "slave-like" conditions. The apartment complex was both dormitory and garment sweatshop – the Chinese Thai operators had lured these migrants, mostly women, to live and to work in the complex, they had procured passports and visas for them, but after arriving in Southern California, they confiscated everything and they threatened to harm the migrants and their family members in Thailand should they refuse to work. Some of the women had been held there for seven years, with little or no contact with their families or with the outside world. The operators sold many of the garments produced in that hellish place to mainstream clothing brands, who in turn sold the clothes at major retailers throughout the region. Unwittingly, American citizens were buying and wearing garments produced through organized crime and slave labor.[15]

Eating chicken or pork, perhaps drinking a glass of milk, or having a strawberry shortcake or a loaf of bread – how often did Americans consider the person at the other end of the butchered cow or pig, or the person doing the milking or the picking or the baking? After 1986, none of this work was supposed to be done by undocumented workers, and yet, without question, they composed a significant fraction of workers in a range of dangerous occupations. Meat processing has always been gross: turning an animal into meat, packaged for sale, is not the most pleasant process to witness. Meat producers relied on modern technologies to do the initial killing and rendering, but because animals come in such distinct shapes and sizes, chopping them up further still required human labor. People still needed to cleave wings from chicken torsos, and to carve hams away from the pigs. They used sharp knives, over and over, many hours a day, using repetitive motions. Fatigue often caused people to make mistakes that could be fatal or maiming. Working in an industrial dairy or bakery was not as dangerous, but this kind of work also involved heavy machinery and repetitive tasks, hours and hours of work to make thousands of gallons of milk or hundreds of thousands of loaves.

In states like North Carolina, Arkansas, and Nebraska, meat processing plants have relied more heavily on immigrant workers since 1986, and in states like New York, Illinois, and California, where immigrant workers had been more common, laboring conditions probably became worse after 1986 than in the period before. Stark health and safety statistics pointed toward those trends: in one national study, immigrant workers, especially those who were out of status, were much more likely to die at work than workers born in the United States. This was because these workers were concentrated in unskilled, dangerous forms of manual labor, and many employers in those industries enlarged their work forces without making similar investments to protect health and safety. Old problems were new again: the United Farm Workers had lobbied hard against the use of certain pesticides in California agriculture since at least the 1950s, when growers would sometimes spray poisons *while* workers were still picking in the fields. Powerful insecticides were common, state and federal regulations seemed non-existent, and thousands of farm workers suffered. Nowadays, scholars have produced a new set of ethnographic and quantitative studies to show that these problems are haunting farmworkers all over again. Injury, illness, and illegality figure together more tightly than before, and simply wishing the undocumented workers away, or pretending that they don't exist, may have made their conditions far worse.[16]

Because many of these workers have faced hyper-exploitation, and because employers have ignored minimum wage rules, immigrant workers have lived in circumstances reflective of a grinding poverty. In recent years, local townships did not react well when large numbers of immigrants moved into areas with less expensive housing. For example, Hazelton, Pennsylvania, once had large mining companies and a garment industry, with many thousands of blue-collar workers, but in the late 1980s, these were declining, and the town was declining, too. In time, though, food processing plants, including two meat processors and an industrial bakery, would draw many unskilled workers to a part of that state where immigration and immigrants just weren't common. In Escondido, California, north of San Diego, a changing mix of industries was also drawing newer immigrants – that area of San Diego had always had a Latino presence, and many immigrants had worked in the citrus and avocado farms, but the opening and expansion of several large-scale industries in and around Escondido changed the demographics of that town rather quickly, just as they did in Hazelton. In 2001, the Pala Indians had opened a casino in North San Diego County, they invested $200 million in that venture, and to their own surprise, thousands of people were headed there every weekend.[17]

In Hazelton, more established residents complained that crime was going up, that the newcomers were unruly, and that they lived too many in one house or apartment. Mayor Lou Barletta complained in public that he could not tell "legal Mexicans from illegal Mexicans," and he also said many other things that caused people to wonder whether he embraced the town's racial diversity. The City Council proposed an Illegal Immigration Relief Act in 2006, the Mayor supported the rule, and so, after it passed, all businesses were required (again) to check for immigration status, and all property owners were to check for the same before they rented or leased properties to any tenant. The Mayor supported another ordinance later that year to make English the official language of Hazelton, and he further intimated that local police would turn over anyone that they'd suspected of being an illegal immigrant. A few years after the rule, the Mayor boasted on a national television show that the Relief Act had "driven away" a sizable fraction of the town's "Hispanics," even though Hispanic residents were suing the city in the federal courts.[18]

In Escondido, later in 2006, Councilwoman Marie Waldron proposed a rental ordinance that she insisted was necessary in the wake of the federal government's failure to enforce immigration rules. The city had commissioned a study that showed how one neighborhood had had an immigrant population exceeding 80 percent, mostly from Mexico. Many were newer immigrants there, and they were living in rental units that were over-crowded. "Illegals are willing to live in horrible conditions," said Ed Gallo, a fellow member of the Council; "This leads to a lot of other issues." Ms. Waldron was more blunt: "Our nation is under siege. Our own federal government has abandoned its constitutional duty, resulting in treason." Her ordinance said that undocumented persons were less likely to report unsafe or unhealthy living conditions, and thus their very presence resulted in "an increased chance that such conditions will multiply in the future." There was talk of crime increasing with the number of immigrants in Escondido, but much of the debate focused more on the quality of life in the town itself, and how the immigrants were making Escondido a less attractive place to live. There were too many kids who didn't speak English in the public schools, there were too many of the older residents who felt as though they couldn't relate to the newcomers, and there was too much traffic from people commuting to and from the large casino, a 30-minute drive north of Escondido. One member of the City Council speculated that at least a quarter of the city's residents were "illegals," and that, in general, these undocumented persons stimulated more "public nuisances."[19]

The bans in Hazelton and in Escondido did not survive the lawsuits filed against them, but this was somewhat beside the point. By then, both ordinances had received national attention, other cities and towns followed, and many people in the United States expressed frustration at the federal government, as well as at the undocumented immigrants. Politicians who were adamantly opposed to further immigration had success pursuing higher office: the Mayor of Hazelton, Lou Barletta, was elected to the United States House of Representatives in

2010, and Marie Waldron, the Councilwoman from Escondido, was elected to the California State Assembly in 2012. Voters across the country were supporting anti-immigrant politicians.

"Having the Wolf by the Ears ..."

Moreover, as these local disputes had gained national attention, the federal government did pass significant new enforcement rules during this same period. President Bush signed the Real ID Act in 2005, which set national standards for identity documents, including state driver's licenses, and he also signed the Secure Fence Act in 2006, a rule that increased funding for all kinds of physical obstacles across the Southern border. Under the first rule, there were new penalties for forging any kind of identity document, and, under the second, metal fences, security cameras, motion sensors, and unmanned aerial drones were all deployed to reduce the number of illegal residents in places like Hazelton or Escondido. Many of the local rules from places like these were challenged and defeated in the federal courts, but the broader political push for harsher immigration enforcement lasted well after. President Bush and moderate Republicans and Democrats attempted broader federal reforms, but a bill in 2005 was mostly enforcement; it passed in the House, but failed in the Senate. A year later, a bill approved in the Senate contained a much tougher path to adjustment than ever before, but because there was a legalization provision at all, it failed in the House. In the 2006 elections, the Republicans lost control of the House and the Senate, as well as a majority of the state governorships.[20]

Blamed for everything, President Bush used existing statutes to set immigration policy. Most significant of all, toward the end of his Administration, with no hope for a comprehensive immigration bill, President Bush authorized the Department of Justice and the Department of Homeland Security to collaborate more closely with local and state law enforcement officials to identify and to remove persons who had been convicted of crimes. In many ways, this policy grew from an earlier crisis in his presidency, after the attacks of September 11, 2001, when President Bush learned that various law enforcement agencies did not necessarily collaborate or work well with each other. Under provisions of the Patriot Act in 2001, all law enforcement agencies were to share intelligence, across federal, state, and local organizations, not just to catch people who did horrifying things, but to prevent future acts of terror and violence. Moreover, with Congressional support, President Bush authorized new methods of surveillance, as well as indefinite forms of detention for non-citizens, under the theory that these methods could yield intelligence against criminal organizations and terrorist groups.[21]

Collaborating, sharing information, detaining a suspect in one law enforcement organization to hand them over to another – these were all elements of Secure Communities, which began as a pilot program with just 14 jurisdictions in 2008. State and local law enforcement officials could request training from their colleagues in the federal government, and, using the latest law enforcement techniques, including the collection of detailed biometric data, they could identify persons eligible for removal and remand them to the proper federal immigration enforcement agencies. The program expanded quickly. When President Obama took office, he ordered that the program be expanded even more, greatly increasing the rate of deportations during his time in office. Presidents Bush and Obama had both indicated support for a comprehensive immigration bill that might resolve some of the tensions in immigration law and policy that had been building for decades now, but they each faced an entrenched opposition in the states and in Congress, and almost exclusively over the fate of illegal immigrants.[22]

Republican leaders demanded that both Presidents do more to reduce illegal immigration and to remove illegal immigrants, particularly those with criminal records. When President Obama came into office, the Republicans indicated that more enforcement was a prerequisite for *any* further discussions about immigration reform. President Obama thus agreed to expand Secure Communities, but he also took the Republicans at their word – he expected Republican leaders in the House and Senate to be open to comprehensive reforms sometime later, after he had enforced existing rules.

Perhaps with his longer, chess-like view of American politics, President Barack Obama felt confident that a comprehensive bill under his presidency would result in many more adjustments and then, in time, many more voters. Some undocumented persons had committed crimes, he conceded, and they ought to be removed. But most people living and working in the United States were not like that, and, should they adjust, President Obama's own party would probably see the largest electoral gains. Democrats had reasons to be optimistic: California, once so red, was now a dark blue, getting bluer still, and this Democratic blueness was very likely related to an infusion of voters of immigrant backgrounds, including many people who were not citizens just a decade ago. Republicans like Pete Wilson may have won re-election in 1994 by being hostile to immigrants, but his rhetoric may have produced a significant backlash, so that Latinos were just not voting for any Republicans anymore. Republicans in California had developed an unfortunate reputation in some quarters for being openly racist, nativist, regressive, and anti-immigrant. President Obama suggested that forward-thinking Republicans should learn from this lesson, avoid Wilson's strategy, legalize Hispanics and Latinos, and then compete for their votes.[23]

But President Obama came to regret an enforcement-first strategy, as he did not anticipate the hostility developing among many Americans for another "amnesty." Nor did he expect such a complete and utter erosion of political power for his own party in Congress – in November 2010, the Republicans won a major electoral victory, taking back control of the House of Representatives. In that election, "Tea Party" activists, including Michelle Bachman in the House and Jim DeMint in the Senate, had had their own differences, but they were growing in power and influence, and almost all of them were firm in their pledge never ever to vote for another "amnesty." President Obama had won a second term in 2012, and in the wake of that election, moderate Republicans pleaded again for a change in tone on immigration. Many Republicans said that the party's hard line was proving a major liability.[24]

Sensing an opportunity, President Obama pushed hard for a comprehensive bill in 2013, but it failed again, and then the Republicans took control of the House *and* the Senate in the midterm elections in 2014. One of the more amazing results came even before that November election, when the House Majority Leader Eric Cantor, the Republican from Virginia, lost in the Republican primaries to an opponent endorsed by the Tea Party Caucus. His opponent Dave Brat had said that Cantor had supported "amnesty for illegals," and that Cantor would put amnesty back on the agenda unless insurgent Republicans stopped him and his "mainstream" Republican allies. There was some truth in Brat's arguments: the House *did* plan to vote on a bill in late June 2014, which would have had legalization provisions, but then, shortly after Cantor lost in the primaries, and then the Republicans took control in November, the Speaker of the House, John Boehner of Ohio, pulled the bill from further consideration.[25]

After November 2014, the political math for a "grand bargain" shifted toward no bargain at all. Perhaps the Republicans, too, were thinking about what had happened to California after 1994: Republican strategists and commentators noted that the party was somewhat trapped by its past – having now opposed legalization or adjustment for over two decades, their chances with Latino or other immigrant constituencies were receding. Mitt Romney had received the lowest support among Latino voters ever in 2012. Few people expected any major party candidate to do worse, until Donald Trump did in fact do worse with Latinos just four years later. Even though the reform bills in 2005, 2006, 2009, and 2013 were ever harsher, so that anyone applying for adjustment would have to apologize, and then risk deportation, fines, and not voting for 10 or 12 years, Republicans knew that they'd face considerable opposition within their *own* party for any type of adjustment. Thus, given that so many Latinos and other immigrant constituencies were becoming hostile to the Republicans for behaving in this way, the Republicans had even more reasons never to adjust undocumented immigrants. More than a few Republicans worried that, after passing into citizenship, the once-undocumented immigrants would be able to vote their anger and to vent the Republicans out of Washington.[26]

This was a strange political deadlock with no obvious ending in sight, and yet it was also familiar to those of us who'd studied American history. Thomas Jefferson once described slavery as having the wolf by the ears: having a firm grasp, the wolf cannot turn and bite, but one simply cannot hold forever. Jefferson had suggested many times that slavery was immoral, even though he owned slaves. His metaphor of slavery, though, was more detached, almost like an empirical observation about slavery. It was dangerous for anyone to hold slaves. And yet the Americans couldn't let go. Ronald Reagan and George W. Bush had insisted that undocumented immigrants could be folded into the Republican Party – if treated with humanity and forbearance, they would blend into American society like other immigrants, and because many of them were otherwise conservative socially, the Republicans had a good chance to win them over. The other, more strident Republican view was that undocumented immigrants represented something like an existential threat to the United States; that if these people now were adjusted, even more would come, and with all of them here, voting, the Americans would lose their character forever. Having considered these persons for so long as "illegals," "wetbacks," "aliens," and "lawbreakers," some Americans might now be unable to consider these same persons as fellow citizens. It was, for them, unthinkable. Again, however, such political and psychological deadlocks were the stuff of American history: as enlightened as he was, Thomas Jefferson considered impossible the possibility of his slaves, people like Sally Hemings and her children, voting in an election in Virginia. He never considered them "citizens" in that way. Besides, even if they could vote, he may have wondered whether they would have voted for him.[27]

In the nineteenth century, even as he tried to save the Union, Abraham Lincoln had imagined removing African Americans from the United States, either back to a portion of Africa or perhaps to Central America. Many other American presidents had harbored the same fantasy, and James Monroe did help to finance free Black settlement in Liberia. Embroiled in crisis, President Lincoln supported colonization more urgently both before and after the Civil War, looking hard for permanent solutions to race-based problems in the United States. To a delegation of African American leaders in 1862, Lincoln observed, "You and we are different races . . . I think your race suffer very greatly, many of them by living among us, while others suffer from your presence. In a word we suffer on each side. If this is admitted, it affords a reason at least why we should be separated." Lincoln acknowledged that slavery was a great sin, and that White people had inflicted upon African Americans sins that only God could forgive. These sins were not just by masters against slaves, they were compounded by a federal government that had tolerated and protected an evil institution through the American Constitution until his presidency. Perhaps he thought these truly were unforgivable crimes, for, throughout his time in office, Lincoln asked Congress for more money, and to imagine with him a permanent separation of Whites and African Americans. If Thomas Jefferson had imagined slavery as a wolf, Lincoln proposed putting this wolf on a ship and sending it away. For Barack Obama, who so often had expressed his admiration for President Lincoln, this particular resemblance to the sixteenth President might be unnerving, for President Obama did remove more people than any of his predecessors.[28]

Tea Parties and Shattered Families

It's hard to pinpoint exactly when mass deportation became such an obvious part of American law and society in our more recent past, but certainly, after the immigration enforcement rules in 1996, the United States was looking more like a "deportation nation." From 1980 to 1990, deportations were about 20,000 to 30,000 persons per year; from 1998 to 2004, deportations approached and then exceeded 200,000 persons per year; and from 2008 to 2012, deportations exceeded 400,000 persons per year. The United States has been deporting more persons every year, year after year, than in ten-year periods. Moreover, in the period before 1996, most of the people being deported had serious criminal convictions, and few if any attachments to American citizens or lawful permanent residents. Proof of those attachments was once grounds for relief, but not anymore. After 1996, the criminal grounds for deportation did not have to be especially egregious, and the law did not care whether the deportee had family members or other meaningful connections in the United States.[29]

Once the law enforcement officials began collaborating more closely, after the Patriot Act in 2001 and then the Secure Communities Program in 2008, so many people were deported so often that this became an unprecedented trend in American law and policy. Local law enforcement officials learned quickly that a lot of people subject to removal had lived in "mixed status" families – the person being removed may be out of status, or a lawful resident with a criminal conviction, but these folks quite often had American citizen spouses or American-born children. In places like Phoenix or El Paso, undocumented families were "shattered families" or "separated families" in the local press, and younger children seemed especially shaken after the deportation of a parent. Many stories themselves were shattering. In San Diego, "[there is a] tiny stretch, measuring no more than fifteen meters wide . . . [where] families are sanctioned to touch fingertips through a steel-mesh fence"; "It is a wafer thin and slowly shrinking no man's land, where border agents will look the other way as Mexican-American families with mixed status convene in the baking sun." In other major border towns, including Brownsville, Texas, and Douglas, Arizona, meeting at the fence has remained a sad and common ritual.[30] We might wonder how these meetings might continue through a wall.

President Obama himself became despondent about what his own Administration was doing, as did many of his supporters. In several public events, even well into his second term, the President was heckled and booed by young people who weren't Republicans, but who were, nevertheless, among the people that his government was likely to deport. In time, President Obama directed his Secretary of Homeland Security, Janet Napolitano, to prioritize only persons with the serious criminal convictions, hoping that this would result in fewer deportations. Secretary Napolitano even suggested that state and local law enforcement agencies might now "opt out" of the Secure Communities Program. But it turned out that this was rather hard, not using the integrated computer systems and databases that had stitched so many law enforcement agencies together. Once that system had been established, few jurisdictions could easily stop relying on it. And so, for most of his presidency, Barack Obama had to witness the steady stream of news stories showing mothers and fathers being deported away from their American-born children – thousands of such instances over many dozens of cities.[31]

During his presidency, many more local governments were declaring themselves "sanctuary cities" once again, or at least saying publicly that they would not cooperate, or no longer cooperate, with federal authorities for immigration enforcement purposes. These cities included Hartford, Connecticut, in 2008, Chicago in 2012, San Francisco in 2013, Boston and New York City in 2014, and New Orleans in 2016. Smaller and larger cities – Seattle, Washington, and Newton, Massachusetts – said that they were "welcoming cities," and that they, too, would not cooperate with immigration enforcement officials. Some cities started issuing identification cards to local residents, as well as helpful pamphlets urging them to "know your rights" should they ever encounter a federal officer. More than a half-dozen states approved rules to allow persons who could not prove lawful status to apply, nevertheless, for a driver's license. By 2015, people in Maryland, Connecticut, Delaware, and Hawaii could drive legally even though they might be living in the United States illegally. In many places, there was clear political pushback against Secure Communities.[32]

Like his predecessor, President Obama may have given up all hope that the Republicans in Congress would ever pass a comprehensive bill that might soften deportation policy or adjust people to protect them from deportation. All of the proposals for immigration reform after 2010 seemed harsher, the very opposite of softening or adjusting, as if the majority of the Republicans in Congress wanted only more fencing, more enforcement, more deportation. In a legislative environment in which compromise seemed no longer a virtue, President Obama signed an executive order, entitled Deferred Action for Childhood Arrivals (DACA), on June 15, 2012, the thirtieth anniversary of *Plyler* v. *Doe*. He ordered the Department of Homeland Security to allow certain undocumented immigrants who'd entered the country as minors to apply for conditional residency. This status would be good for two years, and it would allow the beneficiaries to attend colleges and universities and to work legally. Many leading Republicans immediately denounced the order as an abuse of executive power, an unlawful version of the DREAM Act, the law that had been proposed over ten years earlier by Senators Durbin and Hatch. The Republican candidate for President, Mitt Romney, said that he would probably keep the order in place should he win the election, but his reply did not endear him to more conservative members of his own party. The Tea Party Patriots called Romney a "weak moderate." Romney reassured his friends on the right by saying that, if he won, he would make life so difficult for undocumented persons that they would self-deport.[33]

Mitt Romney did not win. Eric Cantor did not even make it to the November election, and his Republican primary opponent, Dave Brat, took over 60 percent of the vote in Virginia's Seventh Congressional District in November 2012. The Republican Tea Party contingent overall got bigger in 2012. So, shortly after he won a second term, President Obama signed another executive order, this one called Deferred Action for Parents of Americans and Lawful Permanent Residents (DAPA). Under this order, the Department of Homeland Security would grant temporary status ("deferred action") to anyone who'd entered the United States prior to 2010, *and* who had children who were American citizens or lawful permanent residents. During that month, President Obama also expanded DACA. This infuriated the Republican opposition in the House and in the Senate, as well as in many states where the governors were Republicans. The Republican Governor of Texas sued to challenge the executive order, saying that the President of the United States did not get to choose which rules to enforce and which to ignore. He did not get to make law by fiat.[34]

Governor Gregg Abbott and his Attorney General, Ken Paxton, said that the Constitution required that "the President ... shall take care that the laws be faithfully executed." President Obama did not "take care" to enforce the immigration law, or so their lawsuit claimed. A federal judge agreed that the order may have been executive over-reach, and so he blocked the order, although, by then, it was already well into 2015, and over 100,000 people had been granted "deferred action" status under DAPA. The district court said that there would have to be a trial to determine whether in fact Texas and other states were being harmed by DAPA. The Fifth Circuit upheld that decision, and the Obama Administration appealed to the United States Supreme Court.[35]

Justice Antonin Scalia passed away in February 2016, and, two months later, the United States Supreme Court announced that they were divided evenly on the question of whether DAPA was a constitutional exercise of President Obama's executive powers. On the rare occasions that such split votes did occur, the general rule was that the appellate court decision was upheld, without precedent, and so DAPA was thus going to have a full-blown trial in Texas to determine whether it violated the Constitution, and whether it infringed upon the constitutional rights of Texans. Republicans in the House and in the Senate were confident that it did, and they supported the lawsuit against President Obama's attempt "to grant an amnesty without Congress." In March 2016, when President Obama nominated Merrick Garland to fill the vacancy left by Justice Scalia's unexpected passing, the Senate Majority Leader, Mitch McConnell of Kentucky, replied that the Senate would not hold public hearings on this nomination until at least the November election. Now, nothing in the Constitution said that the President wasn't entitled to nominate someone for the Supreme Court in an election year, but Republican members of the Senate noted that *United States* v. *Texas* was a very close case. They also noted that Scalia would probably have upheld the block of President Obama's order, and that Obama's own nominee would probably side with the other four. Almost all of the Senate's Republicans refused to meet with Merrick Garland. They had, of course, other reasons for refusing to meet the President's nominee, but immigration debates certainly added to the tension. The nomination process devolved into a partisan gridlock.[36]

"A Big, Beautiful Wall ..."

Since the mid-1990s, immigration law thus divided Americans more sharply than almost any other issue. It turned routine matters – the nomination of, and then the vetting for, a candidate for the Supreme Court – into acrimonious and bitter fights, unprecedented in their tone and manner. It brought out the worst manners, as when Representative Joe Wilson of South Carolina blurted out "You lie!" while President Obama was speaking to a joint session of Congress in 2009. To gain support for his signature health care bill, President Obama had just assured members of Congress that his law would *not* benefit undocumented immigrants. Joe Wilson accused the President of lying, and he did it in such a way that the President, the Speaker of the House, the Majority Leader, and anyone watching CNN could hear it. He apologized later that evening, President Obama accepted his apology, but in subsequent discussions, Representative Wilson suggested that, although the health care law was written to exclude undocumented persons, it would probably benefit precisely those people in jurisdictions that did not care, or ask, about immigration status.

Wilson and his fellow Republicans learned other things following the outburst: insulting the President during a joint session of Congress did not seem to hurt the Representative, nor was he hurt politically by continuing to claim that the President's bill was going to result "in free health care for illegals." Joe Wilson was such a successful fundraiser in South Carolina that he was raising campaign money not just for himself, but for other Congressional candidates in his state. In 2012, no Democrat opposed him, and so he won the Second District with 96 percent of the vote.[37]

During this same period, entire states moved toward an enforcement model, in ways far more hostile to immigrants than ever before. These movements often began locally: Sheriff Joe Arpaio had always been a colorful figure in Maricopa County, Arizona, a jurisdiction that included Phoenix, one of the largest and most important cities in the American Southwest. Before 2005, he was known mostly for banning pornography among inmates in the county jails, or forcing all of them to wear pink underwear in tents with no air conditioning. They were in jail, he said, and it was supposed to be embarrassing and uncomfortable. After 2005, Sheriff Arpaio agreed with the incoming County Attorney, Andrew Thomas, that illegal immigrants were a threat to the citizens of Phoenix, and so Arpaio deployed his officers in "immigration sweeps," and they rounded up anyone in Phoenix who looked "illegal." Civil rights groups were outraged; they sued repeatedly. But many people in Maricopa County supported Sheriff Arpaio, he became something of a folk hero in Arizona and then across the country, and his willingness to use local law enforcement for immigration purposes became something like a national policy when President Bush authorized Secure Communities in 2008.[38]

When President Obama appointed the Governor of Arizona, Janet Napolitano, to be his Secretary of Homeland Security in 2009, the Secretary of State of Arizona, Jan Brewer, became that state's Governor. Governor Brewer herself was from Maricopa County, having served on the Board of Supervisors there, and then in the State Senate. Her overall record did not suggest a staunch anti-immigrant politician; she had focused on education, and she did not seem to oppose *Plyler* when working to improve the public schools in Arizona. In 2009, however, as Sheriff Arpaio was being sued and then investigated by the federal government for racial profiling, among other charges, his supporters in the state legislature proposed a rule to protect him and other state and local law enforcement officials whenever they acted to enforce immigration rules. Their rule was Senate Bill 1070, or SB 1070, a law that *required* local and state police officers to check for immigration status whenever they had a "reasonable suspicion" that the person whom they were arresting or detaining was out of status. The law also provided for new penalties for anyone who "sheltered, hired, or transported" illegal immigrants, and all immigrants, even the lawful ones, were subject to a misdemeanor citation if they didn't have proper documentation of their legal status. Critics were appalled. Would it not be true, that local and state police officers would claim "reasonable suspicion" when they saw younger brown people in the streets, and not so much when they saw older White ladies at the Scottsdale Fashion Square? The critics said that Arizona was legalizing, and providing legal cover for, racial profiling.

Governor Brewer considered the rule for some time before signing this controversial new law in 2010, which inspired protests throughout the state and throughout the country, in addition to numerous lawsuits in the federal courts. Most of the provisions were eventually struck down by 2012, except for that provision requiring immigration checks during other law enforcement contacts. If the states wanted their police to do that kind of thing, they could order them to do so, according to the United States Supreme Court in *Arizona v. United States* (2012). And so other states followed Arizona: Alabama, Georgia, Indiana, South Carolina, and Utah all approved similar rules requiring state and local police officers to check for immigration status, whenever they might have a "reasonable suspicion" for doing so. Jan Brewer won her own full term as Governor of Arizona in November 2010, and she subsequently published a book about SB 1070 and her approval of it, despite the "unfair liberal media." Sarah Palin, the former Governor of Alaska, and the Vice-Presidential candidate in 2008, wrote the foreword. In 2012, Jan Brewer had a public spat with President Obama about immigration enforcement and immigration policy, after she had signed SB 1070. Some said that yelling and shaking her finger at the President, as she had done, had been so horribly rude. That episode did wonders for her book, though, as it became a bestseller.[39]

The rules in Georgia and in South Carolina sounded similar to the one in Arizona, but the one in Alabama, signed into law in 2011 by Governor Robert Bentley, was quite expansive and much more thorough. There was the "required to check" provision for local and state law enforcement, as in Arizona, but then there were also provisions to bar undocumented students from the public colleges and universities, and more provisions about how public school districts should check for immigration status, too, even though undocumented students were not technically barred from the public schools. Just check whenever students register for school, the law said, and keep track. The law required school districts to report the number of students they believed to be unlawful immigrants in each school. The law also forbade landlords from renting to illegal immigrants and employers from hiring them, and if the illegal immigrants looked for housing or for work, that itself was now a crime in the state of Alabama. Finally, the Alabama law required all voters to show proof of citizenship when registering to vote. The rule inspired half a dozen lawsuits, and President Obama himself supported the Department of Justice in legal actions against HB 56.

The senior Senator from Alabama, Jeff Sessions, criticized the Obama Administration for opposing this state law. Sessions defended HB 56. Donald Trump, an unconventional political candidate for the Republican presidential nomination in 2015, agreed with Senator Sessions – the immigration system was broken, he said, and what the nation needed most was a "big, beautiful wall" running all along the Southern border, so that the "illegals" would never get to Alabama. Donald Trump also said that he would withdraw DACA, DAPA, and any other Obama-era "amnesties." Instead of legalizing anyone, he made bold promises to deport more people than any other President in American history. He also said that the United States should stop admitting so many refugees, and then suspend all immigration from several Muslim countries. These places were infested with terrorists, and so no one should be admitted "until we know what the hell is going on." Donald Trump criticized President Obama and Hillary Clinton, the leading Democratic nominee for President, for wanting to admit more refugees from anywhere, and he also warned that a Clinton victory would mean even more legalizations. The two men, Trump and Sessions, developed a rapport during the campaign, Jeff Sessions was the first Senator to endorse Donald Trump for President of the United States, in February 2016, and less than one year after receiving his endorsement, the new President appointed Sessions to serve as the new Attorney General of the United States. Jeff Sessions became the head of the Department of Justice.[40]

It was the strangest of elections, the one in November 2016. I'm still trying to figure it out, and I will be puzzled by it even by the time you read this. Hillary Clinton received 2.9 million more votes than Donald Trump – in fact, if she could have taken all of the extra votes that she'd received from California and New York, and then spread them across two or three other states, she would have won easily. Why this electoral system, rather than a straight popular vote? I kept thinking of my constitutional law class, many years ago, when my professor laid out the reasons why some of the framers supported an electoral system in 1787 – it was to enhance the political power of the slave states, the ones that had counted African Americans as three-fifths of a person, but let no African Americans vote. In 2016, the electoral math was disturbing, but so was this other math: 12 or 13, or maybe 20, million people who were out of status had no say, as Americans disagreed again about whether these families should remain intact or be ripped apart. How irritating that many of them, here a decade or longer, could not participate, for if half of them could have voted, in states like Michigan or Wisconsin or Florida, where the margins were so narrow, Clinton would have won easily, decisively. Perhaps this possibility, so frightening for some, explained why the one political party not likely to benefit from that math had thus kept so many people out of status for so long. At least for now, the Republicans seemed to have had the wolf by the ears. Yet how long was that going to last? Even as the new President took office, as he was in office, members of his own party might have wondered whether this had been, after all, a good, desirable, or just outcome for their country.

9

THE GREAT DIVIDES

Since the mid-1980s, as law and policy grew harsher for poorer and undocumented immigrants, the migration of the highly skilled continued at a clip. Thus, in many places throughout the United States, the immigrants helped us measure the growing distances between the very well-off and the very poor. In our visceral, nativist debates, it was sometimes easy to forget that many immigrants were quite well-off, if only because the ones who weren't got so much more attention. By 1990, many more immigrants had broad choices about where to live and what kind of life to pursue, while many others faced a greater range of restrictions in their day-to-day lives than ever before. These inequalities, for good and for ill, have all been structured through immigration rules that have privileged the already well-off while disabling the poor, and in ways that tend to trap the immigrant poor in poverty. This chapter presents two settings, in education and in the workplace, to show these trends in greater detail. In both, the experiences of immigrants show how immigration rules might further exacerbate inequalities in American society in the coming years.

Sea Turtles and Wild Geese

Among the social scientists, many scholars now prefer the term "transnational" to describe certain classes of persons who can maintain a significant presence in more than one country. This term might be similar to a more colloquial, older term, "jet-setter," this being a person who can wake up in one country, jet to another, and enjoy a fabulous and fantastic lifestyle. Transnational people also take jets, but many work long hours for a living, and their lives aren't always defined by constant, fantastic forms of recreation. For example, in Taiwan and in South Korea, for over two generations, many younger professionals have taken college degrees from institutions in the United States, and they took away a number of insights from those experiences. It may have been exceptionally difficult for them to attend the University of Wisconsin or Stanford University, back in the day, but while they struggled mightily to get there and then to survive there, they met other kids who didn't struggle so hard or outperform almost everyone in the village for the privilege of attending Wisconsin-Madison or Stanford. Among many international students, it seemed easier to get into an outstanding research university in the United States if you were *from* the United States, instead of applying, say, from Taipei or Seoul.

Even in the late 1980s, immigration scholars saw a trend: it wasn't just that Asian immigrants who'd studied in the United States were staying here permanently, it was also that many Asian immigrants were coming to drop off their wives and kids here, while keeping their jobs in Taipei and in Seoul. Perhaps their wages were higher in Taipei and in Seoul, where glass ceilings or language barriers didn't keep them from senior executive positions, or perhaps business opportunities were just better there than here. Whatever the case, many Asian immigrant families were cycling back and forth, truly "transnational" in the sense that the family members were both here *and* there, getting together during the holidays, even though this could mean Thanksgiving in America, and then the Lunar New Year Festival in Taipei. Many of these families were not especially affluent, fantastic, or fabulous – the kids often went to public schools, although in neighborhoods where the public schools were known to be decent springboards to good colleges. Over the last two decades, people have developed Chinese and Korean idioms to describe these folks, as there were so many of them now: a "haigui" was a "sea turtle," a person who migrated back and forth across vast distances, getting an education in one country, working in another, and having a wife and kids on still another continent. Many more mainland Chinese families now had a sea turtle of one kind or another. In South Korea, similar dads and a few moms were also called sea turtles, but the catchier term was "wild geese," as these birds flew great distances on a regular basis, in predictable, seasonal cycles.[1]

Among members of this migrating middle class, going from here to there was no longer as jarring as it might have been in the years after the Immigration Act of 1965. Then, a flight from Seoul or from Bombay was almost never non-stop – planes weren't that advanced back in 1965, and so taking off and landing, taking off and landing, and taking off and landing was a long, sometimes harrowing, ordeal. My late mother reminded me often that I barfed most of my way to America in 1975, tossing my cookies in Tokyo and again in Honolulu. The flight was also much more expensive, too, as the market for air travel was considerably smaller then compared to now. Flying back and forth from Asia was thus a real commitment – it took forever and cost a fortune. Nowadays, though, there were many non-stop flights from California to dozens of places in Asia, and so it was less difficult to be a sea turtle or a flock of geese. Again, before the major holidays in the United States and in Asia, you can see hundreds of these turtles and geese at LAX or at SFO.

Culturally and otherwise, the transitions were less jarring as well. In 1965, Tokyo and Seoul were once again thriving cities, but the infrastructure, the economy, and other public and private institutions were less developed than in New York or in San Francisco. Only a very few elite families in Seoul could afford piano lessons for their children, as pianists trained in Western classical music were still relatively uncommon in Asia two decades after World War II. By 1980, all of that was changing: many classical musicians had traveled back and forth, not just to the United States, but to Europe as well, bringing back with them violins, cellos, and baby grand pianos, and perhaps enlarging the demand for "refined" forms of Western art. The Yamaha corporation in Japan had been making classical instruments since 1897, but in the postwar period, Yamaha pianos became so popular in Japan and in many other countries, including South Korea, that the company was fast becoming the largest piano-making company in the world. The Japanese and Korean governments may have still had hard feelings toward one another in 1980 or 1990, or even now, but middle-class Japanese and Korean parents have been inflicting similar musical regimens upon their young for a long time.[2]

By 1980, a Korean kid in Seoul could learn how to play Mozart on a Yamaha, while his little sister was learning the violin using the Suzuki method. Finding a music teacher for a reasonable price also wasn't so hard any more, and if the family planned ahead, they might move to Los Angeles to foster the children's education before the eldest turned into a teen. The lessons would continue, but so would development of English proficiency. A handful of these children would become so proficient in the universal language of music, where the try-outs are often pure music, the musicians themselves veiled in curtains from their judges, that some of them transitioned to the Juilliard School or to the New England Conservatory of Music. Their entire families would appear as minor celebrities in the local papers back in Asia. Most of these kids did not, of course, make it to the best music programs, but even those underachievers attended UCLA, NYU, or SUNY Binghamton, thus stimulating anew that epic cycle of sea turtles and wild geese. At the great American conservatories, the faculty and the staff have observed the "Asian music mom," that person whose English may be broken, but whose commitment to her talented baby turtle seemed total. In popular culture, in other variants, this person has appeared as a "tiger mom," like Amy Chua of the Yale Law School, whose own account of tiger motherhood was taken as either a cautionary tale or a how-to manual.[3]

Ah, for love, what wouldn't parents do for their children? In *Plyler*, in 1982, the Supreme Court had said that children who had no legal status should not suffer discrimination, for it was not their fault that they were thus disabled in the law. Instead of getting bogged down in that debate, however, how about simply giving the gift of American citizenship to a child born of foreign parents? That is, why not just get pregnant first, then buy a flight to America, stay through the birth, and leave with an American citizen in your arms? Again, such plans were not new – very affluent people from Saudi Arabia, Iran, Israel, and other parts of the world had done this kind of thing before, as a kind of insurance policy for the kid and for the family should things go badly back home. But, nowadays, "birth tourism" was becoming a thing, a way to confer American citizenship upon the unsuspecting baby, while maybe pulling a fast one on the United States. There were no hard rules against the practice, and, for the most part, only upper-middle-class families could afford this option for now. The market for birth tourism was likely to grow, however, according to our own State Department.[4]

Policies have changed to account for it: the State Department has said that women who appear pregnant, and yet who list "tourism" as the official reason for their visit to the United States, should be considered guilty of fraud. They risked having their visas canceled. Pregnant women can get around this rule by declaring that they intended to use medical facilities in the United States, and that they could offer hard proof that they could pay for them. Chinese companies developed another adaptation for families of more modest means: they encouraged women to travel to the United States earlier, before they showed, during that magic window when they could use the tourist visa, then overstay a little, but not long enough to be barred for three years for having overstayed. It helped to be South Korean: they did not need a visa to come to the United States for tourism, like the citizens of Germany, France, and Japan. For citizens of these countries, our State Department ran a "visa waiver program," primarily to encourage tourism and business travel without the extra hassle of applying for a visa for every trip. Over time, though, many children – who knows how many? – will be transnational right away, while they're still nursing. They were truly the beneficiaries of a "flexible citizenship," able to claim legal belonging here or there, depending upon economic and political circumstances, and not tied to any one place based on some primordial or patriotic tie. These children will be born in the United States, entitled to American passports, and so, for them, traveling back and forth will be even easier than for their parents. They were born as sea turtles, as wild geese.[5]

I myself have taught many privileged migrating children when they were college students. Ever since those budget cuts at the University of California, in 1994, tuition has been going up at the major state universities, both for residents and for non-residents. The cuts to the University of California were so severe that raising tuition only partly addressed the shortfalls. To make up a greater share of that lost state support, administrators at the UC campuses have raised substantial sums of money from private and public sources, and they've also turned to out-of-state and international students, whose families paid much more than in-state residents. California's public universities were not the first or the last to use this approach: when the auto industry cratered in Michigan, for example, and state revenues fell, the University of Michigan began drawing students from out-of-state and from abroad. Colorado, Oregon, Arizona, New York, Virginia, and many other state systems, including California, now all drew more students from out-of-state, too, because the income that these students brought still felt like a financial windfall to the struggling public universities. The University of California was founded in 1868, before air travel, and so drawing students from New York or Arizona or China was not at the forefront of the founders' minds. But now, in the wake of successive budget cuts, out-of-state and international students were very common here and elsewhere. It's as if we were all shuffling our young to make ends meet.[6]

On my campus, it's often easy to spot the affluent Europeans and Asians. Their English skills vary, and not all are hyper-affluent, and yet many speak perfect English and some drive really nice cars for people in that age group. One of my students once waved to me from her Maserati. On the one hand, I am glad that they are here, for they do add to the diversity on my campus, and they offer quite different perspectives in their discussion sections and in the classroom, and they do bring money to rebuild the library and to update the classrooms and to pay the bills. The University of California, Santa Barbara, is a different institution from what it was 20 – even 15 – years ago, when I started as a professor here. Many of my international students are exceptionally well prepared, having had the best tutors and secondary education that money can buy. Having paid so much every year, many have incentives to be more attentive than the California resident, and so they do compare favorably in their academic performance. Also, as these students arrive, while our enrollment targets have remained roughly the same, it's been harder for California residents to get into UCSB, too. We now have a higher concentration of nerds and geeks than ever before.

On the other hand, it seemed sad, that when we sent our campus recruiters to attract applicants from Shanghai or Chicago, we assumed that they wouldn't be pulling from the poorer neighborhoods in those cities. Most families in Shanghai and Chicago couldn't afford the $60,000 per year, the total that my campus charged for tuition, room and board, and other expenses (not including airfare). Yet I would have loved to have had, in my classrooms, a young student of modest background from Shanghai or Chicago, a kid whose family didn't Maserati, to tell her peers what it was like to live as a lower-middle-class or working-class family in one of those cities. The way things were, my faculty colleagues and I will never have her perspective, even though our immigration rules and our admissions policies will ensure that the sons and daughters of the hyper-privileged will always make their way here.

What I've described on my campus is true at all of the UC campuses now, as well as in nearly all of the major public state university systems – we drew from the same small subsection of families in Asia, Europe, and maybe South America, where countries like Brazil have developed enough to justify sending a recruiter there to look for its best *affluent* students. We've all done this because the funding formulas to derive state support, in-state versus out-of-state, were relics of another era before air travel, and so we've simply made do with these rules. We admitted more out-of-state and international students because they paid. We did this even though these policies – implemented over dozens of colleges and universities – were more likely to make the well-off even more well-off, while resulting in a neglect of aspiring young people of modest means around the world, people who might have appreciated even more the unique combination of surfing and libraries on my beautiful campus.

Lives in Limbo

Many administrators at the universities have said that, because we've taken so many out-of-state students, people who have paid so much more, we have been able to preserve access for students of modest means in our own state, just like the great state universities in Wisconsin or in Michigan. There was truth to this argument, and we have had students from extremely modest backgrounds. Because I teach in California, and not in Georgia, Alabama, or South Carolina, the best California "residents," including students who are out of status, have access to the UC campuses, and many of them have also been my students. They can pay in-state tuition, and, after 2011, they were entitled to receive state financial aid, including the Cal grants that had helped to finance my own undergraduate education many years ago. And so, in my large introductory class on immigration law and society after 1965, students who are out of status sit right next to students with Maseratis, and it's an amusing perspective to see them all in that setting. As part of my class, they all read leading social scientists who've studied the "Dreamers," the young people who would have benefitted from the Dream Act that was never passed in Congress. Several scholars have written eloquently about people who have "awakened to a nightmare" when they discovered, often in their early teens, that they had no lawful status, and that a driver's license or college might not be possible. Many of those people found political activism empowering, as when they supported state rules to allow students who were out of status (like them) to access the public colleges and universities. Indeed, my students who are out of status now can read about how another generation of students who were also out of status helped to make college possible for them, which is its own sort of inspirational.[7]

The ones in college, though, were outliers. Most of the social science literature on undocumented youth showed that a larger majority of these young people never made it to college. They dropped out. Being out of status was a like a nightmare from which many people couldn't quite wake up. Young people listened to political debates that portrayed people who were out of status as lawbreakers, bad people, maybe horrible people, who ought to be removed at every chance. In 2010, for example, when Costa Mesa declared itself a "Rule of Law City," its Mayor said that "it's important we state that we do not support illegal immigrants." The grown-ups who participated in these debates might not have considered how a 9- or 10-year-old in the local public schools might absorb these discussions. How might it feel to be a problem, as W. E. B. DuBois once said? How did it feel to listen as the political leaders of your community said that you and your family ought to be deported?

We knew that, for many young people, anti-immigrant speech could take a toll – it could be toxic within the members of a family, and then law and policy could make the pursuit of anything, including a college education, seem pointless. Many of these young people lived lives that were "in limbo," shadowed persistently by the possibility of removal. Even as they were here, they were crippled by an immigration status that has stayed fixed and uncorrectable in the law for over three decades. There was but one provision in the immigration law that could help, and it was called "cancellation of removal." It was widely regarded as an act of mercy: it involved a long, drawn-out application process that could just as easily result in removal as in legal status. To have your removal canceled, you must have been in the United States for longer than ten years, with no criminal record, and then you must show that your removal would result in "exceptional and extremely unusual hardship" to an immediate family member who was a United States citizen. The United States would only approve 4,000 or so petitions every year, and in instances where the petitioners received poor legal advice, they could be put into removal proceedings after filing such a petition, for now our government knew who they were and where they lived. In light of these risks, many people preferred limbo.[8]

The threat of removal haunted everyday life for people who were out of status. New rules appeared more devious: consider that one state rule in Alabama, about how the public schools should keep track of the families who were out of status, while not absolutely prohibiting the students from matriculating there. How could any reasonable person not see such a rule as a trap, as a way for the state to discourage, or perhaps even to betray, the young people who have enrolled in the public schools? That possibility of a sudden, jarring removal was very real in many communities, so much so that making long-term investments in anything – including college – seemed less attractive, less rational. Why spend hours trying to study in a suburb of Atlanta when the best public colleges and universities were closed to you in that state, when the best you could do would be to matriculate into a university system segregated by immigration status? Indeed, for those of us who've studied segregation as part of American history, we noted that segregation had re-appeared in this other context – and if it was true that race-based segregation caused irreparable harm to impressionable African American children, why should we be any less concerned with segregation based on immigration status? American law stigmatized, and it disabled, young people who must learn of this stigma during their most impressionable years.[9]

We might be losing an entire generation of bright young people, as they become "early exiters," their immigration status becoming a kind of "master status" that made daily life and long-term planning exceptionally difficult. Even for the ones who went to college, life could be a struggle – financial aid wasn't available in most states, and, even after a degree, it wasn't clear how or where one might work legally. Still, for the ones who never made it to college, they found low-wage jobs in the shadows of the formal economy, and they relied on incomplete support networks, while always trying to manage the stigma of illegality itself. Not every professor or fellow student was "safe" for students who were out of status, and even though the college campuses had a reputation for being bastions of liberal and lefty people, there were plenty of students and faculty who weren't either. On my campus, some saw the word "TRUMP," scrawled in chalk on a building, as a form of hate speech, and yet I knew of others who saw the same word and voted accordingly. For a moment, we might imagine how hard it would be to be a student, having to go through an institution like this one, unsure of whom to trust.

Comprehensive immigration reform has failed so often, and for so long now, that the social scientists who've followed young people who were out of status as children could now trace them into adulthood, when they were still out of status into that period in their twenties and thirties when other Americans were settling into careers and forming families of their own. Dating, planning to be together, starting a family – for young adults who have no lawful status, they *must* discuss immigration questions as they plot these otherwise routine aspects of their lives. Can you work legally, and, if so, how did you get your papers? How long have you lived out of status? Do your siblings and parents have legal status? Do you have a criminal record? If I marry you and we have children together, what are the odds that you will be deported?[10]

On my campus, in my class, when I've asked my students to consider life after college from this perspective, the students who were out of status pondered these questions from a position that wasn't just academic. They might have been sitting next to a privileged child from Shanghai, whose English was fluent, and whose mother was a sea turtle, but there were great divides between my students. For four years or so, they might have experienced a rough position of equality, but, after they leave here, the student from Shanghai will have choices, the other will experience constraints. We were fooling ourselves to think that their lives would be the same.

Troubled Migrations

Other places in the United States suggested proximity and great distance, shaped by the immigration law. For at least a generation, leading social scientists have written about the "global city," these giant places whose growth has symbolized in late modernity the shift from rural to urban, and then from regional hub to international locations. Global cities were sometimes called world cities, or megacities, or financial capitals, and they contained large numbers of people who've been described as members of the "creative class" or "the knowledge class." Although some members of this class have no obvious merits or achievements, as they may simply have been born into fortunes of one kind or another, the highly educated people who worked for them and managed their money were "the symbolic manipulators," or "the global capitalist elite," or – my favorite – "the masters of the universe." These expressions described venture capitalists, software and hardware designers, corporate lawyers, senior and mid-level executives, financial analysts, investors, app developers, and millionaire hipsters in hoodies and jeans, those people who might not own a tie. Some members of the knowledge class may dress like teens, but most of these folks might also think nothing of a $10 mocha frappuccino, or a single meal for four in the four figures, especially if they have fine wine.[11]

For members of this class, international flights can often be a way of life, and, over time, they could become familiar with other global cities, including Paris, London, Tokyo, or Singapore. Because their social circles often overlap, they might develop the false impression that there are a great many people like them, posting at exotic destinations and making funny faces in Amsterdam one week, in Los Angeles another. Of course, this was true and not true: members of the working class, "the low-wage service class," "the menial class," "the blue-collar class," "the ordinary folk," and "the laboring class" far outnumber the top 2 or 5 percent of the income distribution. However, at least in the United States, people in the top 10 percent also flew around, took vacations in exotic places, and otherwise traveled easily, too, although perhaps not as often. By comparison, most of these folks in the bottom half will never see the inside of an elite college campus, at least not as students, and they might have no idea why anyone would pay $10 for a coffee drink, nor pay in one meal what they might earn in an entire month. The more striking thing was that in the United States, in nearly all of its global cities, very wealthy members of the knowledge class and much poorer members of the service class were both immigrants, and they now encountered each other every day in the most mundane and familiar places.[12]

Immigration rules can explain why New York City or Los Angeles looked the way they did, why every region with high-technology industries also had very high numbers of highly skilled immigrants, and why poorer migrants have flocked to those places, too, often to provide services to members of the other class. In Los Angeles, for example, after the Immigration Act of 1990 liberalized rules for the highly skilled and for the affluent, investors, highly educated workers, and entire corporations from abroad have relocated there. Korean corporations have moved to the Los Angeles region in significant numbers after the riots in 1992 – Hyundai Capital, Nara Bank, and Korean Airlines all now have a significant presence there. Through these corporations, and through the professional workforce that these corporations have brought to the region, Orange County and Los Angeles County were developing into an inter-connected set of Asian ethnoburbs across both counties.[13]

This happened not just on the West Coast. In her book about the South Asian community in Chicago, Sharmila Rudrappa showed how that city also changed after 1990, after waves of highly skilled workers from India settled in and around there. Like many other Asian immigrants, South Asian migrants arrived as students at the University of Chicago, Northwestern, or the University of Illinois at Urbana-Champaign. In time, they settled along the surrounding suburbs of the city and in the city itself, and small business entrepreneurs remade Devon Avenue from an Orthodox Jewish neighborhood into a South Asian one. Highly skilled entrepreneurs would also build significant businesses: Sanjay Shah, the CEO of the Vistex Software and Service Company in Hoffman Estates, bought the most expensive property in Chicago in 2014, the $17 million penthouse in Trump Tower.[14]

More often, though, as urban anthropologists have shown, the Asian immigrants have fanned out. In Morton Grove, it was the Koreans (again), and, farther away, in the surrounding suburbs, Chicago was circled by Filipino, Chinese, and South Asian immigrant enclaves, with more than a quarter of a million persons of South Asian descent in the state of Illinois by 2010. They were concentrated around Chicago, and the professionals commuted inward, while their less affluent co-ethnics lived closer to the city center, where the rent was cheaper and the schools weren't as good. Thus, in recent years, poorer South Asian and other Asian immigrants commuted outward to clean the homes and to take care of the kids of the people who belonged to that privileged class that had fanned out, bought property, and then settled into communities that sat like a circle around Chicago. This pattern would be familiar to any geographer who'd studied race-based segregation, for it resembled closely the "White flight" that took place in the city in the years of the Civil Rights Movement, when White families were leaving for the suburbs in much the same pattern. In the 1980s, urban geographers were talking about vanilla suburbs and chocolate cities, but nowadays, the bananas ("yellow" on the outside, white on the inside) and coconuts ("brown" on the outside, white on the inside) were following that pathway, adding racial diversity to the suburbs while still drawing from the labor of co-ethnics in the city itself.[15]

Scholars could also see similar connections between poorer urban immigrants and affluent suburban co-ethnics farther east, in New York. In Queens, the neighborhood of Flushing became "Flu Shing" after 1990, an area that was now home to one of the largest concentrations of persons of Chinese ancestry in North America. In Xiaojian Zhao's work, the Chinese professionals who lived in Flushing found their Chinese nannies and maids and domestic help through means that most Americans would find impenetrable: the Chinese-language phone book. In the Chinese phonebook, common at nearly all Chinese supermarkets and businesses, Chinese professionals searched for a nanny who spoke Chinese, a maid who wouldn't charge so much for cleaning the apartment, as well as a variety of other services and contacts, including lawyers, doctors, real estate agents, and educational consultants.[16]

In Flushing, speaking English was helpful, but not essential, and for businesspeople from Hong Kong, Taipei, or Beijing, this part of New York was a familiar place with the same kinds of amenities as Hong Kong, Taipei, or Beijing – just maybe a little better, or at least better regulated. In a few of Zhao's ethnographies, her informants have told of how it was still harder to be an affluent or upper-middle-class family in China – you needed to know someone who knew someone to get ahead, and getting the kids into a good school was always a challenge, and even with these basic things squared away, you still couldn't trust the food you ate or the air you breathed, especially not in the major Chinese cities like Beijing.

A lot of people have been trying to get away. In 1993, when the *Golden Venture* ran aground, and nearly 300 Chinese migrants were rescued and then detained, government officials on the East Coast got a sense of what human smuggling and illegal migration looked like. Based on experience, they surmised that, for every crippled ship like the *Golden Venture*, there were probably many other vessels that they weren't finding, steaming along just fine and full of unlawful migrants. Just how many Chinese migrants were being smuggled into the New York area? Difficult to say. Several law enforcement agencies investigated the *Golden Venture*, including the Federal Bureau of Investigation and the Immigration and Naturalization Service (this was before it became Immigration and Customs Enforcement, or ICE). These investigations formed the heart of Patrick Radden Keefe's excellent account of the woman at the top of one of the most unlikely criminal organizations in New York City.[17]

Cheng Chiu Ping was a "snakehead," a human smuggler, but not just any smuggler. She may have started with document forgery, passing small numbers of people from mainland China through Hong Kong, and then into New York, but by 1989, after President Bush denounced the Chinese government for its brutal crackdown against pro-democracy protestors in Tiananmen Square, "Sister Ping" saw a major growth opportunity. She hired brutal street gangs in Hong Kong and in New York, she coordinated several vessels that steamed in all directions from there to here, and she charged at least $15,000 per "customer," on something like a sliding scale. The gangs and smugglers coached their customers before their journeys, the most important element being that part about asking for asylum if the Coast Guard asked who you were and what you were doing. Most of the time, no one asked. Business was booming after 1990.[18]

Among human smugglers, Sister Ping developed a unique reputation that enhanced her criminal business. Not only would she get her person to New York from the more rural areas of Fujian province – from where she herself had emigrated – but also she would make sure that that person found work, either at one of her own businesses or at some other restaurant, garment factory, maid service, nanny service, or a similar Chinese-owned business in Queens, Manhattan, or Brooklyn. Helping them settle in, she surmised, would make them much more likely to repay their debts (to her). If the migrant bailed or attempted to flee before paying his debts, the street gangs would threaten entire families – a few well-publicized murders made sure that this kind of thing didn't happen very often. Sister Ping developed a late-twentieth-century version of indentured servitude. She was an unlikely gangster: she looked rather like my late mother or my aunt, a demure, short, middle-aged Asian immigrant woman who lived in a relatively modest home off East Broadway in Queens. That she did not fit the role of a hard-core criminal mastermind may have explained why she had been in business for over a decade before the authorities caught up with her.

Federal authorities were onto her before the *Golden Venture*, but after that vessel ran aground, and after key members of the street gangs had agreed to testify against her, Sister Ping disappeared from New York. She was arrested in Hong Kong in 2000, she was tried and convicted in 2005, and then she passed away from cancer in a federal prison in Texas in 2014. Federal authorities had evidence that she had smuggled at least 1,000 persons from mainland China to the New York region. Most investigators, though, conceded that this was a profound underestimate, and then no one in law enforcement believed that Sister Ping was the only snakehead in the New York region.

Moreover, boats and vessels were becoming passé in the smuggling business – poorer people in China could be outfitted to look like successful businesspeople or tourists. Criminal organizations in China could pay government officials for false passports. Airplane tickets were cheaper and less risky. And all of this was revolutionizing the illegal migration of Chinese people, even as Sister Ping was paying for her crimes. Her migrant customers were a small and diminishing fraction of unlawful immigrants in the New York region who were Chinese. There were, by 2010, as many as 100,000 persons of Chinese ancestry who were out of status in the five New York City boroughs alone, and an increasing fraction of these folks had "fallen out of status," meaning that they had made an initial lawful entry, as a tourist, a businessperson, or even a student, but then they never returned. It's not especially difficult to pose as a tourist, a businessperson, or a student, to pay a criminal organization in China to bribe the right officials for the right kind of background and passport, and then to apply for a visa and to fly economy class to JFK or Newark. Criminal organizations and legitimate businesses could also arrange for jobs and housing, both in the city center and then also in the more affluent outlying suburbs. Many professional Chinese immigrant and Chinese professional families needed and wanted fellow co-ethnics to watch the kids or to help around the house, and so for poorer migrants who fell out of status, finding work was not especially hard either, and although English was helpful, it wasn't essential.[19]

In 2014, though, there were many people who remembered Sister Ping in ways that other Americans might find familiar. In American history, the heads of criminal organizations sometimes develop a following among members of their own community, even though they victimized many of its members. In death, Sister Ping was celebrated in Flushing – certainly not by everyone, but by a significant group of people who credited her with making a new life possible for them in the United States. They were, at once, the victims of human trafficking, as many of the passengers aboard the *Golden Venture* had claimed, and "customers," people who willingly bought a passage to America when there really was no other way of getting here, at least not legally. Some seemed like happy, grateful customers. They were sad when she passed away. "Without Sister Ping," a Chinese migrant said, "I could never have dreamed of coming here." Other immigrants told of how she sometimes forgave their debts during hard times, or how she paid for the burials of people who had died on the way to New York, although they did not dwell on the conditions that might have caused so many to perish. In the book of condolences, set on a table in the restaurant once owned by Sister Ping, people wrote their names to express their sorrow for her passing. The list was several pages long, most of the names were in Chinese, although some signed in English and in Chinese, a subtle indication perhaps of the life that Sister Ping had made possible.[20]

In Flushing, Brooklyn, and Manhattan, the most prominent Chinese Americans come from families who've spoken at least a dozen major dialects – Fuzhou, Beijing, Suzhou, or Changzhou. That is, to an outsider, they may look the same – they were all Chinese – but their diversity is staggering, from all over China and Taiwan, as well as from the Chinese diaspora in the Americas and from other parts of Asia. Their diversity by class and by immigration status is also impressive – we can find in the three major Chinatowns of New York people who are EB-1s and H-1Bs, highly skilled and well-paid professionals, and then a growing number of EB-5s, the wealthy investors. Even among the EB-5s, there were the $500,000 people and then there were the multimillionaires and a half-dozen billionaires. There were many American citizens, too, like the former City Councilman John Liu, whose father so loved America that he renamed himself Joseph, and then called his other two sons Robert and Edward.[21]

And there were also many thousands of people who had no legal status at all, people who were the victims and/or customers of criminals / folk heroes like Sister Ping. In Benson Hurst and across the Lower East Side, Chinese people on one side of the class divide relied very heavily on the labor of Chinese people on the other side, on the labor of poorer co-ethnics who cooked the food in the restaurants, bussed the tables, and mopped and cleaned up. They also watched the children, cleaned the high-rise apartments, and provided a range of services without which an upper-middle-class, professional, Chinese American or Chinese transnational lifestyle might not be possible. They all appear in Xiaojian Zhao's ethnographies, as well as in several works by the late historian and scholar Peter Kwong, who was long a student of New York Chinatowns. Both scholars have made these connections to illustrate the great divides *among* the Chinese immigrants in a place like New York. The existence of one class of Chinese facilitated the ease of the other class, and for everyone – including the tourists – the restaurants seemed cheaper, the shopping was more colorful, and the other services seemed somehow more affordable. In a way, these New York stories were reflected in every other major global city in the United States after 1990.[22]

Indeed, just on the other side of New York, in New Jersey, we can see these dynamics unfolding at a pace that might be faster than the sociologists or the historians can keep track. In the last ten years, in Fort Lee, New Jersey, across the northwest corner of Manhattan, a visible but relatively small population of Korean immigrants has become a major enclave, so that Fort Lee has looked increasingly like one big Koreatown. Some of the Korean restaurants are amazing, well worth the trip to New Jersey across the George Washington Bridge. Many thousands of Korean American and Korean immigrant professionals have settled in Fort Lee, so that, when the aides to the Governor of New Jersey (and perhaps even the Governor himself?) closed that bridge out of spite in 2013, large numbers of suburban knowledge-class Koreans from Fort Lee were stuck in that horrifying traffic for hours. Korean folks made up about 25 percent of Fort Lee in 2010, and that percentage will probably increase by 2020.[23]

Not 30 minutes away, in Jersey City, near the southwestern corner of Manhattan and the Holland Tunnel, South Asians were settling into one of the largest concentrations of South Asian people in North America. By 2015, persons of South Asian ancestry composed about 15 percent of Jersey City, and for several years, the residents have hosted at India Square one of the largest outdoor festivals in New Jersey every fall. Around September, visitors can find statues of Devi – large and small – triumphant over the water-buffalo demon, plus fantastic curries, sweets, and naan everywhere, for blocks and blocks. Hindu temples anchor the street festival. Children and families in colorful clothing walk up and down, eating and shopping. I think that Devi, being a female goddess, might make the festival more attractive to the South Asian American yuppies and hipsters. As they tended to their professional jobs in Manhattan, perhaps confronting older White male executives who sometimes resembled the evil water-buffalo demon, the ancient festival replayed in New Jersey could have for them a special and contemporary spin. For a few days, India Square became the center of civic life for thousands of South Asians throughout the greater New York region.[24]

The best studies and complex ethnographies of places like Fort Lee and Jersey City have yet to be written. There have been excellent scholarly books about South Asian Americans, but these urban places have been so dynamic, and their changes have been so abrupt, that book-length dissertations and books about them have not yet been published. That remains one of the best arguments for why my best students should go to graduate school, to give us all a better sense of these tremendous changes in our major cities. As immigration rules continue to favor the affluent and the skilled, and as poorer folks continue to come despite formidable barriers – falling out of status rather than coming across the border – we can see how immigration rules will continue to play a greater role in structuring and in shaping inequality. If we looked closely at Fort Lee or Jersey City, and if we looked past the hipsters and doctors and college-educated folks on their iPhones, we could see working-class people, too – very hard-working people. In these enclaves, on the edges of these global cities, they labor in the restaurants, they care for the smaller children in the public parks, and they otherwise tend to the necessities of life, giving time and rest to people who are more privileged and do other kinds of work, but who are just like them in terms of race or ethnicity. Nowadays, more than other aspects of identity, immigration status and immigration policy are only the starting points that can help in understanding the great divides within these growing immigrant ethnic enclaves.[25]

Unruly Immigrants, Precarious Claims

In the global cities, as in many other regions, transnational businesses and entrepreneurs have remade the urban landscape. In 2017, Korean Air finished the tallest building west of the Mississippi River in Los Angeles, the Wilshire Grand Center, a mega-complex that contained a hotel, a shopping mall, commercial office space, and several restaurants and nightclubs, all within a series of stunning interior plazas. For those of us familiar with Asian American history in Southern California, the building and the company behind it have both represented a significant shift in the Asian American presence in Los Angeles. The Wilshire Grand Center was not in Japantown or in Koreatown, but along the Figueroa Street corridor, near the heart of downtown. How amazing: Asian American entrepreneurship for most of the 1970s through the 1990s consisted of people running small businesses in the garment industries, and then gas stations, delis, laundries, and liquor stores, all along the peripheries of the city centers. Things were different now: when I was a kid, none of my aunts, uncles, or their church friends had attempted a $1.2 billion project of steel and glass on the scale of the Wilshire Grand Center.[26]

Of course, any project of this size took years to plan, and the Thomas Properties Group, the main partner with Korean Air on this project, had spent hundreds of thousands of dollars on studies of the project's environmental and economic impact well before construction could begin. The trickiest negotiations, however, were over labor, particularly the hundreds of people who would work in the hotel, in the restaurants, and otherwise clean the entire building and keep the place running. Between 1992, the year of the riots, and 2016, when construction was coming to an end, Los Angeles had changed a great deal, from a place that had been hostile to immigrants to a city where immigrant activism had wrought significant gains for some of the city's least well-off.[27]

Several of the most intense disputes had happened in Koreatown: in October 1997, for example, labor organizations and their allies, including the Korean Immigrant Workers Advocates (KIWA), protested outside one of the most popular and successful restaurants in the city. The owners of the Chosun Galbi restaurant were Korean American entrepreneurs, and so they did not expect a labor organization led by people with names like Bong Hwan Kim, Roy Hong, or Danny Park to move in such a public way against them. Koreans were supposed to keep their disputes from spilling into the *Los Angeles Times*, or at least that was the expectation among many older Korean immigrants. We did not air our grievances in public. To have other Koreans complain about labor abuses – including college kids from UCLA, carrying signs urging people not to eat at Chosun Galbi – took many Korean immigrant entrepreneurs by surprise, even though some of the more unscrupulous among them had often paid less than $3 an hour to some their own workers in 1997.[28]

Progressives in the city saw that kind of casual exploitation as a significant moral and economic problem. Formed in the wake of the riots, KIWA was a "worker's center" – it wasn't a traditional labor union, nor was it a conventional non-profit social service agency. KIWA had elements of both: drawing support from donations and private philanthropies, KIWA assisted low-wage workers with a variety of social services, including placements for low-income housing and affordable childcare. But it also had a significant labor organization component: in Koreatown, where many people were out of status and working in jobs that were not unionized, KIWA encouraged their "clients" to be apprised of their rights even when they were out of status. KIWA organized workers that conventional unions were wary of organizing. There should be dignity in all forms of work, KIWA's organizers had said, and no one should exploit another or take advantage of an employee just because they thought that they could get away with it. KIWA wrote letters to employers for alleged abuses, often reminding them of state and federal minimum-wage rules. Although KIWA was originally formed to help low-wage Korean workers, the organizers there recruited people who could speak fluent Spanish, and they continued to do outreach to all low-wage workers in Los Angeles.[29]

In 1997, in the dispute at Chosun Galbi, KIWA's remonstrative letters hadn't worked in over six months, and KIWA's clients were still being fired for complaining about the long hours and harsh working conditions. No one was paid overtime. In a restaurant where workers were stoking and then carrying hot coals to individual tables, or shaving hunks of frozen meat onto giant trays so that the customers could grill these at their own tables, Chosun Galbi should have paid special attention to health and safety codes. Many workers said they really didn't. Some of his friends suggested that the owner, Won Tek Park, should call the immigration authorities to have his own workers deported, and so, in response, members of KIWA organized daily picket lines at the restaurant. Members of KIWA also participated in a ten-day hunger strike on the public sidewalk outside, within sight of the people grilling and eating Korean barbecue inside. They took care to watch for immigration officials, but they also called the press, the major television news stations, the *Los Angeles Times*, and the *Korea Times*, all to demand an end to "wage theft" and other abuses at Chosun Galbi.

Mr. Park never admitted how much money these protests were costing him, but the bad publicity was terrible for business, a kind of on-going nightmare for his restaurant. They never knew when the protests would pop up. Rumors were that the Parks regretted not taking the initial KIWA settlement offer for $12,000 to cover back wages for their clients. This, it turned out, would have been the cheaper option. Other Korean entrepreneurs said that KIWA was a pack of gangsters, that this was a form of extortion, while mainstream labor unions in Southern California watched this dispute with great interest. In the established labor unions, leaders could not always agree about whether undocumented workers should join as members, or whether they shouldn't be working at all. Many labor unions had, after all, supported the Immigration Reform and Control Act in 1986, which was supposed to do away with "illegal labor," and yet no one in the unions thought that this law was working. And so, when poorer immigrant workers were getting injured or maimed, when they were working for incredibly low wages, or even having their wages stolen, the progressives did not embrace summary deportations.[30]

At the end of six months, Mr. Park settled with KIWA to pay tens of thousands of dollars in back wages, lost wages, and unpaid wages. He agreed to rehire some employees. All workers would be offered help with health insurance, and some of the settlement money would go toward a new Restaurant Workers Association to help other businesses become more informed about city, state, and federal labor laws and state health and safety codes. Not everyone was happy about this – Korean American entrepreneurs expressed "fear and loathing" of KIWA and its leftist allies. Other scholars have written extensively about similar kinds of labor disputes, in Oakland, in New York, and in Chicago, where progressive activists have often used colorful tactics to engage in "public shaming," almost like street theater, where the activists and performers humiliated a business or restaurant publicly for abusing people who were some of the most vulnerable residents of the city. It didn't always work.[31]

Not having legal status remained a huge disability. A year after the Chosun Galbi settlement, Syngman Rhee and his family made a massive investment in what would become a chain of supermarkets in the United States, including one in Koreatown Los Angeles. The Assi Supermarkets were part of an international food conglomerate based in South Korea, heavily capitalized and with plans to move well beyond California. In South Korea, Mr. Rhee had developed a reputation for being a hard-charging businessman; in the United States, he was Steve Rhee, and he was determined to dominate the Korean ethnic supermarket business, starting in Los Angeles. In 1998, he made it very clear that he would not tolerate anything like a labor union among any of his workers. And so, his managers and the legal owner of the store in Los Angeles, Daniel Rhee, Steve's brother, seemed to have hired workers who were out of status, mostly Koreans and Latinos, people whom they thought would work willingly for low pay, and without complaint.

The new Assi Supermarket was just a few blocks from KIWA's offices. Steve and Daniel Rhee had been warned about KIWA, but when they were embroiled in their own labor disputes with many more of KIWA's "clients," they didn't expect members of KIWA to show up at their church or in their neighborhood in the Pacific Palisades, denouncing them both for being among the worst employers in Southern California. KIWA and allied workers' organizations picketed the Assi Supermarket on and off for four years. They filed lawsuits. The Rhee brothers countersued. In one horrible day in 2002, Daniel Rhee fired 56 workers, nearly half of his workforce, and then he threatened all of them with deportation. In many ways, this second labor dispute was even more horrible for everyone, as it did result in the deportation of several employees. The Rhee brothers had sent the names and addresses of their own employees to immigration enforcement officials, so that these workers would be deported. This antagonized KIWA and its allies no end, and this only prolonged the agony for everyone. Through many months and then over years, the dispute exhausted all of the participants, including the members of KIWA, the managers of the Assi Supermarket, and dozens of immigrant employees. Former employees at Assi had to rely on donations and to support themselves. Many had taken other jobs.[32]

By the time that the Rhee brothers settled several of their lawsuits at once, in 2007, for $1.457 million, middle-class Koreans and Korean Americans had more grocery choices anyway, including the Hannam Chain, the Galleria supermarkets, or the H Mart. They didn't need to shop at Assi, mired as it was in this dreadful public labor dispute. Assi Corporation survived the lawsuits and it did settle for far less than the damages alleged against it, but the supermarket did not survive. The grocery store on West 8th closed in 2015. In a sense, no one won. Few could claim "victory" for the people who had been deported, and even the settlement wasn't very much, spread over many families, some of whom had lost years' worth of wages.[33]

It's all becoming repetitive: in 2003, yet another new and fantastic restaurant opened to great acclaim in Beverly Hills, west of downtown Los Angeles. Hiroyuki Urasawa brought with him from Japan an already amazing reputation, Urasawa got two stars in the famed *Michelin Guide*, and if you could get a table there, you would be among the beautiful people who could pay $400 for the most super fabulous omakase dinner of your life, right at Two Rodeo Drive. Chef Urasawa sprinkled gold flakes on some of his dishes, "for the iron," and we might just imagine a starlet or other self-important person just dying to eat some gold for the iron, if only to be able to post the experience on social media. For several years, Urasawa made a fortune, but, as in the other stories in this chapter, things didn't end so well.

Staff members complained about being over-worked, about how no one was getting overtime pay or sick days. A prep cook said that he worked 75 hours per week, as hard as any lawyer, but not even at minimum wage and without overtime or breaks. One staff member alleged an assault involving chopsticks, another said he had to urinate in a disposal sink, as he wasn't allowed to take a bathroom break for several hours. When Urasawa abruptly fired one worker and then refused to pay him the for the hours he had already worked, the worker called KIWA and became a client. Protests followed. The publicity was awful. Customers asked for reservations, but then they asked strange things, like did the restaurant have a back entrance? Others wondered whether they might dine in complete confidentiality, so that no one would know that they were eating at Urasawa. Having regularly booked all of the rooms and tables weeks in advance, the restaurant people suddenly got anxious calls inquiring about labor protests on the day of their reservations. Are the picketers there? Many people canceled, even when the answer was "no" or "not yet." The labor troubles didn't go away.

And then, during an inspection with the California State Labor Commissioner, Chef Urasawa said something incriminating: "employees don't take breaks, it's Japanese style." The Labor Commissioner that day, Julie Su, was very probably unsympathetic to that argument, because, years earlier, in 1995, she had been among the lead attorneys for the Thai garment workers who'd been held in slave-like conditions in El Monte, not 30 miles from Urasawa. One can almost imagine her face when the chef said what he was alleged to have said. In 2013, Ms. Su issued fines against Urasawa for about $68,000. Friends reported that Chef Urasawa was about to close his restaurant and move back to Japan. Some tried to console him by offering perspective: another famous chef, Mario Batali, the Iron Chef America, had settled with his own workers at several restaurants in New York City for $1.15 million just a year ago, and those were a lot more gold flakes. Urasawa stayed open after all.[34]

Just Cities

Because these kinds of labor problems happened so often, progressives in many cities have moved toward more aggressive forms of regulation, to impose rules on all employers to benefit all employees. They've cobbled together unlikely coalitions, including fast-food workers in New York and restaurant workers in Seattle. In many of these cities, especially in places with a relatively high cost of living, an increase in the minimum wage has proven politically popular. The City of Seattle voted to raise the minimum wage in 2014, using a formula that accounted for the size of companies, and that phased in the increase over several years. By 2017, larger businesses with more than 500 employees will see an hourly wage of $15; by 2021, smaller businesses would also raise the hourly wage to $15. New York City approved of a similar rule in 2015, so that, by 2018, the hourly wage will be $15. The state of New York passed one, too, but only for fast-food employees in the state who were working in larger franchise restaurants like McDonald's or KFC. Their wages will rise to $15 by 2021.

On this issue, California cities have been the most active. San Francisco's hourly wages will rise to $15 by 2018, as will Mountain View's and Sunnyvale's. San Jose, Los Altos, Cupertino will have $15 by 2019. In Los Angeles, the City Council agreed in June 2016 to raise the minimum wage to $15 by 2021. In addition, in that same city ordinance, the City of Los Angeles mandated paid sick leave, applicable to all employees. The city ordinance also stipulated penalties for employers who intimidated or retaliated against employees who pressed their rights under the city law, just as they did in similar rules in San Francisco and in Oakland. In March 2016, the Governor and Legislature in California agreed to increase the state's minimum wage to $15 by 2022, over the objections of several Republican State Senators and Assembly members. Of course, the fate and economic fortunes of immigrants weren't the only reasons that these rules were approved, but it's notable that these rules in California and elsewhere disqualified no one solely because of immigration status. Every employee in Los Angeles was to be paid $15 per hour by 2021, without exception. In several major cities, by 2016, public officials had extended the principle to other labor regulations, as well as access to city services, so that all persons could expect basic protection and services in ways far more egalitarian than the federal immigration law might suggest. Indeed, citing Los Angeles and San Francisco as especially bad examples, many Republicans argued that the local political leaders and their ordinances in those cities often undermined immigration enforcement.[35]

But California was an unusual place in 2016, as the Democrats controlled the Governor's office and both chambers of the Legislature. Both of California's candidates for Senator were Democrats, as no Republican even made it to the run-off in November. That is, in November 2016, in the United States Senate race, California voters got to choose between one Democrat and another Democrat. Senator Kamala Harris was elected the first African American *and* Asian American Senator to represent the state, and she had been very much in favor of the minimum wage increases popping up there. In her campaign, she indicated that federal policies around immigration were threatening too many California families, and that comprehensive immigration reform would be among her top priorities. This was before she or many other people in California knew what the November elections would produce, at least in the Presidential race. In the absence of comprehensive immigration reform, Senator Harris said subsequently, the states must do what they can, and passing and supporting statewide rules to protect workers was what Californians should do. In not very subtle ways, like many city and state officials throughout her state, Senator Harris was suggesting that immigration status alone should not be so important, and it shouldn't disqualify someone from pressing a legitimate claim against an unscrupulous employer.[36]

Thus, the Wilshire Grand Center opened in a very different regulatory environment from the one that had existed in California or in Los Angeles when this project was first conceived. So far, everything has gone well – perhaps because it will be the tallest building west of the Mississippi River, the developers and the managers seemed mindful of that higher level of visibility. They arranged for labor contracts with the hotel workers well in advance. They've said publicly that they will honor the city's minimum wage ordinance, even though it'll be double the federal minimum wage in just a few years. In their manner and tone, they seemed wholly willing to do whatever was reasonable to avoid embarrassing forms of street theater when the building opened. As the building is finished, the architects will install that Korean Air logo, bolted onto the sides of this massive structure. It was so fascinating, how one group of Koreans financed and conceived this thing while another group will watch it carefully for any signs of labor trouble.

In the coming decades, if comprehensive reform of the immigration law continues to fail, the greatest divide among Americans might be between those who obey the law, and those who willingly ignore it, or even break it. In many jurisdictions, Americans already enforced some rules and not others. We thus lived in a confusing time, when federal law said one thing, and state and local rules said another. Immigration law and marijuana law were similar these days: under federal law, marijuana was illegal everywhere, and yet, in many of the states and local jurisdictions, it was legal, more potent than ever, and available for sale every few blocks. Just looking at the federal law alone, and then concluding from it that no one smoked pot legally in the United States, would have been a big mistake. Similarly, federal immigration rules were but one set of rules now; many people were frustrated that they don't work, and that they may in fact be counterproductive. They've passed other rules in the states and in the cities, and these rules have suggested that all persons were deserving of dignity irrespective of their immigration status. Other states and local jurisdictions have pushed hard to push away all immigrants, especially the "illegals." All of this was precarious and unstable, a constant, bitter contest between Americans working through different levels of government. We will need the social scientists for many years more to tell us about our great divides, the fights that will happen again and again, with no clear end in sight.[37]

10

THE FUTURE OF AMERICAN MIGRATIONS

Ourselves, in the Fullness of Time

Having been a student of the immigration law for most of my life, I am quite certain that Congress did not mean to worsen many of the divisions we've seen, nor did the American presidents design intentionally the many dilemmas discussed in this book. I also think that many reasonable members of Congress would concede that the consequences of some of our immigration laws were good for no one, including us and our political system. For example, even some Republicans might acknowledge that it's just bad for any republic to hold elections when a significant fraction of the people affected by the results have no right to vote. Perhaps for lack of anything better, the prevailing solution of their party – to "remove," or to deport, as many of these people as possible – will probably have unintended consequences, too, even in the best of circumstances. Taking people away from family members, and from communities where they've lived for many years, will anger many people, not to mention harm irreparably the people who are thus removed. In response, as we have seen for some time, many well-meaning Americans will refuse to participate in any enforcement, to the point where they will break the law rather than uphold it. To enforce the law as it was, American citizens risked even more repression against immigrants, and then against themselves.

The other solution, though, an amnesty, or a legalization, or an adjustment – whatever we call it – will also prove a limited one: good for now, for the people who have been here already for some time, but not a permanent answer to the on-going patterns of migration we've seen in the world. As Ronald Reagan and his successors have learned, legalizing 1 or 3 million people now, without addressing the conditions that caused people to migrate in the first place, will not stop 1 or 3 million more people from coming unlawfully. Yet another group of unlawful migrants will settle in, too; they will develop connections to more lawful residents and citizens – perhaps have one, or a few, citizen children themselves. Thus, they will create over time yet another need for another amnesty, legalization, or adjustment.

Even if we could, by some magic, eliminate low wages, political instability, or states that fail, we are still almost guaranteed to see irregular migrations, if only because the world is just more interconnected, and a great many people who are out of status now aren't desperately poor or looking for asylum or crossing a major river at night to get to America. Flying has become so easy, and falling out of status is easier, too. Millionaires and highly skilled people have already enjoyed a relatively borderless world; they have enjoyed a "flexible citizenship," as well as political affiliations based on economic and social choices rather than blood and soil attachments. They really were freer than ever before, and few liberal states were moving to limit their free movement.[1]

For poorer migrants, we have seen proposals for something between enforcement and amnesty – some combination of both approaches – and these have characterized nearly all of the comprehensive reforms proposed since 1996, ever since the spate of immigration enforcement and welfare reform rules enacted during that year. But because amnesty has proven politically fatal for nearly any Republican who has proposed it, few if any have continued to do so, and, instead, we have had even greater enforcement, no amnesty, and guarantees of future stalemates. We have seen complex state and local rules that reflected defiance of federal immigration law, especially when they concern education or labor regulations, and these rules also captured an acrimony and defiance toward federal policies. In the United States, during and after the presidential election of 2016, no one could doubt the central place of immigration policy in American law and politics. Many of the biggest cheers for the winning candidate were for a wall, that big beautiful wall, and yet if just a fraction of the people offended by that same wall could have voted, too, that same candidate would have lost by a larger, more staggering margin in the popular vote.

It's quite likely that the Donald Trumps of America's future will continue to be among the primary beneficiaries of paralysis in this area of law, if only because the people who find such candidates the most offensive and vulgar will be denied a say, year after year, election after election. Because immigrants can't vote – especially not the illegal ones – we might see this disenfranchisement as nothing special, when, in fact, it is a major and growing democratic crisis, a deep flaw in light of how this political system *ought to* function. Other people have been disenfranchised in American history, but we tend to think of these periods with regret. Perhaps the most misogynistic and unrepentant racists among us regret nothing but their disappearance, and maybe they still long for another time: once, not long ago, women and people of color could not vote. It might seem so unreal now that this was true. I explained to my own three daughters, when they were younger, that they would not have been able to vote for most of American history, because they were women and people of color. My children asked excellent questions during this discussion: Were they stupid, the men who didn't want women to vote? Didn't they know that many women are smarter than many men? And were they evil or blind, the ones who didn't want people of color to vote? Did White people *actually* think that White people were better people? At least *we* agreed, at the end of these discussions, that, whatever the reason, disenfranchising so many people had been an irrational and horrible flaw in American political history.

Again, in the early twenty-first century, many Americans might think that there was nothing wrong with keeping 10, or 12, or however many million people from voting in *our* elections. In the fullness of time, though, we wonder what other Americans in the future will make now of our casual indifference to our own democratic principles, of the people and the political parties that willfully, stubbornly disenfranchised many more people. They will observe that most Americans did nothing to "deserve" the right to vote – they just fell into it at birth. Other Americans, as well as people who aren't Americans, might also believe in the future that this disenfranchisement of immigrants nowadays was even more heinous when they learn that rich people, and their spoiled children, and those fortunate enough to have schooling and skills, were not all so excluded. To state this bluntly, it wasn't that Americans had disenfranchised all immigrants the same – just the poor ones. It's hard to see how our descendants might find any of this just or fair, if we imagine a nation across a temporal space, having a past and a future, and so we can only wonder what our descendants will make of all this in the fullness of time.

Fenced In

Among my professional colleagues who study immigration, no one believes that a wall – no matter how tall – will stop poorer and desperate people from coming in numbers significant enough to justify building it. A few of my colleagues have argued quite persuasively, I believe, that our existing obstacles and walls and fences have functioned much more like traps rather than as barriers. Because getting across was becoming so hard, people who crossed once did not want to bother going back and then trying it again, especially not on foot. For those who'd fallen out of status, they could not fly back and forth, lest they be subjected to three- or ten-year bars, and so they didn't go back either. They were "fenced in." They simply stayed on this side, our side, and then spent many years not seeing their family members and loved ones, many of whom they were supporting on the other side. Money moved more freely across boundaries than people, and so they've been sending record amounts of money back home.[2]

A wall will wall in as much as it walls out, and a wall, even if it is super tall, is not as hard to overcome as some might promise. In 1943, the Mexican government declared that Mexico City's Central Airport would be the first truly international airport in Mexico, with regular flights at least once every week to Los Angeles. By 2010, Mexico had at least 50 international airports. There were, on average, about 30 flights to Mexico City International Airport from just LAX every day, and, if one planned ahead, some of these flights cost less than $250. The planes nowadays carry two or three times as many passengers as the ones in 1943, the great irony being that many of the travelers were Americans taking holidays in Mexico. These numbers were modest compared to other places.

The government of China had planned five dozen new airports to be completed by 2020, and, by 2015, over 100 million Chinese people were leaving every year to see the world as tourists. It's curious how people who demanded a wall didn't consider flying.[3]

Many other public officials did think about flying. Indeed, the professionals in our government in charge of drug enforcement and interdiction have said that drug traffickers from Mexico and other countries have moved people and drugs increasingly by air, as well as by sea and through tunnels *under* the Southern border. Single drug organizations were like any other capitalist organization: they took multiple approaches to minimize their risks. The Sinaloa cartel hired master tunnel builders, they bought small and large submarines and boats, they bought light and medium-sized planes, they sprinkled cocaine over dozens and dozens of donuts to look like powdered sugar, and they also built giant mobile catapults, similar to the ones that Hulegu, Genghis Khan's son, had used in the siege of Baghdad in 1258. Drug traffickers thought that Sinaloa catapults could fling well-packaged bundles of cocaine across remote, fenced portions of the Southern border, and then their associates on the Arizona or California side would come to pick these up. Sinaloa lieutenants received permission to use any and all of these systems to get people across the border, too, as this human trafficking could be lucrative as well, although some techniques were obviously better for transporting people than others. Planes were the best, all-purpose method, they agreed, and so they continued to invest in a fleet of small planes that was, in number, comparable to some international airlines by 2010. All of this experimentation had paid off: from 2009 to 2011, the head of the Sinaloa, Joaquin Guzman, nicknamed "El Chapo," was named by *Forbes* magazine as the tenth-richest man in Mexico, whose personal fortune exceeded at least $1 billion.[4]

Aside from even more evidence that a wall would not necessarily work, the Sinaloa cartel and El Chapo offered insights into how the drugs and people coming from Mexico to the United States was rather an American problem, not so much a Mexican problem or a border problem. That is, despite numerous rules and billions of dollars spent on enforcing them, Americans still demonstrated a robust demand for Mexican workers, and then lots and lots of demand for drugs, too. Cocaine was not produced in Mexico until maybe 2010 – before then, cartels in Colombia, more than in any other country, made cocaine, and then shipped it directly to the United States or through Mexico. They made fortunes. Our own drug enforcement agencies have estimated that slightly less than 3 percent of Americans used cocaine at least once every year, starting in the 1970s. Independent researchers have said that Americans have used up to 300 metric tons of pure cocaine every year since at least 2000.

Others insisted that this figure was too low. Biologists and chemists have tested the waters from the Hudson River near New York City and from the River Rhine near Dusseldorf – the human body produces trace chemicals during cocaine consumption, which remain even in treated sewage, and so, by detecting their concentrations, the chemists can get a sense of how much cocaine people have been using. The chemists said that people around the River Rhine basin used about 11 tons per year by 2000; the people around New York City did over 16. Extrapolated across the country, Americans might be snorting and smoking and shooting up as much as 500 metric tons of cocaine per year.[5]

Drug problems were like immigration problems – more enforcement, more interdiction, more heavily armed local police and federal drug marshals; none of these have curbed the American appetite for drugs. The drug business has always been violent, just like the alcohol business during the Prohibition Era, and yet because this business was exponentially larger, and measured in the billions of dollars and tens of metric tons, many thousands of people were willing to kill and to terrorize each other for access to this lucrative market. The Sinaloa, the Cali, the Medellin, the Juarez Cartel, the Felix Brothers of the Tijuana Cartel – they have all been ultraviolent over the last two decades, and they have targeted government officials, local and federal authorities, journalists, and hundreds of civilians. By far, though, their members have killed one another, targeting associates within vast criminal organizations at an alarming and horrifying rate, and turning entire cities into macabre spectacles of death. In Cuidad Juarez, across from El Paso, the cartels employed other, Genghis Khan-like tactics, such as hanging bodies from public places or butchering people into little pieces and then having them delivered to loved ones. Smaller, upcoming organizations used torture and public assassinations to let the established ones know that they were "serious." By 2005, the annual murder rate in the United States was about 6 persons per 100,000 people. In Mexico, it was four times higher – over 20 people killed per 100,000 inhabitants, or over 20-25,000 murders each year. One might wonder how these organizations maintained these horrifying levels of murder, year after year.[6]

The United States had sent billions of dollars in military aid to Mexico and to other countries to fight the drug trade, especially after President Reagan had declared a war on drugs. But, since 1986, the United States has been sending deportees from here to Mexico and to other Central American countries every year, year after year, hundreds of thousands of people; most of them were men with criminal records. What were these Americans doing in Mexico or in El Salvador or in Guatemala? During George W. Bush's presidency, several Central American governments protested not just the method of deportation – the deportees were simply dropped off at the airports, our officials having given no warning about the arrival of these people to the governments of El Salvador or Honduras – but also the sheer numbers of American deportees, hundreds every month. Many of these deportees did not speak Spanish, and they had no idea what they would do in San Salvador or Guatemala City. Yet because so many of them were coming all at once, they found among themselves people they knew, including fellow members of street gangs from Los Angeles or Phoenix. The Maras were especially notorious.[7]

Mara Salvatrucha originated around the Pico-Union area of Los Angeles, but American deportation policies helped to make them an international criminal organization. The sons and daughters of Central Americans who'd fled to the United States had formed some version of the Maras since the late 1970s and early 1980s, largely in opposition to the Mexican Mafia and to other street gangs in Los Angeles. By 1980, the Maras were an organized and well-armed criminal organization, and their members had a significant presence within the

California state prison system. Many of them were deported, "removed" not just because of their criminal activity, but also because so many of them had never passed into American citizenship. An American-born gangster of Mexican ancestry cannot be "removed," for he is an American citizen, and yet the kid who came with his parents from El Salvador when he was 5 years old can be deported more easily than ever before, even though he is in all respects indistinguishable from his Mexican American peers. Many people have been deported to countries that they couldn't remember – so many that the Maras now ran the prisons in Central America. They may have single-handedly increased the urban murder rates of several Central American cities. As long as the United States keeps removing such persons, American deportees will continue to replenish the cartels, to form new ones, and, with their laptops and cell phones, to develop novel methods of delivering drugs and people back to the United States. They themselves often came back "home." We know this because, these days, drug busts in California or in Texas yield gangsters who've been deported once or twice before.[8]

We wonder how or when the leading policy-makers in the United States might re-think all of this, as it seems self-defeating, perhaps even pointless, to the government officials and scholars who've kept track of these trends. Again, I am certain that Presidents Reagan, Bush, Clinton, Bush, and Obama did not expect or want deportation policies to create these strange new diasporas, connected still to the United States in ways that are so violent and disturbing, and yet this seems precisely to be the result. It has now become embedded into the future of American migrations. We will see this trend for a long, long time, as there has been no political support to stop the pace of removal, or to consider in a more compassionate way the impact of all of these deportations on the "receiving" countries, places like El Salvador and Guatemala, still recovering from decades of civil war. In Mexico, American deportation policies have challenged and strained the government for over two decades, just as the economy of Mexico produced more, and was itself producing a stable middle class. If Mexico became unlivable, a significant fraction of that middle class would move here, and there was already some evidence that this had been an unfolding pattern. Like their Asian peers, Mexican professionals were wild geese, too, dropping off their spouses and children in Texas or in Arizona so that they might have better schools and far less drug violence in their day-to-day lives. Again, it seemed to many of us in this field unrealistic to think that we could wall off Mexico's problems while making many of them worse.[9]

Things were deteriorating. Between 2013 and 2014, for example, the United States experienced a surge in unlawful border crossings by children, unaccompanied by their parents. Children from Central America and Mexico were traveling across vast distances through Mexico, most on trains, others on buses, and they represented a 90 percent increase in the number of such persons detained by the United States Border Patrol. About 60,000 children were being held in United States detention facilities in 2014. Most agents said that this figure represented less than half of the children attempting to cross during those two years. Scholars wondered whether the children detained by our government were the lucky ones or not – local and federal officials found the corpses of children not far from major cities and small towns along the border.

Even for the most hardened Border Patrol agents, this migration was so disturbing. Locking up children to process their removal was just disturbing. Many civic organizations and academics interviewed these children, and some of these children then said that their parents had told them to go, and that this was because their homes were violent and unlivable. The parents had encouraged many of these children to find one or more loved ones in the United States, relatives who might also be living here, legally or illegally, so that they might avoid the seasons of death that were becoming so common in Mexico and in Central America. Many children reported that they had no surviving parents. President Barack Obama was shaken by the numbers of unaccompanied children in the federal detention facilities. He urged all parents to stop giving this kind of advice to their children. He sent Vice President Joe Biden to visit governments in Central America to facilitate the quick and safe transport of minors back to their home countries, if just to show people there that the United States would not tolerate this dangerous and often tragic pattern of behavior.[10]

Obama's critics said that this migration was his fault: the Democrats were "soft" on immigration, they didn't mind offering free public schools or even college to "illegals," and they were talking about "amnesty" whenever they could, even governing by executive fiat in DACA and in DAPA. No wonder these people were sending their children. The two Democratic candidates for President in 2016 disagreed sharply about President Obama's policy – Hillary Clinton said that Central American and Mexican children under US custody should be sent back, and that this was the humanitarian thing to do, because it discouraged subsequent attempts, ultimately saving these children from needless death and suffering. Senator Bernie Sanders said that they should all be granted asylum, that sending them back into drug-infested lives was just cruel. The Republican candidates were less divided – deport all of them, they said, the bad hombres, the rapists and criminals, the killers and the drug dealers, the people who had been protected by DACA or DAPA. They all blamed Obama, while taking no responsibility for their own support of those deportation policies that were making these problems worse.[11]

And there was to be no asylum for those Central American and Mexican children: in January 2017, President Trump issued an executive order to halt the admission of certain people into the United States, including the citizens of Syria, Iraq, Iran, Libya, Somalia, Sudan, and Yemen, for at least 90 days. President Trump had insisted that this order was primarily about national security, and that it was quite necessary to stop the potential migration of terrorists. Yet a significant portion of the order blocked the admission and resettlement of all refugees in the United States, including children who might have had one or both parents in the United States already. In late 2014, President Obama's Administration had allowed for "humanitarian parole" in cases where a minor in immigration detention could be released to his or her parents or legal guardians while applying for asylum. President Trump's order attempted to eliminate that policy. The federal courts blocked this first executive order, and then they blocked a similar revision issued in March 2017, but no one could mistake his desire to block and to remove more people than any previous President, just as he had promised during his campaign.[12]

Exclusion, deportation, drug trafficking, horrifying levels of violence, the flight of children and their detention here – they have all been interrelated. They suggested that a nation pursuing its narrow self-interest may not, in the end, serve its own interests. Our deportation policies and the criminal diasporas that they've created were almost certainly making our own problems worse, while not helping at all the countries to our south. As conditions deteriorate in those countries, more people will take their chances and attempt to fly, tunnel, and cross their way here, forming again populations of illegal people. Policies that did not comprehend this inter-relatedness were doomed to fail, and, in profound ways, Americans were the source of these endless cycles of misery. In the United States, people who used drugs, whether they were using recreationally, once in a while, or much more often, were probably not thinking about how a single line of cocaine contributed to pain and misery and cultures of death far from where they were snorting or smoking and getting high. It might even blow the high, to think of dead children in the desert, or gang members dismembering one another to get that cocaine to that place where you were snorting, so that you might forget and enjoy yourself for a while. That casual, off-handed failure to see the interconnectedness of things, over millions of users and hundreds of metric tons, caused all of us to be worse off, and to create intractable problems well into our future, for which there were not going to be any easy solutions. We ourselves appeared fenced in by our own bad habits, and by our own repetitive, self-defeating patterns of behavior.

Weak States and Climate Change

For the most vulnerable, for whom immigration controls have been the most harsh, the underlying conditions for emigration may have grown worse, either because of continued indifference, or because of too much attention of the wrong kind. Low wages might get lower in many countries, and more governments might fail in the near future. Just in the last two decades, the list of "failed states" has grown long indeed: Somalia, Sudan and South Sudan, Liberia, Uganda, Burundi, Nigeria, Libya, Haiti, Venezuela, Iraq, Afghanistan, and Syria, just to name a few. A child born into any one of these countries will be born into dangerous, unstable circumstances, even when – or perhaps because – the American military arrived there. Because of our efforts to stop terrorism, to engage in "regime change," or to do both, Iraq and Afghanistan will remain chaotic for the foreseeable future, and they will generate many thousands of migrants, even as hundreds of thousands have already left. The United States has spent billions of dollars in Iraq and Afghanistan, but no one would mistake these places for stable, secure, or safe places to live.[13]

Some chaotic countries have banned emigration, but they were often no more successful in this than countries that banned certain classes of immigrants. By many measures, for example, North Korea was a failed state, too, although its political leaders behaved as though they were not, and were united in their efforts to build nuclear weapons and to missile them at the United States. North Korea appeared to be among the most dangerous states, even to its own citizens. Between 1994 and 1998, at least 500,000 people died during a period of severe droughts and then massive flooding, an astonishing loss of life that reflected a criminal level of ineptitude within the North Korean state. Ever since those terrible years, North Korea has had emigration problems instead of immigration problems – no one wanted much to go there; most people were looking to leave. As many as 300,000 North Koreans were "hiding" in China by 2000, because it's illegal to leave North Korea and yet quite unbearable to live there. Wracked by internal dissent, threatened with disintegration, the North Korean state retrenched: it took food aid and other material support from South Korea, its mortal enemy, and then from the United States, too, and, without question, it used this to rededicate itself to developing nuclear weapons. It has been blackmailing the world ever since. The North Koreans showed how a weak state was still very dangerous.[14]

Other states that weren't quite failing weren't quite "successful" either: Russia, the Philippines, Turkey, Egypt, Cuba, and Nicaragua, to name a few, have been difficult to govern, they were dangerous places for their own citizens, and, although they have ostensibly strong leaders, they also had very weak economies and civil societies, and they experienced periods of political chaos, economic privation, or both. Emigration has been a way of life for these places for many, many years, and a catastrophic political or economic crisis in any one of these countries could produce more refugees and displaced people than any single state or international organization could handle.

Moreover, various kinds of environmental catastrophes might cause so many people to lose their homes that what we now consider "mass migration" could seem quaint in 50 or 100 years. The climate has been changing; it was not some "hoax." Already, from Florida through the Gulf Coast, from Fujian province to Bangladesh and India, and across the Sahara Desert in Africa, surface temperatures have never been so high so consistently for so many years, and all with graph lines going up. In the poles, North and South, temperatures have been rising faster, so that the polar ice caps were melting at an alarming rate. Coastal flooding and erosion were already-present problems by 2010, not ones that were forecasted to happen by the end of the century. The concentrations of greenhouse gases in the Earth's atmosphere – carbon dioxide, methane, nitrous oxide, ozone, and water vapor – were higher in 2000 than at any time in the planet's history, and ten years later, they were ever higher. They will be continuing to rise by the time you read this sentence. When the ice caps melt, when the major cities flood or burn, or when there is no water or way too much water, what will happen to human migrations? I must admit, 25 years ago, when I started driving and putting gasoline into my car, I didn't think that that mundane and boring chore was related to epic droughts, scary heat waves, ferocious storms, and mass extinctions, including the death of polar bears and monarch butterflies. The monarchs were especially beautiful, hanging from the eucalyptus trees in Santa Barbara. On the West Coast, those fragile and beautiful creatures had flown hundreds of miles from northern Mexico to southern and central California, before the Americans, the Mexicans, the Spaniards, and even the Chumash lived here, but they may cease to exist in part because of the gasoline in my car.

My single contribution to greenhouse gas production was minuscule, of course – unlikely to change anything. But 350 million Americans like me, plus all of those Europeans and Asians and everyone else, each contributing their modest amounts of carbon dioxide, and using coal and other fossil fuels – all this meant that the planet was headed for big trouble. Not only were human beings capable now of ending the world suddenly, through nuclear weapons, we were changing the Earth's atmosphere through millions and millions of slower burns, generation after generation, ever since the Industrial Revolution. Perhaps the Greek gods were right to have punished Prometheus, for we were learning now that human beings truly were incapable of managing their fires after all.[15]

And a great chunk of the world's population lives between the Tropic of Cancer and the Tropic of Capricorn, that vast belt that will experience the worst storms, the highest rise in sea levels, the most uncontrollable fires, and the most severe droughts. Most of the world lives in a band between 20° north and 20° south of these lines, respectively. Where will these people go? Already, we have seen how the combinations of drought or fires or flooding can overwhelm weaker states, how they can cause people to embrace drastic and dangerous measures, and how politically unstable places can spiral out of control. In Syria, for instance, the governments of Hafez al-Assad and then of his son Bashar al-Assad were among the more stable in that region of the world, although neither of these leaders was a paragon of democratic virtue.

Syria was like other states in the Middle East, cobbled together in the wake of Western imperialism, with ethnic groups thrust together even though they had experienced intense animosity toward one another during the colonial period, long before the state of Syria existed. Under the Assad regimes, Sunni elites did well, but the Alawite sect of Shia Muslims did even better. Poorer Sunnis, many Christians, the Kurds, the Yezidis, and the Assyrians, among other ethnic groups, had reasons to dislike and to distrust the Assads, these people who never bothered to hold free and fair elections. When Bashar al-Assad was elected President in 2000, he reportedly received 99.7 percent of the vote, he being the only candidate. The government said that the turnout was 94.6 percent of eligible voters. These were not persuasive lies to many people in Syria.[16]

Still, Syria functioned, Assad pursued economic reforms, and, as a statesman, he tried magnanimous gestures, such as receiving Iraqi refugees, to broaden his base of support. In 2006, however, when the Syrian economy was still growing, and when many people seemed to be accepting Assad's regime, a serious drought threatened agricultural production. This was not a minor problem – nearly a third of all production in Syria was tied to agriculture, and that sector employed about 40 percent of all workers. The drought dragged into another year, and then another, and yet another. After five years of drought, agricultural production fell so much that unemployment rose to frightening levels, food prices skyrocketed, and water shortages were common and, in many cases, fatal in more remote areas. Some said that Assad's government only helped its own supporters, while letting others suffer and die. They demanded democratic reforms, and they protested in demonstrations that grew larger and more strident.[17]

Their protests coincided with the Arab Spring, during which the people of many nations demanded democratic reforms across the Middle East. In Syria, the protests turned violent – the Syrian civil war began with a set of protests that turned into armed uprisings in March 2011. The violence quickly escalated when the Syrian Army fractured, between those who supported Assad and those who defected and formed the Free Syrian Army. President Assad certainly never had over 90 percent of his country's support, and whatever support he may have had abroad disappeared when his forces bombed civilian targets with no obvious military purpose, and with callous disregard for human life. In 2013, the United States and European governments accused Assad of using sarin gas, chlorine bombs, and other chemical weapons. The civil war has dragged on longer than the drought, and it has produced millions of displaced people, as well as a massive refugee crisis in Europe.

Many armed men have flocked to Syria to join the fighting, including members of the Islamic State of Iraq and the Levant, commonly known in the West as ISIS. They have made this war far more complex and multidimensional. From the perspective of Western liberal democracies, it was hard to imagine a more repellent group of extremist men – at least 40,000 armed Sunni militants, all devoted to jihad. From President Assad's perspective, ISIS fighters were terrorists who should be expelled from eastern Syria, but only after he had defeated the Syrian rebels in the major western cities, in Aleppo and Homs, and within Damascus. From the perspective of ISIS, ISIS was the only legitimate government in the region, and they would willingly have beheaded and replaced Assad if they had had the chance. From the perspective of the Syrian rebels, Assad's entrenched position and ISIS' hold in Western Iraq made any reasonable peace unlikely, as if they had to choose between two different devils. The Russian and Iranian governments supported Assad, the Americans supported the rebels, and many diplomats accused Sunni leaders in Saudi Arabia, as well as elements of the Turkish government, of supporting ISIS – at least ideologically, if not materially. And so the war has dragged on.[18]

In this highly inter-connected world, we've learned also that this war in one place could have profound repercussions closer to our own homes. Many of the young men who'd joined ISIS had come from elsewhere – Europe, the United States, and other parts of the Middle East. They had radicalized on-line: they were consumers of videos produced by jihadists who, on the one hand, rejected all aspects of the decadent West, and yet who also used Western technologies to grow their movement. They recorded the beheading of prisoners and posted the executions on social media, they used the "dark web" and other encrypted forms of internet communication to coordinate their activities, and, through these methods, they called upon fellow Muslims to find purpose and meaning by blowing up and killing Westerners, either in the major cities of the West, or by traveling to Syria or Iraq to fight and to die for an Islamic utopia. ISIS offered citizenship in a state that didn't exist, and they spoke directly to the troubled young men who felt no deeper attachments to the Western nations in which they'd lived or were born. In San Bernardino, Boston, Orlando, New York, London, Paris, Stockholm, and Berlin, the "home-grown" terrorist, the person who was a citizen or long-time resident, could very well be the radical, cold-blooded killer, having crossed no physical international boundary to cause chaos or mayhem. These persons, and the methods through which they were inspired to kill, both posed serious and significant challenges for all governments.[19]

In Syria, at least 60,000 people have died thus far in direct military engagements, and yet the more telling figure might be 470,000, the number of people that the United Nations has estimated have perished from 2011 until the end of 2016. The country was literally decimated in just five years. Syria was not a well-functioning democracy, it had had an autocratic system of government, with what was essentially a hereditary presidency, and it had many other problems. And yet, Syria had an infrastructure, it had a middle class and a professional class, and, until 2011, it was a place that received refugees and displaced persons, not a place that produced so many of them. Persons from very different religious traditions once coexisted in Syria without killing each other. But in 2006 and 2007, in the first two years of drought, many Syrian farmers could not remember another time when the rains failed so much, so horribly; and then in the next two years, everything had dried up and just died, things turning to dust as if in some Old Testament nightmare.

Scientists in the West said that the Syrian drought may have been the worst in over 500 years. Climate researchers at NASA reported that the drought in that region was well outside what could be explained as part of a natural climate cycle. Lebanon, Syria, and Israel were moving into an unusual, unpredictable climate pattern as part of broader changes in the eastern Mediterranean Sea, where surface temperatures have never been higher. As early as 1993, the scientists were predicting a drier, more arid eastern Mediterranean, with periods of severe heat waves and multiyear droughts in the Levant. Water would become the scarcest of resources. In Syria, since 2011, to add to the cruelty of this war, and as a weapon of war, all of the combatants have been preoccupied with controlling and destroying water supplies. They bombed water trucks, they destroyed water treatment facilities, and they bombed and killed aid workers rushing to assist civilians. They have wanted their enemies to die of thirst and then those diseases caused by lack of sanitation. They did not appear to mind or to care that this kind of strategy destroyed entire communities, including and especially the very young, the elderly, and the infirm.[20]

How many more Syrias will there be in our future? The math is terrifying – count the number of autocratic states, weak states, and failed states, then add climate change, and this could be awful indeed. And just as climate change is a global problem, its symptoms, including forced human migrations, will become global and unavoidable as well. This problem will make every other worse. It may seem tempting for some to see this future as an occasion to embrace nationalism and patriotism, perhaps become even more parochial and narrow: our nation and our people above all others, our nation first, America First. Will it be possible, though, to wall ourselves away and disengage from the world, and tend simply to ourselves? Is it even morally tenable to keep burning fossil fuels, while walling ourselves away and disengaging from the world, simply tending to ourselves? Won't other people around the world *see* what we are doing, perhaps complain that the United States has burned more carbon-based fuels than any other nation, thus contributing the most to this global problem, even while they are retreating into themselves, tending only to themselves?

The essence of thinking is that ability to see the world from another person's perspective, to see the world through a perspective that isn't your own. The future of the United States might lie in that same direction, to see migration problems from the perspective of the immigrants, not so much the citizens, and to consider the responsibilities of the United States not from a narrow, interior point of view, but from a broader, global point of view. This engagement with the world, made ever more possible through transportation and communication technologies, may be the only tenable moral position, the one best for us and for others, including polar bears and monarch butterflies, too. They have as much right to exist as we do, and we certainly have no right to cause them to become extinct. A global, engaged perspective might be the only one that inspires others to support and to join us, rather than wish for our demise. No one likes a self-absorbed narcissist. We might also consider this perspective not just because it is more moral – and ultimately more beautiful, too – but because, in the long run, it's probably the only one that will work.

Epilogue

At the end of every class, my students have submitted written evaluations, and many of them have said that the class was interesting and compelling, but rather short of solutions. "You never tell us what we should *do* about these problems," complained one student. In response, in recent years, I've indicated in advance that this class wasn't an occasion where I, as The Professor, gave directions about law and policy; where I behaved as though everything would be better if Everyone Just Listened to Me. We lived in a liberal democracy, I've said, and so, to ensure long-term changes, the people of the United States had to engage one another over many years of public debate, and with respect for the opinions of fellow-citizens who disagreed profoundly with the positions that others might hold dear. Sure, I had developed some ideas that I've felt were more likely to work in law and in policy, and I was willing to offer them (after class), but I was also sure that most of my suggestions wouldn't be practical policy positions – at least, not yet.

I had to glean this insight myself: I once gave a briefing to the staff members of my local Congresswoman; they sat politely through my 90-minute presentation about the two revolutions, but then they never contacted me again. It occurred to me later that Ms. Lois Capps, my Congresswoman, would have had a hard time keeping her committee assignment if she had declared, on the floor of the House of Representatives, that national sovereignty was perhaps an outmoded form of political organization in light of the kinetic, interwoven nature of the world, and that hard boundaries between nations would never work, and that birth-right citizenship was morally unjustifiable because it privileged American citizens in a medieval and archaic way. Alas, her political fortunes would have been dimmer after such a speech. And so, as Emily Dickinson might say, we academics should tell the truth, but tell it slant. I've written the next few paragraphs in that spirit.

Rules that acknowledged the inter-connectedness of the world were more just and likely to work than rules that promoted narrower, nationalistic self-interests.

Rules that protected the residents of a jurisdiction might be better than the ones that protected only citizens, native-born or otherwise. Rules that gave residents more rights and opportunities based on the length of their residency would work better than rules that disregarded the long-term attachments that residents could make in one place, over time. Rules that taxed all residents, and rules that taxed wealthier residents more than poorer ones, were more likely to work, and to appear as just. Rules that taxed all persons, but then denied some residents the services that their taxes still supported, solely because they were not citizens, were unfair. Rules that further victimized people abused at work were far less just or fair than rules that punished unscrupulous, amoral employers. Rules that disenfranchised long-term residents were simply antithetical in any functioning democracy. They generated perverse incentives for political parties to exclude people rather than appealing to them. The very pursuit of such rules made the system *less* democratic and participatory. And rules that treated some children as somehow more worthy than other children – just because they were born on one side of a political line – were neither just nor fair. Such rules relied on brute chance; they resembled other rules long rejected as immoral in our own political system, because they privileged *and* disabled persons based upon morally arbitrary reasons.

Rules that punished people proportionately, based on the infraction that they'd committed, were more just, compared to rules that punished people based on some strange combination of their infraction *and* their status. Removing someone from her home and from her family for a minor infraction did not comport with our considered judgments about justice or fairness. Moreover, removing lots of people who'd committed very serious crimes, hundreds of thousands of such persons, was akin to sending away *our* social problems, in ways that could cripple other countries, and in ways that might cause us much more harm than good in the long run. It defied reason that any American would want larger, more complex, and better-connected drug trafficking organizations, all made possible because of our own deportation policies and our own drug consumption habits. They were also naïve, those rules that had been premised on this idea that, once we removed someone, they were out of our lives forever.

Rules that recognized the lives of others, even in far-off places, were more likely to appear just and fair than rules about building walls, or rules designed to close ourselves off. Rules that promoted civic engagement, here and abroad, were far more just and just more practical. If, for example, rules about progressive taxation, decent working conditions, robust political participation, adequate forms of public assistance, basic equality among persons, and proportionality in crime and punishment – if these were good rules for us, then maybe all people around the world should enjoy these rules, too, wherever they were. Perhaps, as Americans, we should do even more to persuade people around the world to support the poorer people in their midst, to pay a decent wage always, to share political power with all the residents in a jurisdiction, and to acknowledge basic human rights and dignity under all circumstances. By thus engaging with the world, and by promoting democratic values, Americans might reduce the more horrifying and traumatic migrations that we've witnessed. We might thus support the further development of conditions that make migration seem unnecessary. If a good and decent life in one's place of birth was possible, then, really, there would be no desperate reason to leave.

Americans had done this kind of thing before: in the ashes of war, in Europe and in Asia, the United States did not punish the "losers" after 1945. Instead, the United States worked to promote liberal governments in Europe and in Asia, and the Americans spent billions of dollars to rebuild these former adversaries. As a result, people in Germany or in Japan could live decent lives, and so we did not see, even after 1965, Germans and Japanese migrants fleeing their own countries in disappointment or in fear. Stability and shared prosperity tended to dampen emigration. Perhaps, if we could learn from that experience – and in conjunction with other wealthy nations, including our friends in Germany and in Japan – we all might craft another Marshall Plan, to lift the rest of the world as we once lifted our enemies.

Americans did this once to fight communism, but perhaps we must do it again, to combat terrorism and other forms of dismay, and to address more directly those conditions that spawned virulent ideologies and hatred for the liberal democracies. Troubled and angry people were prone to attack civilians in the West, and they will no doubt continue to materialize and to reach our homes – just a few clicks away across our very small world – and to cause their mayhem without even crossing an international boundary. Instead of only planning to kill and to hunt them, perhaps we needed to offer a better way – another life. This will require engagement. Most of all, we ought to support rules that acknowledged, in a more profound way, that we had no choice but to share this world with others. Rules that allowed industries to pollute with no care were not good rules – they will never be good rules. Rules that required all persons and states to care for complex ecologies, so that everyone might do their part in protecting all of the persons, plants, and animals in them, were the only ones that will ever appear as just or fair in this world.

★ ★ ★ ★ ★

Progressive solutions might be difficult to embrace in a world that was changing so quickly, and, in such chaotic times, it might have been understandable that many people clung to the stable and the familiar. Perhaps it's human nature to want things the way they were. Some scholars have said that nostalgia arises from a lack of proper mourning, as we all tend to long for the very thing that we can't quite accept as gone. We see this in our daily lives: in Santa Barbara, middle-aged men will buy fast cars, hoping to recover their youth, even though all that speed and power will never grow back their hair or reduce their paunch. We look upon such men and feel sad, for they will not be young again, no matter how hard they wish for it. Perhaps communities and societies were the same way: in portions of the United States, as cities like New Orleans or Charlottesville removed their confederate monuments, so many people fought and screamed for those objects, as though hostile outsiders were wresting away a past and a heritage for which they still had a longing. They seemed to want those good old days, when Robert E. Lee stood in marble, when deindustrialization was not yet a reality, when they were the only citizens – perhaps, for them, those *were* the days when America was great.

These Americans seemed filled with a painful longing, for a past that they could not accept as past. The very phrase, "Make America Great Again," has a middle-aged, older-person quality to it (does it not?), as though buying a flashy new car, or taking up with a younger woman, or bringing coal back, or erecting a wall, could somehow magically return the nation's virility to what it once was. This nostalgia seemed so strong, so profound, even though, in that other time when America may have been great (for some), women couldn't vote, African Americans weren't legally people, Mexicans were wetbacks, and Asians couldn't come to America at all. Perhaps, for Americans who suffered from this kind of nostalgia, the Immigration Act of 1965 *was* a catastrophe, the beginning of the end, the start of a time when their collective sense of an American identity was thrown into a crisis from which it might never "recover."

As I watched the last presidential campaign, with that one candidate promising walls, bans, and America First, as though he alone could solve the nation's problems, and his crowds so large and raucous, I was reminded of another time, when other Americans were mourning for their lost world. In the late nineteenth century, in the Far West, a spiritual leader claimed that, during a solar eclipse in 1889, he had had a sacred vision, and that, if other Native Americans followed him and joined in his sacred Ghost Dance, miracles could happen. Wovoka insisted that his followers had to be righteous men and women – they could not lie or steal, and they had to work to support themselves – but when they came together, dancing for hours in a sacred, turning circle, they could restore through the ritual their identities and themselves, even as they mourned collectively all that they had lost. The Ghost Dance attracted thousands of adherents among the torn communities of Native Americans, especially on the large reservations from Oklahoma to Nevada and into the Dakotas. Many people embraced it as though it were a new religion, adding symbols and meaning to the ceremonies that drew hundreds of people.

Because so many Native Americans were bereft, they vested the powerful ritual with elements of nostalgia. Some said that the Ghost Dance could bring back the buffalo, the revered animal driven to extinction by White men. Parents sought out the Ghost Dance because they had heard that, through the ceremony, they could *see* and speak to their beloved dead, especially their children, as well as the many other loved ones that the Dakota Sioux and the Paiute lost so recently, also murdered by the White men. Perhaps, some said, the Ghost Dance could cause the White people to disappear from this earth. It began as a rumor: a few Native American men worked for the federal government as police officers within the reservations, and some of these men suggested that the Ghost Dancers were praying fervently and rapturously for all White men to be taken away by floods or consumed by fire. The Ghost Dancers were wishing for the White people to be cast away, they said, for only then could the land heal itself and be returned to a condition like before the White men ever came. Dakota Sioux warriors had fashioned Ghost shirts, which were rumored to make them impervious to bullets, so that no White man could kill them, while they could kill as many White men as they wished.

This was frightening talk – these claims unnerved especially the White agents assigned to guard the Sioux reservations established in the Dakota Territory.

The agents called for reinforcements; the United States Army brought several mounted guns. It wasn't as though the armed White men believed this mythology (or perhaps they did), but, having seen these people mourn their dead, and knowing that their loved ones were never coming back, they worried about the fervor of the Ghost Dancing, these hundreds of men, women, and children, with their drums and tribal music, perhaps all wishing the White men dead and gone, perhaps all of them hoping for a return to a time when the Native Americans could be whole again. These Native Americans danced for many days, Sioux, Paiute, Crow, and Caddo, and although they were once enemies, they seemed united now in their common loathing for the Americans who were pushing them from their lands, taking their children to boarding schools, forcing them to beg for rations, and talking constantly about their White Jesus, even as they were killing Native Americans with impunity.

Not all Native Americans embraced the Ghost Dance or the religious and spiritual ideas surrounding it. Some prominent chiefs said that the Ghost Dance was "worthless," and that the aspirations that others had attached to it were hopeless. The great buffalo herds were never coming back, the beloved dead were not coming back either – nor would the earth swallow or flood or burn the White men. The White men were not leaving. Even more were likely to come. Native Americans had to mourn now for what they had lost, for what was never coming back, but then they had to move on, even if that meant a life alongside the White men that they'd once hated – the White men who did, in fact, make impossible a way of life that had lasted for as long as any one of them could remember. Even these Native Americans joined the Ghost Dance on occasion, but not to wish ill upon the White men. Rather, they danced and turned with other Native Americans to mourn and to accept with them what had passed, the world that they had lost. They engaged the ceremony to feel "Indian" again, and to help them adjust, however bitterly, to the new reality, and to try sincerely to live in peace with the newcomers. Wovoka himself had worked as a laborer for a White man, and he had encouraged younger Native Americans to attend the White schools. He grew alarmed by the rumors spreading about the Ghost Dance in the Dakota Territory. And when he had heard how the United States Army had opened fire on a Sioux camp near Wounded Knee Creek in South Dakota, he was horrified. In the winter of 1890, to defend themselves against charges that they had committed an indiscriminate, indefensible massacre, Army officials reported that the Sioux victims had been hostile Ghost Dancers.[1]

★ ★ ★ ★ ★

We cannot undo or uninvent the two revolutions. We cannot uninvent televisions or computers, any more than we can undo international commerce or abolish shipping containers. We cannot, by building a wall, stop people from flying over it, nor can we wish away airplanes, interstate highways, railroads, and cars. Most of us cannot even put down our cell phones; nor should we believe that these devices will be the end of things, because other wonders and miracles will continue to perplex us and make us feel old. Altogether, these things were just parts of a new reality. Even if this White savior could wall away the very poor, which he could not, the highly skilled and the affluent will still arrive here

– even the poor will find ways to fly – and then their growing numbers and ethnoburbs and strange foods and religious practices will continue to challenge the members of this once White Christian nation. Devout members of that nation might become so despondent that they will attend political rallies, large and riotous, simply to be among thousands of others who wished as fervently as they did for another America, when things were great. They may have even acknowledged that the man at the head of their gatherings may have been less than Christian by his own admission, but God worked in mysterious ways. Together, they behaved as though they were the only people in the history of this most kinetic nation to have experienced a sudden, jarring sense of displacement.

Yet if the point of supporting their man was to turn things back, then they will have a hard time achieving their desires, if only because there are now millions of new Americans who are entrenched here, just as they are. Many of these foreigners have had and will have children here, and so, naturally, many of those children now already considered this land as *their* home, too. Why should we leave, they might ask, for we were the winners of spelling bees, and we can play the violin and do math, too, better than you? Why should we leave, those of us who, despite all odds, and with no legal status, finished degrees at the major research universities? Why should we leave, the people who've toiled and sacrificed here? Indeed, these newcomers – these immigrants and their children – often had that sense of having achieved and done things that then tied them to this place, much more strongly than just birth or chance. This may have been something that any Native American might have recognized among the many Whites who'd settled upon their lands, making it their own. That attitude suggested that they were not going away, at least not without a fight. We worry about what the last election may have unleashed in this violent and beautiful country, and we wonder what troubles may come when some Americans might attempt to drive others from their homes. In American history, these dangerous circumstances have never ended well.

★ ★ ★ ★ ★

And so, to avoid the terrible and to learn from history, we might agree with one another that there is a sorrow inherent to the two revolutions, and maybe we should all of us just acknowledge it, no matter when we came to this land, and whatever our circumstances. We live in a world that is interconnected, but that world also tends to separate us from the people we love, and no family or community or region or country is safe from sudden changes – such vast changes – that might render each of us strangers in those very places that should feel familiar. As much as we might wish for our families and our communities to remain somehow fixed, that is now less possible in a world as kinetic as ours. The changes are so intimate: the children that we love and that we raise will likely leave us and live far away in this world in which we live. We will see them and speak to them from time to time, but it's unlikely that they'll live as close or be as near as when we once had them close, in our own homes. In addition, when they fall in love and form families of their own, it's much more likely now that they'll meet and love people who will seem unfamiliar to us, people who do not share the same race or ethnicity or religion or culture, so that our very own descendants may look nothing like us, nor share our values. We should all empathize with one another, especially those of us for whom these changes cut to the heart of who they were, and made them want to mourn for a world that they'd lost, for there *is* a sorrow possible in all of these changes, and in this world, all of this is possible.[2]

We should mourn what we've lost in the midst of this unsettling modernity. Then perhaps, after some weeping, and after accepting that this is how things just are, we would be in a better position to embrace the world as it is, chaotic and so full of movement. After a proper mourning, we would no longer be captivated by imprudent men who promised things that were simply unrealistic. We might also be better able to welcome and to greet with humanity those strangers who come among us, whether we've wanted them or not. The persistent, constant arrival of strangers has, in fact, long been part of the new reality, especially after the Immigration Act of 1965. No amount of wishful thinking will change things back to the way they were, nor sweep away this new country composed now of so many different people.

Notes

1 The Two Revolutions

1 These topics appear again in this volume in chapter 6, but for a general, comparative look at the migration of the privileged and the highly skilled, see RICHARD FLORIDA, THE FLIGHT OF THE CREATIVE CLASS (2005).
2 These topics appear in this volume, in chapters 5 and 7, but for an accessible, general account of displaced people and refugee movements, see PATRICK KINGSLEY, THE NEW ODYSSEY (2017).
3 For Chris Christie's suggestion, see *Chris Christie Proposes Tracking Immigrants the Way FedEx Tracks Packages*, N.Y. TIMES (Aug. 29, 2015). The United States Department of Commerce and the United States Department of Homeland Security maintain websites that track the number of immigrants, international visitors, and other "non-immigrants" to the United States every year, through tabulations of the I-94 form. From about 2010 through 2016, around 68 million non-immigrants entered the United States every year, although in 2015, over 76 million entered with an I-94.
4 For a readable account of cell phones, their history, and what they might be doing to us, see HEATHER HORST and DANIEL MILLER, THE CELL PHONE (2006).
5 For useful discussions of immigrant families separated over time, see IMMIGRATION AND THE FAMILY (Alan Booth et al., eds., 2016), as well as LEISY ABREGO, SACRIFICING FAMILIES (2014) and JOANNE DREBY, EVERYDAY ILLEGAL (2015). For an interesting discussion of how immigration into, and migration from, rural communities have caused anxiety among White families in the United States, see ARLIE HOCHSCHILD, STRANGER IN THEIR OWN LAND (2016).
6 I'm inclined to think it's nostalgia, and I'd recommend SVETLANA BOYM, THE FUTURE OF NOSTALGIA (2002) to those who might also regard political nostalgia as a key way through which to understand the national elections in the United States and in Europe in 2016. Boym passed away in 2015, but her work can help us

understand, perhaps, that political appeal to "make America great again," a theme that appears in the Epilogue of this volume.

7 For a broad, general history of American imperialism, see RICHARD IMMERMAN, EMPIRE FOR LIBERTY (2012).

8 For an in-depth study of American and Korean relations after World War II, see GREGG BRAZINSKY, NATION BUILDING IN SOUTH KOREA (2009).

9 Many outstanding scholars in media and in communications studies have offered nuanced theories of the internet age, as well as our (in)ability to comprehend the data produced every day, day after day. To make sense of this field, I've benefitted from NICHOLAS CARR, THE SHALLOWS (2011), and NEIL POSTMAN, AMUSING OURSELVES TO DEATH (2005).

10 For instructive, readable accounts of the history of electronic communications, "hacking," and cyberwarfare, see FRED KAPLAN, DARK TERRITORY (2017), and MICHAEL HAYDEN, PLAYING ON THE EDGE (2017). Kaplan is a journalist, Hayden the former Director of the National Security Agency.

2 The Kinetic Nation

1 Several scholars have published excellent overviews of American immigration history. See, for example, ROGER DANIELS, COMING TO AMERICA (2002); PAUL SPICKARD, ALMOST ALL ALIENS (2007); ARISTIDE ZOLBERG, A NATION BY DESIGN (2008); and RONALD TAKAKI, A DIFFERENT MIRROR (2008). For excellent thematic overviews of American immigration law in the late nineteenth and early twentieth centuries, during that period when the federal government began to manage immigration directly, see: JOHN HIGHAM, STRANGERS IN THE LAND (2002); HIROSHI MOTOMURA, AMERICANS IN WAITING (2007); and MAE NGAI, IMPOSSIBLE SUBJECTS (2014).

2 Since the late 1980s, scholars of immigration and citizenship have focused on immigrants from Europe and their efforts to confront and to reinforce White racial identity as a prerequisite for American citizenship. The best examples of that scholarly work include: NOEL IGNATIEV, HOW THE IRISH BECAME WHITE (1995); MATTHEW FRYE JACOBSON, WHITENESS OF A DIFFERENT COLOR (1999); and DAVID ROEDIGER, WORKING TOWARD WHITENESS (2006). Relying on insights from social theory, particularly MICHAEL OMI and HOWARD WINANT, RACIAL FORMATION IN THE UNITED STATES (1986, 2014), most social scientists and historians now agree that courts and legislatures had to define and to redefine "White" as a racial concept over time. Certainly, for Europeans arriving in North America, "White" was a nonsensical identity. Like all racial categories, its meaning was fluid, it changed over time. When Congress used the term in early American public law, as it did in the Naturalization Act of 1790, which stipulated that only "free white persons" could naturalize into American citizenship, it did not itself define what "white" meant. Well into the twentieth century, the federal courts continued to debate its meaning. See, for example, IAN HANEY LOPEZ, WHITE BY LAW (1996, 2006).

3 For a general history of the first contacts between Europeans and Native Americans, see DAVID STANNARD, AMERICAN HOLOCAUST (1992); JAMES WILSON, THE EARTH SHALL WEEP (2000); and DANIEL RICHTER, FACING EAST FROM INDIAN COUNTRY (2001).

4 For histories and accounts of King Philip's War, see JILL LEPORE, THE NAME OF WAR (1999); SO DREADFULL A JUDGMENT (Richard Slotkin and James Folsom, eds., 1999); and DANIEL MANDELL, KING PHILIP'S WAR (2010).

5 For a study of European emigration to the North American colonies during this period, see BERNARD BAILYN, THE BARBAROUS YEARS (2013).
6 For a study of how Native Americans encountered Christianity and then reframed their own identities in response to the Europeans, both before and after King Philip's War, see KRISTINA BROSS, DRY BONES AND INDIAN SERMONS (2004).
7 For a general history of the Virginia colonies, see JAMES HORN, A LAND AS GOD MADE IT (2006), and BENJAMIN WOOLLEY, SAVAGE KINGDOM (2008).
8 For a history of Bacon's Rebellion and its aftermath, see JAMES RICE, TALES FROM A REVOLUTION (2013).
9 For histories of early Virginia and Maryland, including discussions of religious and racial tensions, see MAURA FARRELLY, PAPIST PATRIOTS (2012); ALAN TAYLOR, THE INTERNAL ENEMY (2014); and ROBERT CURRAN, PAPIST DEVILS (2014).
10 For histories of the Carolinas, see KIRSTEN FISCHER, SUSPECT RELATIONS (2001), and DANIEL TORTORA, CAROLINA IN CRISIS (2015).
11 See, for example: PETER WOOD, BLACK MAJORITY (1996); MARK SMITH, STONO (2005); and PETER HOFFER, CRY LIBERTY (2011).
12 For histories of colonial Florida, see JANE LANDERS, BLACK SOCIETY IN SPANISH FLORIDA (1999); PAUL HOFFMAN, FLORIDA'S FRONTIER (2002); ANDREW McMICHAEL, ATLANTIC LOYALTIES (2008); and DAVID NARRETT, ADVENTURISM AND EMPIRE (2015).
13 For histories of slave revolts and of internal migrations before the American Revolution, see JILL LEPORE, NEW YORK BURNING (2006), and TIMOTHY SHANNON and DAVID GELLMAN, AMERICAN ODYSSEYS (2013).
14 For histories of the French and Indian War and its impact on the American Revolution, see FRED ANDERSON, CRUCIBLE OF WAR (2001); WALTER BRONEMAN, THE FRENCH AND INDIAN WAR (2007); and ROBERT MIDDLEKAUFF, THE GLORIOUS CAUSE (2007).
15 In a provocative new history, Professor Gerald Horne has argued that the Americans pushed for independence to preserve and to protect slavery, during a time when the British were moving to abolish it. Horne's account provides a study of the rhetoric of slavery on both sides of the Atlantic in the years leading up to the Revolution. GERALD HORNE, THE COUNTER-REVOLUTION OF 1776 (2016). See also KATHERINE DuVAL, INDEPENDENCE LOST (2015), whose history of the revolutionary period also considered this era from the perspective of people who were not land-owning, White, or free.
16 For a general history of this period after the Revolution, see GORDON WOOD, EMPIRE OF LIBERTY (2011).
17 See, for example, SIMON SCHAMA, ROUGH CROSSINGS (2007), and MAYA JASANOFF, LIBERTY'S EXILES (2012).
18 For histories of slavery in the late eighteenth and early nineteenth centuries, see EDMUND MORGAN, AMERICAN SLAVERY, AMERICAN FREEDOM (2003); PETER KOLCHIN, AMERICAN SLAVERY, 1619-1877 (2003); and EDWARD BAPTIST, THE HALF HAS NEVER BEEN TOLD (2016).
19 For a history of Native Americans in the Great Lakes region, see RICHARD WHITE, THE MIDDLE GROUND (1991, 2010). For a history of how European encroachment was causing violence and conflict *among* Native Americans throughout the nineteenth century, see NED BLACKHAWK, VIOLENCE OVER THE LAND (2008).

20 For thorough discussions of how the states attempted to regulate internal migrations of people of color after the Revolution, see LEON LITWACK, NORTH OF SLAVERY (1965), and CHERYL LaROCHE, FREE BLACK COMMUNITIES AND THE UNDERGROUND RAILROAD (2013).
21 For a biography of Andrew Jackson and his broad influence on Indian removal and westward expansion, see JOHN MEACHAM, AMERICAN LION (2009).
22 For detailed histories of Texas during this period, see T. R. FEHRENBACH, LONE STAR (2000), and H. W. BRANDS, LONE STAR NATION (2005). For the history of slavery in Texas, both before and after the Mexican-American War, see RANDOLPH CAMPBELL, AN EMPIRE FOR SLAVERY (1991).
23 For general histories of Chinese Exclusion, see RONALD TAKAKI, STRANGERS FROM A DIFFERENT SHORE (1989, 1998); SUCHENG CHAN, ASIAN AMERICANS (1991); and ERIKA LEE, THE MAKING OF ASIAN AMERICA (2016). For a discussion of the racial politics in California in the second half of the nineteenth century, see TOMAS ALMAGUER, RACIAL FAULT LINES (1994, 2008).
24 For histories of fugitive slaves, see JOHN HOPE FRANKLIN and LOREN SCHWENINGER, RUNAWAY SLAVES (1999), and ERIC FONER, GATEWAY TO FREEDOM (2016).
25 For histories of Chinese migration during the exclusion period, see LUCY SALYER, LAWS HARSH AS TIGERS (1995); MADELINE HSU, DREAMING OF GOLD, DREAMING OF HOME (2000); and XIAOJIAN ZHAO, REMAKING CHINESE AMERICA (2002).
26 See ERIC FONER, THE FIERY TRIAL (2011).
27 For thorough histories of Reconstruction, see LEON LITWACK, BEEN IN THE STORM SO LONG (1980), and DOUGLAS BLACKMON, SLAVERY BY ANOTHER NAME (2009). For a contemporary account of the internal migrations of African Americans after Reconstruction, see ISABEL WILKERSON, THE WARMTH OF OTHER SUNS (2011).
28 See, generally, JOHN HIGHAM, SEND THESE TO ME (1984), and NELL IRVIN PAINTER, THE HISTORY OF WHITE PEOPLE (2011).
29 See, generally, ROEDIGER (2006) and JACOBSON (1999).
30 For an interesting history of the flag salute, public education, and new European immigrants, see RICHARD ELLIS, TO THE FLAG (2005).
31 For histories of anti-Asian racism in the first half of the twentieth century, see EIICHIRO AZUMA, BETWEEN TWO EMPIRES (2005); SHELLEY LEE, A NEW HISTORY OF ASIAN AMERICA (2013); LON KURASHIGE, TWO FACES OF EXCLUSION (2016); and SARAH WALLACE, NOT FIT TO STAY (2017). For a general history of American nativism in the late nineteenth and early twentieth centuries, see ROGER DANIELS, NOT LIKE US (1998). Shortridge's statement appeared in the SACRAMENTO UNION (Sept. 28, 1921), on 1.
32 For histories of Filipino exclusion, see CATHERINE CHOY, EMPIRE OF CARE (2003), and RICK BALDOZ, THE THIRD ASIATIC INVASION (2011).
33 For a history of refugees and state policies toward displaced persons in the twentieth century, see PETER GATRELL, THE MAKING OF THE MODERN REFUGEE (2015).
34 See, generally, GEORGE HERRING, FROM COLONY TO SUPERPOWER (2011) and IMMERMAN (2012).
35 For overviews of American foreign policy during the Cold War, see JOHN LEWIS GADDIS, THE COLD WAR (2006), and ODD WESTAD, THE COLD WAR (2017).

36 For histories that have tied the Cold War to the American Civil Rights Movement, see THOMAS BORSTELMANN, THE COLD WAR AND THE COLOR LINE (2003), and MARY DUDZIAK, COLD WAR CIVIL RIGHTS (2011).
37 These themes appear in JOHN LEWIS GADDIS, STRATEGIES OF CONTAINMENT (2005), and ODD WESTAD, THE GLOBAL COLD WAR (2007).
38 I've made this point in my last book: JOHN PARK, ILLEGAL MIGRATIONS AND THE HUCKLEBERRY FINN PROBLEM (2013).

3 The Immigration Act of 1965

1 In addition to BORSTELMANN (2003) and DUDZIAK (2011), both cited in the last chapter, I would recommend MARY GINSBERG, COMMUNIST POSTERS (2017), as this work contains stimulating visual examples of how the communists in China and in the Soviet Union imagined themselves, and the United States and its allies.
2 For a study of how American White supremacy provided disturbing templates for Nazis and other White supremacists around the world, see GEORGE FREDERICKSON, WHITE SUPREMACY (1982); ANTHONY MARX, MAKING RACE AND NATION (1998); and JAMES WHITMAN, HITLER'S AMERICAN MODEL (2017).
3 For histories of racial segregation and Jim Crow law, see C. VANN WOODWARD and WILLIAM McFEELY, THE STRANGE CAREER OF JIM CROW (2001); RICHARD KLUGER, SIMPLE JUSTICE (2004); and MICHAEL KLARMAN, FROM JIM CROW TO CIVIL RIGHTS (2006).
4 See DAVID GARROW, BEARING THE CROSS (2004), and TAYLOR BRANCH, AT CANAAN'S EDGE (2007).
5 For a biography of Senator Pat McCarran, including a discussion of his role in the Immigration Act of 1952, see JEROME EDWARDS, PAT McCARRAN (1982). McCarran's remarks appear in CONG. REC. (Mar. 2, 1953), on 1518.
6 For a "prehistory" of the Immigration Act of 1965, including Harry Truman's veto of the rule in 1952, see IMMIGRATION AND THE LEGACY OF HARRY S. TRUMAN (Roger Daniels, ed., 2010). For a discussion of the Immigration Act of 1965, see THE NEW AMERICANS (Mary Waters and Reed Ueda, eds., 2007), and THE IMMIGRATION AND NATIONALITY ACT OF 1965 (Gabriel Chin and Rose Cuison Villazor, eds., 2015).
7 See, generally, Edward Kennedy, *The Immigration Act of 1965*, 367 ANN. AMER. ACAD. POL. & SOC. SCI. 137 (1966). Kennedy's remarks appear in US SENATE, SUBCOMMITTEE ON IMMIGRATION AND NATURALIZATION (Feb. 10, 1965), on 8.
8 For a discussion of Johnson's strategy for immigration reform, see JOSEPH CALIFANO, THE TRIUMPH AND TRAGEDY OF LYNDON JOHNSON (2015).
9 Lyndon Johnson, *Remarks at the Signing of the Immigration Bill* (Oct. 3, 1965). The entire text of this speech can be found on-line, at the American Presidency Project based at University of California, Santa Barbara.
10 For an overview of the American military presence in Asia in the twentieth century, see MICHAEL HUNT and STEVEN LEVINE, ARC OF EMPIRE (2012). For a discussion of how racist attitudes toward Mexico and Latin America had shaped American foreign policy in that region, see LARS SCHOULTZ, BENEATH THE UNITED STATES (1998). We can see there how American policy-makers saw Mexican nationals primarily as racially inferior people and as cheap sources of labor.

11 DAVID REIMERS, STILL THE GOLDEN DOOR (1992), and Gabriel Chin, *The Civil Rights Revolution Comes to Immigration Law*, 75 N.C. L. REV. 273 (1996).
12 CHOY (2003). For an instructive, comparative discussion of other forms of labor throughout the American Empire, see MAKING THE EMPIRE WORK (Daniel Bender and Jana Lipman, eds., 2015).
13 For a general discussion of the Act, see Karen Weingarten, *The Inadvertent Alliance of Anthony Comstock and Margaret Sanger*, 22 FEM. FORM. 42 (2010).
14 See, generally, David Pivar, *The Military, Prostitution, and Colonial Peoples*, 17 J. SEX RES. 256 (1981).
15 For an overview of the United States military abroad, including detailed discussions about the regulation of gender relations and sexual contact between Americans and foreign women, see OVER THERE (Maria Hohn and Seungsook Moon, eds., 2010). For discussions about birth control in general within modern states, see ROBERT JUTTE, CONTRACEPTION (2008).
16 For a thorough discussion of the wars in Europe, and of Nazi "family" policies, see RICHARD EVANS, THE THIRD REICH IN POWER, 1933-1939 (2005). For a broad discussion of Japanese politics and domestic policies before and during World War II, see JAPANESE REFLECTIONS ON WORLD WAR II AND THE AMERICAN OCCUPATION (Edgar Porter and Ran Porter, eds., 2017). For accounts of sexual violence during the war, see J. LILLY, TAKEN BY FORCE (2007); MARIAM GEBHARDT, CRIMES UNSPOKEN (2017); YOSHIAKI YOSHIMI, COMFORT WOMEN (2002); and C. SARAH SOH, THE COMFORT WOMEN (2009).
17 See, generally, MARY ROBERTS, WHAT SOLDIERS DO (2014); MARIA HOHN, G.I.S AND FRAULEINS (2002); BARBARA FRIEDMAN, FROM THE BATTLE FRONT TO THE BRIDAL SUITE (2007); JENEL VIRDEN, GOODBYE, PICCADILLY (1996); and KATHARINE MOON, SEX AMONG ALLIES (1997).
18 For a discussion of how military service shaped domestic immigration law, including the War Brides Act, see Philip Wolgin and Irene Bloemraad, *"Our Gratitude Toward Our Soldiers,"* 41 J. INTERDISC. HIST. 27 (2010); and CATHERINE LEE, FICTIVE KINSHIP (2013).
19 JOHN DOWER, EMBRACING DEFEAT (2000), on 130. See also, John Lie, *The State as Pimp*, 38 SOC. QTLY 251 (1997).
20 MOON (1997) and SOH (2009) both address these issues to some extent. This remains a controversial, tense topic between Korea, China, and Japan. See also GEORGE HICKS, THE COMFORT WOMEN (1997); YUKI TANAKA, JAPAN'S COMFORT WOMEN (2001); and PEIPEI QIU, CHINESE COMFORT WOMEN (2014).
21 JI-YEON YUH, BEYOND THE SHADOW OF CAMPTOWN (2004). See also GRACE CHO, HAUNTING THE KOREAN DIASPORA (2008); Na Young Lee, *The Construction of Military Prostitution in South Korea during the U.S. Military Rule, 1945-1948*, 33 FEM. STUD. 453 (2007); and John Lie, *The Transformation of Sexual Work in 20th Century Korea*, 9 GEND. & SOC. 310 (1995).
22 See, generally, Sonya Rose, *The '"Sex Question" in Anglo-American Relations in the Second World War*, 20 INT. HIST. REV. 884 (1998); PAMELA WINFIELD, MELANCHOLY BABY (2000); and FRIEDMAN (2007).
23 YUH (2004) traces this migration pattern from South Korea to the United States in some detail.
24 For a general overview, see MARCIA ZUG, BUYING A BRIDE (2016).

25 See, for example: Roland Tolentino, *Bodies, Letters, Catalogs*, 48 SOC. TEXT 49 (1996); NICOLE CONSTABLE, ROMANCE ON A GLOBAL STAGE (2003); Christine So, *Asian Mail-Order Brides, the Threat of Global Capitalism, and the Rescue of the U.S. Nation-State*, 32 FEM. STUD. 395 (2006); and ERICKA JOHNSON, DREAMING OF A MAIL-ORDER HUSBAND (2007). In recent years, immigrant men have sought brides abroad as well; see, for example, HUNG CAM THAI, FOR BETTER OR FOR WORSE (2008).

26 Christina Snyder, *Andrew Jackson's Indian Son*, in THE NATIVE SOUTH (Tim Garrison and Greg O'Brien, eds., 2017).

27 PAUL CARLSON and TOM CRUM, MYTH, MEMORY, AND MASSACRE (2012).

28 For comprehensive accounts of the Indian Wars in the late nineteenth-century United States, see PETER COZZENS, THE EARTH IS WEEPING (2016); BRIAN DeLAY, WAR OF A THOUSAND DESERTS (2009); and PEKKA HAMALAINEN, THE COMANCHE EMPIRE (2009). For scholarly accounts of the Indian boarding schools, see DAVID ADAMS, EDUCATION FOR EXTINCTION (1995); BRENDA CHILD, BOARDING SCHOOL SEASONS (2000); and JOHN GRAM, EDUCATION AT THE EDGE OF EMPIRE (2016).

29 For histories of the Holts and of transnational adoptions from South Korea to the United States, see SOOJIN PATE, FROM ORPHAN TO ADOPTEE (2014); ELEANA KIM, ADOPTED TERRITORY (2010); and ARISSA OH, TO SAVE THE CHILDREN OF KOREA (2015). For histories of transracial, international adoption in the twentieth century, see CULTURES OF TRANSRACIAL ADOPTION (Toby Volkman, ed., 2005); CATHERINE CHOY, GLOBAL FAMILIES (2013); SARA DOROW, TRANSNATIONAL ADOPTION (2006); and LAURA BRIGGS, SOMEBODY'S CHILDREN (2012).

30 For studies of Korean adoptees in the United States, see JOHN PALMER, THE DANCE OF IDENTITIES (2010); KRISTI BRIAN, REFRAMING TRANSRACIAL ADOPTION (2012); and KIM PARK NELSON, INVISIBLE ASIANS (2016). For a discussion of contemporary South Korean policies, see KIM (2010).

31 See, for example, JANE TRENKA, FUGITIVE VISIONS (2009); KATY ROBINSON, A SINGLE SQUARE PICTURE (2002); and ELIZABETH KIM, TEN THOUSAND SORROWS (2000).

32 See, generally, ROBERT McKELVEY, THE DUST OF LIFE (1999); STEVEN DeBONIS, CHILDREN OF THE ENEMY (2013); and ALLISON VARZALLY, CHILDREN OF REUNION (2017).

33 See, generally, Kay Johnson, *Politics of International and Domestic Adoption in China*, 36 L. & SOC. REV. 379 (2002); Peter Selman, *Intercountry Adoption in the New Millennium*, 21 POP. RES. & POL'Y REV. 205 (2002); and Andrew Brown, *International Adoption Law*, 43 INT. LAWYER 1337 (2009).

34 Ethan Kaplan, *The Baby Trade*, 82 FOR. AFF. 115 (2003). See also Lynette Clementson, *Working on Overhaul, Russia Halts Adoption Applications*, N.Y. TIMES (Apr. 12, 2007); Ellen Barry and Andrew Roth, *Russians Rally Against Adoption Ban in a Revival of Anti-Kremlin Protests*, N.Y. TIMES (Jan. 13, 2003); and Andrew Roth, *Mother Asks Putin to Return Second Son After Death in Texas*, N.Y. TIMES (Feb. 21, 2013).

35 For excellent histories on the Bracero Program, see KITTY CALAVITA, INSIDE THE STATE (2010) and DEBORAH COHEN, BRACEROS (2013).

36 See RONALD MIZE and ALICIA SWORDS, CONSUMING MEXICAN LABOR (2010), and S. DEBORAH KANG, THE INS ON THE LINE (2017).

37 See, for example, DONALD WORSTER, THE DUST BOWL (2004).
38 For histories of the American economy that discuss these themes, see PAUL KENNEDY, ENGINEERS OF VICTORY (2013); PAUL KOISTINEN, ARSENAL OF WORLD WAR II (2004); and DAVID KENNEDY, THE AMERICAN PEOPLE IN WORLD WAR II (2003). On the shift in California agriculture, see MARK ARAX and RICK WARTZMAN, THE KING OF CALIFORNIA (2005).
39 On the changes to the Bracero Program in the 1940s, see COHEN (2013).
40 See KANG (2017).
41 Many scholars have drawn these connections. See, for example, Kelly Hernandez, *Mexican Immigration to the United States*, 23 OAH MAG. HIST. 25 (2009), and Rafael Alarcon, *U.S. Expansionism, Mexican Undocumented Migration, and American Obligations*, 9 PERSPECT. POL. 563 (2011). JOHN HART, EMPIRE AND REVOLUTION (2016), has considered how Mexican and American histories were too intertwined to be disentangled.
42 For historical overviews of Mexican American immigrants and Mexican immigration, see MANUEL GONZALES, MEXICANOS (2009); ZARAGOSA VARGAS, CRUCIBLE OF STRUGGLE (2010); and NEIL FOLEY, MEXICANS IN THE MAKING OF AMERICA (2014). For Mexican Americans within major regions and states, especially in the Southwest, see DAVID MONTEJANO, ANGLOS AND MEXICANS IN THE MAKING OF TEXAS, 1836–1986 (1987); GEORGE SANCHEZ, BECOMING MEXICAN AMERICAN (1995); LAURA GOMEZ, MANIFEST DESTINIES (2008); and ARNOLDO DE LEON, MEXICAN AMERICANS IN TEXAS (2009).
43 See, generally, MICHELLE KELLS, HECTOR P. GARCIA (2006); Carlos Blanton, *The Citizenship Sacrifice*, 40 WEST. HIST. QTLY. 299 (2009); and JACQUES LEVY, JACQUELINE LEVY, and FRED ROSS, CESAR CHAVEZ (2007).

4 The Multiracial State

1 For more thoughts on Mill with regard to imperialism, and the distances between advanced and less advanced nations, see Beate John, *Barbarian Thoughts*, 31 REV. INT. STUD. 599 (2005), and Robert Kurfirst, *John Stuart Mill's Asian Parable*, 34 CAN. J. POL. SCI. 601 (2001). In an earlier book, I addressed themes in classical liberal theory, nationalism, and pluralism: see JOHN PARK, ELUSIVE CITIZENSHIP (2004).
2 Violence is a dominant theme in American history, as noted, for example, in Professor Slotkin's renowned trilogy of historical essays. I've borrowed heavily from these volumes: RICHARD SLOTKIN, REGENERATION THROUGH VIOLENCE (1975, 2000); THE FATAL ENVIRONMENT (1985, 1994); and GUNFIGHTER NATION (1992).
3 See, generally, MARK TUSHNET, THE AMERICAN LAW OF SLAVERY, 1810–1860 (1981); SLAVERY AND THE LAW (Paul Finkelman, ed., 1998); and SUE PEABODY and KEILY GRINBERG, SLAVERY, FREEDOM, AND THE LAW IN THE ATLANTIC WORLD (2007). White owners routinely inflicted violence upon their slaves, not the other way around, and the law was almost always on the side of the owners. See, for example, ANDREW FEDE, HOMICIDE JUSTIFIED (2017).
4 For historical accounts of violence against early Asian immigrants, see JEAN PFAELZER, DRIVEN OUT (2008), and YONG CHEN, CHINESE SAN FRANCISCO, 1850–1943 (2002).

5 For historical accounts of Japanese American internment, see PETER IRONS, JUSTICE AT WAR (1993); ROGER DANIELS, PRISONERS WITHOUT TRIAL (2004); and GREG ROBINSON, A TRAGEDY OF DEMOCRACY (2010). For first-hand accounts, see MARY GRUENEWALD, LOOKING LIKE THE ENEMY (2005); LAWSON INADA, ONLY WHAT WE COULD CARRY (2000); and LAST WITNESSES (Erica Harth, ed., 2003).

6 On *Brown* and the aftermath of *Brown*, see JAMES PATTERSON, *BROWN* v. *BOARD OF EDUCATION* (2002); KLUGER (2004); CHARLES OGLETREE, ALL DELIBERATE SPEED (2005); and DERRICK BELL, SILENT COVENANTS (2005).

7 On the Watts riots, see GERALD HORNE, FIRE THIS TIME (1997), and ROBERT BAUMAN, RACE AND THE WAR ON POVERTY (2008). For a biography of George Wallace, see MARSHALL FRADY, WALLACE (1996).

8 Details of this case appear in Theresa Ford, *United States v. Hanigan*, 6 CRIM. JUST. J. 1 (1982), and *United States v. Hanigan*, 681 F.2d 1127 (9th Cir. 1982).

9 The case appears in detail in HELEN ZIA, ASIAN AMERICAN DREAMS (2001), and in *Racial Violence Against Asian Americans*, 106 HARV. L. REV. 1926 (1993). The two federal cases are *United States v. Ebens*, 800 F.2d 1422 (6th Cir. 1986) and *United States v. Ebens*, 654 F. Supp. 144 (E.D. Mich. 1987).

10 For an account of how civil rights lawyers pressed the federal government to prosecute race-based crimes in the early days of the Civil Rights Movement, see RAWN JAMES, ROOT AND BRANCH (2013). For a set of essays about David Duke and his political career, see DAVID DUKE AND THE POLITICS OF RACE IN THE SOUTH (John Kuzenski et al., eds., 2006). On Duke's involvement in the Hanigan case, see Ray Ybarra, *Thinking and Acting Beyond Borders*, 3 STAN. J.C.R. & C.L. 377 (2007).

11 William Stevens, *Klan Inflames Gulf Fishing Fight Between Whites and Vietnamese*, N.Y. TIMES (Apr. 25, 1981).

12 See, generally, Gregory Padgett, *Racially Motivated Violence and Intimidation*, 75 J. CRIM. L. & CRIMINOLOGY 103 (1984), and Mari Matsuda, *Public Response to Racist Speech*, 87 MICH. L. REV. 2320 (1989). The federal case appears as *Vietnamese Fishermen's Association v. Knights of the Ku Klux Klan*, 518 F. Supp. 993 (S.D. Tex. 1981).

13 For a defense of this position, one that extends the idea to cover crimes of violence against women, see Christopher Wellman, *A Defense of Stiffer Penalties for Hate Crimes*, 21 HYPATIA 62 (2006).

14 See, generally, TERRYLYNN PEARLMAN, SANCTIONING BIAS CRIME (2008), and PHYLLIS GERSTENFELD, HATE CRIMES (2013). Scholars have differed widely on these issues; see, for example, JAMES JACOBS and KIMBERLY POTTER, HATE CRIMES (2000), and JEREMY WALDRON, THE HARM IN HATE SPEECH (2014).

15 For a discussion of federal and state rules, as well as their enforcement against perpetrators of color, see JEANNINE BELL, POLICING HATRED (2004), and BARBARA PERRY, HATE CRIMES (2009).

16 For scholarly discussions of violence against Arab Americans, especially after September 11, see MICHAEL WELSH, SCAPEGOATS OF SEPTEMBER 11TH (2006), and ANNY BAKALIAN and MEDHI BOZORGMEHR, BACKLASH 9/11 (2009). For a scholarly discussion of "lone wolf" terrorist attacks, like the ones at Fort Hood in 2009 or in Orlando in 2016, see Risa Brooks, *Muslim "Homegrown" Terrorism in the United States*, 36 INT. SEC. 7 (2011).

17 These cases appear in: *The Cultural Defense in the Criminal Law*, 99 HARV. L. REV. 1293 (1986); Kay Levine, *Negotiating the Boundaries of Crime and Culture*, 28 L. & SOC. INQ. 39 (2003); ALISON DUNDES RENTELN, THE CULTURAL DEFENSE (2005); Melissa Demina, *Fictions of Intention in the "Cultural Defense,"* 110 AMER. ANTHRO. 432 (2008); and Sigurd D'Hondt, *The Cultural Defense as Courtroom Drama*, 35 L. & SOC. INQ. 67 (2010).

18 For this in the context of similar controversies, see Alison Dundes Renteln, *Corporal Punishment and the Cultural Defense*, 73 L. & CONT. PROB. 253 (2010).

19 This case appears in Sujatha Jesudasan, *Local and Global Undivided*, in BODY EVIDENCE (Shamita Das Dasgupta, ed., 2007).

20 See, generally, *Female Genital Mutilation Outlawed in the United States*, 313 BRIT. MED. J. 1103 (1996); Elizabeth Boyle, Fortunata Songora, and Gail Foss, *International Discourse and Local Politics*, 48 SOC. PROB. 524 (2001); and Elizabeth Boyle and Sharon Preves, *National Politics as International Process*, 34 L. & SOC. REV. 703 (2000). For a compelling account of an immigrant family struggling with a child's illness, through culture and difference, see ANNE FADIMAN, THE SPIRIT CATCHES YOU AND YOU FALL DOWN (1998, 2012).

21 For a summary of the political dimensions of the cultural defense, see SARAH SONG, JUSTICE, GENDER, AND THE POLITICS OF MULTICULTURALISM (2007). Patrick Buchanan, the former speechwriter for President Nixon, and himself a presidential candidate several times, has written several anti-immigrant books offering a "nationalist" perspective. See, for example, PATRICK BUCHANAN, STATE OF EMERGENCY (2007).

22 Some critics of the cultural defense have suggested that these strategies repackage the worst stereotypes of an older colonial discourse. See, for example, CAROLINE BRAUNMUHL, COLONIAL DISCOURSE AND GENDER IN U.S. CRIMINAL COURTS (2014). For an extended discussion of how multiculturalism has been challenged as a political ideal, see CHRISTIAN JOPPKE, IS MULTICULTURALISM DEAD? (2017). (The short answer is "no.")

23 See, generally, David Haldane, *Culture Clash or Animal Cruelty?* L.A. TIMES (Mar. 13, 1989); Mary Curtius, *Culture Clash Over Sale of Live Animals for Food*, L.A. TIMES (Aug. 12, 1996); Ming-Han Liu, *Reconsidering Animal Rights*, 6 DICK. J. ENV. L. POL. 279 (1997); Peter Kilborn, *In Rural Enclaves of U.S., Cockfights Are Flourishing*, N.Y. TIMES (June. 6, 2000); and Frank Wu, *The Best "Chink" Food*, 2 GASTRONOMICA 38 (2002).

24 On the Zoot Suit riots, see EDUARDO OBREGON PAGAN, MURDER AT THE SLEEPY LAGOON (2003).

25 For this political perspective on Chinese Exclusion, see LIPING ZHU, THE ROAD TO CHINESE EXCLUSION (2013).

26 For scholarly discussions of Los Angeles before the riots, see IVAN LIGHT and EDNA BONACICH, IMMIGRANT ENTREPRENEURS (1991); READING RODNEY KING / READING URBAN UPRISING (Robert Gooding-Williams, ed., 1993); MANUEL PASTOR, LATINOS AND THE LOS ANGELES UPRISING (1993); and NANCY ABELMANN and JOHN LIE, BLUE DREAMS (1997).

27 Professor William Julius Wilson has published classic studies of deindustrialization and race relations in the United States after 1970. They are: WILLIAM JULIUS WILSON, THE DECLINING SIGNIFICANCE OF RACE (1980, 2012); THE TRULY DISADVANTAGED (1987, 2012); and WHEN WORK DISAPPEARS (1997).

28 For discussions of American foreign policy in Central and South America, see, generally, WALTER LaFEBER, INEVITABLE REVOLUTIONS (1993); STEPHEN

KINZER, BLOOD OF BROTHERS (2007); GREG GRANDIN, EMPIRE'S WORKSHOP (2007); and STEPHEN RABE, THE KILLING ZONE (2015).
29 For scholarly accounts of Central Americans in Los Angeles and in the United States, see NORMA HAMILTON and NORMA CHINCHILLA, SEEKING COMMUNITY IN A GLOBAL CITY (2001), and U.S. CENTRAL AMERICANS (Karina Alvarado et al., eds., 2017).
30 For discussions of Korean Americans, particularly Korean American entrepreneurship, see LIGHT and BONACICH (1991); PYONG GAP MIN, CAUGHT IN THE MIDDLE (1996); KYEYOUNG PARK, THE KOREAN AMERICAN DREAM (1997); and JENNIFER LEE, CIVILITY IN THE CITY (2006).
31 See, generally, CLAIRE JEAN KIM, BITTER FRUIT (2003); PATRICK JOYCE, NO FIRE NEXT TIME (2003); and LEE (2006).
32 BRENDA STEVENSON, THE CONTESTED MURDER OF LATASHA HARLINS (2013).
33 STEVENSON (2013), on 236.
34 For a discussion of rap music and rap artists of this era, see BEN WESTHOFF, ORIGINAL GANGSTERS (2017). For Ms. Karlins, see *Joyce Karlins Fahey Named to Courthouse Corporation*, MET. NEWS ENTER. (Apr. 21, 2000), and Angel Jennings, *Black Teen's Killing Sent Ripples Across South L.A.*, L.A. TIMES (Mar. 19, 2016).
35 For scholarly accounts of the riots and their aftermath, see LOS ANGELES – STRUGGLES TOWARD MULTIETHNIC COMMUNITY (Edward Chang and Russell Leong, eds., 1994); DARNELL HUNT, SCREENING THE LOS ANGELES "RIOTS" (1996); MIN SONG, STRANGE FRUIT (2005); and READING RODNEY KING (1993).
36 For a discussion of state and national politics after the riots, see George Sanchez, *Face the Nation*, 31 INT. MIG. REV. 1009 (1997); Robert Chang and Keith Aoki, *Centering the Immigrant in the Inter/National Imagination*, 85 CALIF. L. REV. 1395 (1997); and Tamara Nopper, *The 1992 Los Angeles Riots and the Asian American Abandonment Narrative as Political Fiction*, 6 NEW. CENT. REV. 73 (2006).
37 For Donald Trump's positions on immigration and crime, see Vivian Yee, *For Grieving Parents, Trump is "Speaking for the Dead" on Immigration*, N.Y. TIMES (June 25, 2017), and *Trump's Speech to Congress*, N.Y. TIMES (Mar. 1, 2017). For scholarly discussions about immigration and crime based on empirical social science evidence, see IMMIGRATION AND CRIME (Ramiro Martinez and Abel Valenzuela, eds., 2006).
38 The full transcript of President Donald Trump's remarks, made during a press conference in the lobby of Trump Tower on August 15, 2017, appears in *Full Transcript and Video of Trump's News Conference in New York*, N.Y. TIMES (Aug. 15, 2017). The incidents that preceded his remarks occurred in Charlottesville during the weekend of August 12.

5 Common Wealth

1 Several political theorists have explored these themes, including: BONNIE HONIG, DEMOCRACY AND THE FOREIGNER (2003); SEYLA BENHABIB, THE RIGHTS OF OTHERS (2004); and DAVID MILLER, STRANGERS IN OUR MIDST (2016).
2 See, generally, THEDA SKOCPOL, PROTECTING SOLDIERS AND MOTHERS (1995).

3 MICHAEL KATZ, IN THE SHADOW OF THE POORHOUSE (1986), and WILLIAM TRATTNER, FROM POOR LAW TO WELFARE (1998).
4 *Edwards* v. *California*, 314 U.S. 160, on 173-4 (1941). The Court quoted from *Baldwin* v. *Seelig*, 294 U.S. 511 (1935), on 523.
5 See, generally, IRA KATZNELSON, FEAR ITSELF (2014); DAVID KENNEDY, FREEDOM FROM FEAR (2001); and MELVYN DUBOFSKY and JOSEPH McCARTIN, LABOR IN AMERICA (2017).
6 In discussing the "strains of commitment," the late Professor Rawls was speaking more generally about the *possible* demands of others within a constitutional democracy, after persons have considered one another in an "original position," behind "a veil of ignorance." If all of this sounds mysterious to people not familiar with Rawls' over-arching work, I would recommend Jeremy Waldron, *John Rawls and the Social Minimum*, 3 J. APP. PHIL. 21 (1986). For the entire work, see JOHN RAWLS, A THEORY OF JUSTICE (1971).
7 Many wealthy and influential people did not care for President Roosevelt or for his New Deal. See, generally, H. W. BRANDS, TRAITOR TO HIS CLASS (2009).
8 Perhaps the most popular statement of a libertarian position in popular politics is by DAVID BOAZ, THE LIBERTARIAN MIND (2015). For a statement about the differing conceptions of liberty, the best essays are still by ISAIAH BERLIN, FOUR ESSAYS ON LIBERTY (1969, 2002).
9 GERALD NEUMAN, STRANGERS TO THE CONSTITUTION (1996). For histories of African Americans during this period, see HARVARD SITKOFF, A NEW DEAL FOR BLACKS (2008), and JOE TROTTER, FROM A RAW DEAL TO A NEW DEAL (1996). For restrictions against immigrants during this period, see LEE (2016) and NGAI (2014).
10 GOTZ ALY, PETER CHROUST, and CHRISTIAN PROSS, CLEANSING THE FATHERLAND (1994), and JONATHAN HUENER and FRANCIS NICOSIA, MEDICINE AND MEDICAL ETHICS IN NAZI GERMANY (2004).
11 See, generally, EDWIN BLACK, WAR AGAINST THE WEAK (2012); ADAM COHEN, IMBECILES (2017); and THOMAS LEONARD, ILLIBERAL REFORMERS (2017). The case appears as *Buck* v. *Bell*, 274 U.S. 200 (1927).
12 See, generally, CHRISTOPHER BROWNING, ORDINARY MEN (1998); SAUL FRIEDLANDER, NAZI GERMANY AND THE JEWS, 1939–1945 (2008); and TIMOTHY SNYDER, BLOODLANDS (2012). For histories of the Nuremberg trials and the prosecution of Nazis, see MICHAEL MARRUS, THE NUREMBERG WAR CRIMES TRIAL, 1945–1946 (1997), as well as HANNAH ARENDT, EICHMANN IN JERUSALEM (1963).
13 On racial integration in the United States military, see WILLIAM TAYLOR, MILITARY SERVICE AND AMERICAN DEMOCRACY (2016); on Japanese American soldiers during World War II, see ROBERT ASAHINA, JUST AMERICANS (2006).
14 For histories of the postwar economic boom in the United States, see MARC LEVINSON, AN EXTRAORDINARY TIME (2016), and ROBERT GORDON, THE RISE AND FALL OF AMERICAN GROWTH (2016).
15 For histories of this period, see JUAN GARCIA, OPERATION WETBACK (1980), and KELLY HERNANDEZ, MIGRA! (2010).
16 See, for example, Blanton (2009).
17 For a discussion of the origins of the public charge provision, see Douglas Baynton, *Defectives in the Land*, 24 J. AMER. ETH. HIST. 31 (2005), and CHRISTINA

McPHERSON, AMERICANIZATION IN THE STATES (2010). For a discussion of the rule in 1952 and 1965, see Joyce Vialet, *Welfare Entitlement*, 20 IN DEFENSE OF THE ALIEN 1 (1997), and THE IMMIGRATION ACT OF 1965 (2015).

18 *City of San Diego v. Viloria*, 80 Cal. Rptr. 869 (1969). See also Liza Cristol-Deman and Richard Edwards, *Creating a Permanent Underclass of Immigrants Residing in the U.S.*, 9 STAN. L. & POL'Y REV. 141 (1998).

19 *Graham v. Richardson*, 403 U.S. 365, on 370 (1971). For the broader political context behind this case, see Gerald Rosberg, *Discrimination Against the "Non-Resident" Alien*, 44 U. PITT. L. REV. 399 (1983).

20 For a studied overview of these refugee movements, see GATRELL (2015). See also: VLADISLAV ZUBOK, A FAILED EMPIRE (2009); MARIFELI PEREZ-STABLE, THE CUBAN REVOLUTION (2011); YEN LE ESPIRITU, BODY COUNTS (2014); and MICHAEL AXWORTHY, REVOLUTIONARY IRAN (2013).

21 See, generally, Arnold Leibowitz, *The Refugee Act of 1980*, 467 ANN. AMER. ACAD. POL. & SOC. SCI. 163 (1983), and CARL BON TEMPO, AMERICANS AT THE GATE (2015). For a conceptual discussion of refugee laws in the late twentieth century, see ZYGMUNT BAUMAN, STRANGERS AT OUR DOOR (2016).

22 See, generally, HELENE HAYES, U.S. IMMIGRATION POLICY AND THE UNDOCUMENTED (2001).

23 I've relied on H. W. BRANDS, REAGAN (2016), to map the President's views on the Cold War as it appeared to him in Central America. See also WILLIAM LeoGRANDE, OUR OWN BACKYARD (2000).

24 MARIA GARCIA, SEEKING REFUGE (2016).

25 Barbara Yarnold, *Politicized Judicial and Congressional Asylum Policymaking, 1980–1987*, 17 JUST. SYST. J. 207 (1994), and KATHLEEN HAWK, RON VILLELLA, and ADOLFO VARONA, FLORIDA AND THE MARIEL BOAT LIFT OF 1980 (2014).

26 ANN CRITTENDEN, SANCTUARY (1988); SUSAN COUTIN, THE CULTURE OF PROTEST (1993); and HILARY CUNNINGHAM, GOD AND CAESAR AT THE RIO GRANDE (1995). For a discussion of how refugee policies became more restrictive during this period across several states, see REBECCA HAMLIN, LET ME BE A REFUGEE (2014).

27 Els de Graauw and Shannon Gleeson, *Immigrant Labor Rights Advocacy in San Francisco and Houston*, in THE CITY IS THE FACTORY (Miriam Greenberg and Penny Lewis, eds., 2017), and Cecilia Menjivar, *Immigrant Kinship Networks and the Impact of the Receiving Context*, 44 SOC. PROB. 104 (1997).

28 For a full account of the rule, see Wilbur Finch, *The Immigration Reform and Control Act*, 64 SOC. SCI. REV. 244 (1990).

29 See Katherine Donato, Jorge Durand, and Douglas Massey, *Stemming the Tide?* 29 DEMOGRAPHY 139 (1992), and SUSAN BAKER, THE CAUTIOUS WELCOME (1990).

30 The quotes are from Ronald Reagan, *Statement on Signing the Immigration Reform and Control Act of 1986* (Nov. 6, 1986). For more about Reagan and the Act of 1986, see Thomas Maddux, *Ronald Reagan and the Task Force on Immigration, 1981*, 74 PAC. HIST. REV. 195 (2005).

31 Many conservative critics were severe; see, for example, NICHOLAS LAHAM, RONALD REAGAN AND THE POLITICS OF IMMIGRATION REFORM (2000).

6 The Privileged Classes

1 JAMES GIMPEL and JAMES EDWARDS, THE CONGRESSIONAL POLITICS OF IMMIGRATION REFORM (1998).
2 For detailed discussions of these provisions, see Princeton Lyman, *New Developments in the Areas of Immigration and Asylum*, 14 IN DEFENSE OF THE ALIEN 105 (1991); Anna Law, *The Diversity Visa Lottery*, 21 J. AMER. ETHN. HIST. 3 (2002); Ines Miyares et al., *The Interrupted Circle*, 2 J. LATIN AMER. GEOGR. 74 (2003); Margot Canaday, *Who Is Homosexual?* 28 L. & SOC. INQ. 351 (2003); Margaret Stock, *Immigration and Naturalization Law*, 41 INT. LAWYER 555 (2007); and Marc Stein, *All the Immigrants Are Straight, All the Homosexuals Are Citizens, But Some of Us Are Queer Aliens*, 29 J. AMER. ETHN. HIST. 45 (2010).
3 For scholarly reviews of these debates, see Lucie Cheng and Philip Yang, *Global Interaction, Global Inequality, and Migration of the Highly Trained to the United States*, 32 INT. MIG. REV. 626 (1998); THE INTERNATIONAL MIGRATION OF THE HIGHLY SKILLED (Wayne Cornelius et al., eds., 2001); EDWARD PARK and JOHN PARK, PROBATIONARY AMERICANS (2005); and Michael Ewers, *Migrants, Markets and Multinationals*, 68 GEOJ. 119 (2007).
4 For an early, influential account of this process, see BARRY BLUESTONE and BENNETT HARRISON, THE DEINDUSTRIALIZATION OF AMERICA (1984). See also BEYOND THE RUINS (Jefferson Cowie and Joseph Heathcott, eds., 2003), and STEVEN HIGH and DAVID LEWIS, CORPORATE WASTELAND (2007).
5 For concise histories, see MARC LEVINSON, THE BOX (2008), and ALEXANDER KLOSE, THE CONTAINER PRINCIPLE (2015).
6 See PARK and PARK (2005).
7 See LEVINSON (2016).
8 See, generally, LEO CHING, BECOMING JAPANESE (2001); THE DYNAMICS OF HIGHER EDUCATION DEVELOPMENT IN EAST ASIA (Deane Neubauer et al., eds., 2013); and INTERNATIONALIZING HIGH EDUCATION IN KOREA (Yeon-Cheon Oh and Rennie Moon, eds., 2016). For scholarly discussions of Japanese economic development, see JAMES VESTAL, PLANNING FOR CHANGE (1994), and PENNY FRANCKS, JAPANESE ECONOMIC DEVELOPMENT (2015).
9 This point is taken from JOSEPH NYE, SOFT POWER (2005). Other nations, like China, were catching on: JOSHUA KURLANTZICK, CHARM OFFENSIVE (2008).
10 Some of these themes appear in HIGHER EDUCATION IN EAST ASIA (Gregory Poole and Ya-Chen Chen, eds., 2009).
11 For a history of Korea that discusses this period of political turmoil, see BRUCE CUMINGS, KOREA'S PLACE IN THE SUN (2005). For an overview of chain migration, see Fred Arnold, *Unanswered Questions about the Immigration Multiplier*, 23 INT. MIG. REV. 889 (1989). This article introduces several others concerning chain migration that were published in this same volume. See also BIN YU, CHAIN MIGRATION EXPLAINED (2007).
12 For histories of Taiwan and of the Philippines during this period, see DENNY ROY, TAIWAN (2002); DAFYDD FELL, GOVERNMENT AND POLITICS IN TAIWAN (2012); STANLEY KARNOW, IN OUR IMAGE (1990); and LUIS FRANCIA, HISTORY OF THE PHILIPPINES (2013).
13 For migration and return migration, see, generally, HUIYAO WANG and YUE BAO, REVERSE MIGRATION IN CONTEMPORARY CHINA (2015); and

JOON NAK CHOI and GI-WOOK SHIN, GLOBAL TALENT (2015). For conceptual discussions about the migration of highly skilled people across the world, see SASKIA SASSEN, THE GLOBAL CITY (2001); Aylet Shachar and Ran Hirschl, *Recruiting "Super Talent,"* 20 IND. J. GLOB. LEG. STUD. 71 (2013); and UGO ROSSI, CITIES IN GLOBAL CAPITALISM (2017). For a story about the President of China and his daughter, see Evan Osnos, *What Did China's First Daughter Find in America*, NEW YORKER (Apr. 6, 2015).

14 See, generally, EZRA FOGEL, DENG XIAOPING AND THE TRANSFORMATION OF CHINA (2013); YUEN YUEN ANG, HOW CHINA ESCAPED THE POVERTY TRAP (2016); and BRUCE DICKSON, THE DICTATOR'S DILEMMA (2016). For histories of China under Mao, see FRANCIS DIKÖTTER, MAO'S GREAT FAMINE (2011); DIKÖTTER, THE TRAGEDY OF LIBERATION (2013); and DIKÖTTER, THE CULTURAL REVOLUTION (2017).

15 See, generally, ZHOU JI, HIGHER EDUCATION IN CHINA (2006); Zuoyue Wang, *Science and State in Modern China*, 98 ISIS 558 (2007); Yu Xie et al., *China's Rise as a Major Contributor to Science and Technology*, 111 PROCEED. NAT. ACAD. SCI. U.S. 9437 (2014); and CHINA'S GLOBAL ENGAGEMENT (Jacques Delisle and Avery Goldstein, eds., 2017).

16 See, generally, Dingxin Zhao, *Foreign Study as a Safety Valve*, 31 HIGHER ED. 145 (1996); Heike Alberts, *Beyond the Headlines*, 68 GEOJ. 141 (2007); MEREDITH OYEN, THE DIPLOMACY OF MIGRATION (2015); and REED UEDA, CROSSCURRENTS (2016).

17 ROBYN MEREDITH, THE ELEPHANT AND THE DRAGON (2008); REFORMS AND ECONOMIC TRANSFORMATION IN INDIA (Jagdish Bhagwati and Arvind Panagariya, eds., 2012); and JAGDISH BAGWATI and ARVIND PANAGARIYA, WHY GROWTH MATTERS (2014)

18 See, generally, ROSS BASSETT, THE TECHNOLOGICAL INDIAN (2016).

19 Suranjan Das, *Higher Education in India and the Challenge of Globalization*, 35 SOC. SCI. 47 (2007), and LOKANATH MISHRA, HIGHER EDUCATION IN INDIA (2013). For an interesting discussion of how young people in India have coped with limited educational and economic opportunities, see CRAIG JEFFREY, TIMEPASS (2010).

20 See generally, Victor Johnson, *U.S. Openness to International Students*, 25 IN DEFENSE OF THE ALIEN 47 (2002); John Douglass, *Can We Save the College Dream?* 1 BOOM 25 (2011); Hao Wei, *An Empirical Study on the Determinants of International Student Mobility*, 66 HIGHER ED. 105 (2013); and Robin Shields, *Globalization and International Student Mobility*, 57 COMP. ED. REV. 609 (2013). For a history of the University of California, see JOHN DOUGLASS, THE CALIFORNIA IDEA AND AMERICAN HIGHER EDUCATION (2007).

21 For a discussion of these themes, see MADELINE HSU, THE GOOD IMMIGRANTS (2017).

22 See, generally, NAZLI KIBRIA, FAMILY TIGHTROPE (1995); SUCHENG CHAN, THE VIETNAMESE AMERICAN 1.5 GENERATION (2006); and KARIN SAN JUAN, LITTLE SAIGONS (2009). See also Susan Eckstein and Thanh-Nghi Nguyen, *The Making and Transnationalization of an Ethnic Niche*, 45 INT. MIG. REV. 639 (2011).

23 Dae Young Kim, *Stepping Stone to Intergenerational Mobility?* 40 INT. MIG. REV. 927 (2006); PYONG GAP MIN, ETHNIC SOLIDARITY FOR ECONOMIC SURVIVAL (2008); Tamara Nopper, *The Globalization of Korean Banking and Korean Immigrant Entrepreneurship in the United States*, 16 RACE, CLASS, &

GEND. 248 (2009); and ROBERT FAIRLIE and ALICIA ROBB, RACE AND ENTREPRENEURIAL SUCCESS (2010).

24 Nopper (2009), and Edward Park, *From an Ethnic Island to a Transnational Bubble*, 38 AMERASIA 43 (2014).

25 James Flanigan, *Coming to the West Coast Ready to Make a Deal*, N.Y. TIMES (Oct. 20, 2005); Roger Vincent, *California Market Purchase Completed*, L.A. TIMES (Apr. 30, 2005); and Soyoung Ho, *Bankers, Grocers, and Lots of Kims*, FORBES (Jan. 2, 2009).

26 JAMIE LEW, ASIAN AMERICANS IN CLASS (2003), and MUN WOO LEE, EARLY STUDY-ABROAD AND IDENTITIES (2015). See also Martrin Kaste, *Korean Families Chase Their Dreams in the U.S.*, NPR (July 11, 2012), and Teresa Watanabe, *Families Are Choosing This L.A. School*, L.A. TIMES (Oct. 25, 2015).

27 For nuanced, inter-related studies of younger Asian Americans in these circumstances, see VIVIAN LOUIE, COMPELLED TO EXCEL (2004), and LOUIE, KEEPING THE IMMIGRANT BARGAIN (2012), as well as LISA PARK, CONSUMING CITIZENSHIP (2005).

28 TIMOTHY FONG, THE FIRST SUBURBAN CHINATOWN (1994); JOHN HORTON, THE POLITICS OF DIVERSITY (1995); and LELAND SAITO, RACE AND POLITICS (1998).

29 See, generally, PARK and PARK (2005). For a comparative perspective, see WANTED AND WELCOME? (Triadafilos Triadafilopoulos, ed., 2013).

30 For a recent study of Asian American suburbanites, especially near information technology regions, see WILLOW LUNG-AMAM, TRESPASSERS? (2017). Also, see generally, THE MASSACHUSETTS MIRACLE (David Lampe, ed., 1988); WILLIAM ROHE, THE RESEARCH TRIANGLE (2011); and BARRY KATZ and JOHN MAEDA, MAKE IT NEW (2017).

31 For interesting scholarly discussions about open borders, see KEVIN JOHNSON, OPENING THE FLOODGATES (2009), and RYAN PEVNICK, IMMIGRATION AND THE CONSTRAINTS OF JUSTICE (2014).

32 REUEL ROGERS, AFRO-CARIBBEAN IMMIGRANTS AND THE POLITICS OF INCORPORATION (2006); IRA BERLIN, THE MAKING OF AFRICA AMERICA (2010); and CHRISTINA GREER, BLACK ETHNICS (2013). See also Alex Asieudu, *Some Perspectives on the Migration of Skilled Professionals from Ghana*, 53 AFRICAN STUD. REV. 61 (2010).

33 For the idea that skilled immigrants were more similar to "refugees" than not, see Ji-Yeon Yuh, *Moved by War*, 8 J. ASIAN AMER. STUD. 277 (2005).

7 Out of Status

1 I've made these arguments in some detail in PARK, ILLEGAL MIGRATIONS (2013).

2 For an overview of illegal immigration along these themes, see AVIVA CHOMSKY, HOW IMMIGRATION BECAME ILLEGAL (2014).

3 For an account of the federal cases arising from this crisis, see BRANDT GOLDSTEIN, STORMING THE COURT (2006). For the Haitian refugee crisis more generally, see HAITI AND THE HAITIAN DIASPORA IN THE WIDER CARIBBEAN (Phillipe Zacair, ed., 2010).

4 PATRICK KEEFE, THE SNAKEHEAD (2010).

5 LEVY et al. (2007).

6 The case appears as *De Canas* v. *Bica*, 424 U.S. 351 (1976). For a recent study about the implications of *De Canas*, see Stephen Lee, *Private Immigration Screening in the*

Workplace, 61 STAN. L. REV. 1103 (2009), and Mark Walsh, *Raising Arizona*, 96 ABA J. 20 (2010).

7 This case appears as *Plyler* v. *Doe*, 457 U.S. 202 (1982). Comments and reflections about the case appear in CARLOS SOLTERO, LATINOS AND AMERICAN LAW (2006).

8 Other scholars have dealt with the case in central ways. For example, see MICHAEL OLIVAS, NO UNDOCUMENTED CHILD LEFT BEHIND (2012), and HIROSHI MOTOMURA, IMMIGRATION OUTSIDE THE LAW (2014).

9 For more about these perspectives, see IRA KATZNELSON, WHEN AFFIRMATIVE ACTION WAS WHITE (2006), and NANCY DOWD, THE MAN QUESTION (2010), as both works deal with legal and structural aspects of privilege and discrimination in public law. See also Steven Farough, *Structural Aporia and White Masculinities*, 10 RACE, CLASS, & GEND. 38 (2003); Michael Messner, *The Privilege of Teaching About Privilege*, 54 SOC. PERSPECT. 3 (2011); and Su Boatright-Horowitz et al., *Teaching Anti-Racism*, 43 J. BLACK STUD. 893 (2012). For a broader philosophical discussion of privilege, see JONATHAN WOLFF and AVNER DE-SHALIT, DISADVANTAGE (2013).

10 For this perspective, see AYELET SHACHAR, THE BIRTHRIGHT LOTTERY (2009), and JOSEPH CARENS, THE ETHICS OF IMMIGRATION (2015). For a novel take on the right to be admitted, see BAS SCHOTEL, ON THE RIGHT OF EXCLUSION (2012).

11 See, generally, Amy Sorkin, *The Anchor Baby Question at the G.O.P.*, NEW YORKER (Sep. 15, 2015). For discussions about this issue, see Robin Jacobson, *Characterizing Consent*, 59 POL. RES. QTLY 645 (2006); Margaret Tebo, *Who's A Citizen?* 93 ABA J. 30 (2007); Mark Shawhan, *The Significance of Domicile in Lyman Trumbull's Conception of Citizenship*, 119 YALE L. J. 1351 (2010). For a novel take on this debate, see Elizabeth Cohen, *Reconsidering U.S. Immigration Reform*, 9 PERSPECT. POL. 575 (2011). The long-standing precedents for birthright citizenship would include *United States* v. *Wong Kim Ark*, 169 U.S. 649 (1898).

12 See, for example: Elliott Barkan, *Return of the Nativists?* 27 SOC. SCI. HIST. 229 (2003); John Ayers et al., *Is Immigration a Racial Issue?* 90 SOC. SCI. QTLY 593 (2009); Gil Epstein and Avi Weiss, *The Why, When, and How of Immigration Amnesties*, 24 J. POP. ECON. 285 (2011); and Jennifer Merolla et al., *"Illegal," "Undocumented," or "Unauthorized,"* 11 PERSPECT. POL. 789 (2013). Several popular accounts frame immigration issues more pungently, at least in national politics– see, for example, Ryan Lizza, *Getting to Maybe*, NEW YORKER (June 24, 2013).

13 For a scholarly discussion of these types of political appeals, see IAN HANEY LOPEZ, DOG WHISTLE POLITICS (2015).

14 For a discussion of these elections with respect to Pat Buchanan, see Owen Harries, *Pat's World*, 43 NAT. INT. 108 (1996), and Robert Rowland and John Jones, *Entelechial and Reformative Symbolic Trajectories in Contemporary Conservatism*, 4 RHET. PUB. AFF. 55 (2001). For interesting accounts of the Republican Party before and during these years, see LAURA KALMAN, RIGHT STAR RISING (2010), and PATRICK ALLITT, THE CONSERVATIVES (2010).

15 See, generally, RUTH GILMORE, GOLDEN GULAG (2007), and JONATHAN SIMON, GOVERNING THROUGH CRIME (2009), as both studies give thick accounts for this turn toward mass incarceration. For a broader discussion of mass incarceration within American race relations, see MICHELLE ALEXANDER, THE NEW JIM CROW (2012).

16 See, generally, Daniel Mitchell, *"Duke, Is There Perhaps Something You Forgot to Tell Me?"* 90 S. CA. QTLY 379 (2008).

17 See, generally, CHRISTOPHER NEWFIELD, UNMAKING THE PUBLIC UNIVERSITY (2011), and JAMES VIGIL, A RAINBOW OF GANGS (2002).
18 For recent studies about the economics of immigration and their relationship to immigration politics, see CYNTHIA BANSAK et al., THE ECONOMICS OF IMMIGRATION (2015); GEORGE BORJAS, WE WANTED WORKERS (2016); and TOM WONG, THE POLITICS OF IMMIGRATION (2017).
19 See, generally, ROBIN JACOBSON, THE NEW NATIVISM (2008), and ANDREW WROE, THE REPUBLICAN PARTY AND IMMIGRATION POLITICS (2008).
20 See, generally, Philip Martin, *Proposition 187 in California*, 29 INT. MIG. REV. 255 (1995); Kitty Calavita, *The New Politics of Immigration*, 43 SOC. PROB. 284 (1996); and Adrian Pantoja and Gary Segura, *Fear and Loathing in California*, 25 POL. BEHAV. 265 (2003). For a broader discussion of the criminal justice aspects of immigration politics, see GOVERNING IMMIGRATION THROUGH CRIME (Julie Dowling and Jonathan Inda, eds., 2013).
21 See, generally, Corinne Lain, *Outraged Over Immigration*, 82 VA. L. REV. 987 (1996).
22 For multiple perspectives about Proposition 187, see Otto Santa Ana, *"Like an Animal I Was Treated,"* 10 DISC. & SOC. 191 (1999); Michael Alvarez and Tara Butterfield, *The Resurgence of Nativism in California?* 81 SOC. SCI. QTLY 167 (2000); and Andrea Campbell et al., *"Racial Threat," Partisan Climate, and Direct Democracy*, 28 POL. BEHAV. 129 (2006).
23 For an aftermath of that election in California, see KENT ONO and JOHN SLOOP, SHIFTING BORDERS (2002), and WROE (2008).
24 See, generally, James Lai et al., *Asian Pacific American Campaigns, Elections, and Elected Officials*, 34 PS. POL. SCI. & POL. 611 (2001). See also, Claire Spiegel and Connie Kang, *The Fast, Rocky Rise of Jay Kim*, L.A. TIMES (Oct. 27, 1993).
25 See, generally, NIGEL HAMILTON, BILL CLINTON (2007).
26 JAMES GIMPEL, LEGISLATING THE REVOLUTION (1996).
27 All of these rules are discussed in GOVERNING IMMIGRATION THROUGH CRIME (2013). For further studies that discuss the impact of welfare reform on immigrants, see ALEJANDRA MARCHEVSKY and JEANNE THEOHARRIS, NOT WORKING (2006); LYNN FUJIWARA, MOTHERS WITHOUT CITIZENSHIP (2008); MICHAEL FIX, IMMIGRANTS AND WELFARE (2009); and LISA PARK, ENTITLED TO NOTHING (2011).
28 For more on "crimmigration," including a summary of the scholarly literature, see DORIS MARIE PROVINE and MONICA VARSANYI, POLICING IMMIGRANTS (2016); AMADA ARMENTA, PROTEST, SERVE, AND DEPORT (2017); and CESAR HERNANDEZ, CRIMMIGRATION LAW (2017). See also Michael Light et al., *Citizenship and Punishment*, 79 AMER. SOC. REV. 825 (2014), and Hannah Gurman, *A Collapsing Division*, 69 AMER. QTLY 371 (2017).
29 On that election, see HAMILTON (2007). For the weirdness of that election and that scandal, see JEFFREY TOOBIN, A VAST CONSPIRACY (2000).
30 For this era of mass deportation, see DANIEL KANSTROOM, DEPORTATION NATION (2010); KANSTROOM, AFTERMATH (2012); BILL ONG HING, DEPORTING OUR SOULS (2013); TANYA GOLASH-BOZA, DEPORTED (2015); and SUSAN COUTIN, EXILED HOME (2016).
31 See, generally, Maria Hwang and Rhacel Parrenas, *Not Every Family*, 78 INT. LAB. & WORK. CLASS HIST. 100 (2010); Kerry Abrams and Kent Piacenti, *Immigration's Family Values*, 100 VA. L. REV. 629 (2014); and IMMIGRATION

AND THE FAMILY (Alan Booth and Ann Crouter, eds., 2016). For a broader discussion of family reunification and its changing nature in the immigration law, see LEE (2013). For scholarly discussions of remittances, see HUNG CAM THAI, INSUFFICIENT FUNDS (2014), and SARAH LOPEZ, THE REMITTANCE LANDSCAPE (2015).

8 Local, State, and Federal

1 For an overview of that scholarly literature, see PRATHEEPAN GULASEKARAM and KARTHICK RAMAKRISHNAN, THE NEW IMMIGRATION FEDERALISM (2015).
2 For the rules in Kansas, see Gary Reich and Ayala Mendoza, *"Educating Kids" Versus "Coddling Criminals,"* 8 STATE POL. & POL'Y QTLY 177 (2008).
3 See MARGUERITE ARCHIE-HUDSON, PROPOSITION 187 (1994). See also IMMIGRANTS OUT! (Juan Perea, ed., 1996), and JANET LOPEZ, UNDOCUMENTED STUDENTS AND THE POLICIES OF WASTED POTENTIAL (2010).
4 The cases from California appear as: *Leticia A.* v. *Regents of the University of California*, No. 588982-4 (May 7, 1985); *Regents of the University of California* v. *Superior Court of Los Angeles*, 225 Cal. App. 3d 972 (1990); and *American Association for Women* v. *Board of Regents*, 38 Cal. Rtpr. 2d 15 (1995).
5 See, generally, PARK (2013).
6 See, generally, WALTER NICHOLLS, THE DREAMERS (2013), and EILEEN TRAUX, DREAMERS (2015).
7 NICHOLLS (2013).
8 See, generally, Georgina Rojas-Garcia, *Transitioning from School to Work as a Mexican 1.5er*, 648 ANN. AMER. ACAD. POL. & SOC. SCI. 87 (2013).
9 Leisy Abrego, *Legitimacy, Social Identity, and the Mobilization of Law*, 33 L. & SOC. INQ. 709 (2008); and Neidi Dominguez et al., *Constructing a Counternarrative*, 52 J. ADOLES. & AD. LIT. 439 (2009); and Evelyn Nakano Glenn, *Constructing Citizenship*, 76 AMER. SOC. REV. 1 (2011).
10 See, generally, NICHOLLS (2013).
11 See, generally, Una Newton and Brian Adams, *State Immigration Policies*, 39 PUBLIUS 408 (2009); Maria Carabelli, *Whose Children Are These?* 84 INT. SOC. SCI. REV. 115 (2009); and ALEJANDRO RINCON, UNDOCUMENTED IMMIGRANTS AND HIGHER EDUCATION (2010). The California Supreme Court case upholding AB 540 appeared as *Martinez* v. *Regents of the University of California*, 50 Cal. 4th 1277 (2010).
12 *California Extends In-State Tuition Benefits to Undocumented Aliens*, 115 HARV. L. REV. 1548 (2002); Alejandro and Nathan Alleman, *Status Convergence*, 57 J. COLL. STUD. DEV. 990 (2016); and Emily Greenman and Matthew Hall, *Legal Status and Educational Transitions for Mexican and Central American Immigrant Youth*, 91 SOC. FORCES 1475 (2013).
13 See, generally, Rhys Williams, *Immigration and National Identity in Obama's America*, 42 CANAD. REV. AMER. STUD. 322 (2012); Haley Swenson, *Anti-Immigration as Austerity Policy*, 27 FEM. FORM. 98 (2015); and Raymond Mohl, *The Politics of Expulsion*, 35 J. AMER. ETH. HIST. 42 (2016).
14 The federal case appears as *Hoffman Plastic Compounds* v. *National Labor Relations Board*, 535 U.S. 137 (2002). For commentary, see Orrin Baird, *Undocumented Workers and the NLRA*, 19 LAB. LAW. 153 (2003); Nhan Vu and Jeff Schwartz, *Workplace Rights and Illegal Immigration*, 29 BERK. J. EMPLY. & LAB. L. 1 (2008);

and Ming Chen, *Where You Stand Depends on Where You Sit*, 33 BERK. J. EMPLY. & LAB. L. 227.

15 See, generally, Rachel Shigekane, *Rehabilitation and Community Integration of Trafficking Survivors in the United States*, 29 HUM. RIGHTS. QTLY 112 (2007), and Richard Sullivan and Kimi Lee, *Organizing Immigrant Women in America's Sweatshops*, 33 SIGNS 527 (2008).

16 For some of the best work on immigrant workers and the conditions of work, across a range of industries and workplaces, see PETER KWONG, FORBIDDEN WORKERS (1999); ANGIE CHUNG, LEGACIES OF STRUGGLE (2007); JENNIFER CHUN, ORGANIZING AT THE MARGINS (2011); HELEN MARROW, NEW DESTINATIONS DREAMING (2011); LEISY ABREGO, SACRIFICING FAMILIES (2014); SHANNON GLEESON, PRECARIOUS CLAIMS (2016); SARAH HORTON, THEY LEAVE THEIR KIDNEYS IN THE FIELDS (2016); ANGELA STUESSE, SCRATCHING OUT A LIVING (2016); and JONATHAN ROSENBLUM, BEYOND $15 (2017).

17 JAMES LONGAZEL, UNDOCUMENTED FEARS (2016); Clifton Gruhn, *Filling Gaps Left by Congress or Violating Federal Rights*, 39 U. MIAMI INTER-AMER. L. REV. 529 (2008); and Karla McKanders, *Sustaining Tiered Personhood*, 26 HARV. J. RACIAL & ETHNIC JUST. 163 (2010).

18 See LONGAZEL (2016).

19 See Kai Bartolomeo, *Escondido's Undocumented Immigrant Rental Ban*, 17 S. CAL. REV. L. & SOC. JUST. 855 (2008), and Hayden O'Brien, *Municipal Over-reaching*, 14 TEX. HISP. J. L. & POL'Y 69 (2008).

20 See, generally, Ramon Gutierrez, *George W. Bush and Mexican Immigration Policy*, 113 REV. FRAN. D'ETUD. AMER. 70 (2007); WROE (2008); and John Skretny and Micah Gell-Redman, *Comprehensive Immigration Reform and the Dynamics of Statutory Entrenchment*, 120 YALE L.J. ONL. 325 (2011). For the legislative bills signed into law, see Anna Ni and Alfred Ho, *A Quiet Revolution of a Flashy Blip*, 68 PUB. ADMN. REV. 1063 (2008); *United States Secure Fence Act of 2006*, 45 INT. LEG. MAT. 1409 (2006); and Sara Ibrahim et al., *United States Border Control and the Secure Fence Act of 2006*, 59 ADMIN. L. REV. 569 (2007).

21 See generally, Jasmine Farrier, *The Patriot Act's Institutional Story*, 40 PS. POL. SCI. & POL. 93 (2007), and Mary Wong, *Electronic Surveillance and Privacy in the United States After September 11, 2001*, SINGAPORE J. LEG. STUD. 214 (2002).

22 Margaret Dorsey and Miguel Diaz-Barriga, *Senator Barack Obama and Immigration Reform*, 38 J. BLACK STUD. 90 (2007); Jennifer Chacon, *Overcriminalizing Immigration*, 102 J. CRIM. L. & CRIMIN. 613 (2012); and Adam Cox and Thomas Miles, *Policing Immigration*, 80 U. CHIC. L. REV. 87 (2013).

23 For a discussion of immigration in national politics in this era, see Rogers Smith, *From a Shining City on a Hill to a Great Metropolis on a Plain?* 77 SOC. RES. 21 (2010), and LOUIS DeSIPIO and RODOLFO DE LA GARZA, U.S. IMMIGRATION IN THE TWENTY-FIRST CENTURY (2015).

24 See, generally, Loren Collingwood et al., *Revisiting Latino Voting*, 67 POL. RES. QTLY 632 (2014), and Leonie Huddy et al., *Political Identity Convergence*, 2 RSF J. SOC. SCI. 205 (2016).

25 On Congressional politics after the 2014 elections, see Holly Fechner, *Managing Political Polarization in Congress*, 2014 UTAH L. REV. 757. For a study of the origins of the Tea Party, see THEDA SKOCPOL and VANESSA WILLIAMSON, THE TEA PARTY AND THE REMAKING OF REPUBLICAN CONSERVATISM (2012).

26 For similar discussions about immigration politics and immigration policy, see

Michael Light and Dimeji Togunde, *The Mexican Immigration Debate*, 34 INT. REV. MOD. SOC. 279 (2008); George Hawley, *Political Threat and Immigration*, 92 SOC. SCI. QTLY 404 (2011); and Gyung Ho Jeong, *Congressional Politics of U.S. Immigration Reforms*, 66 POL. RES. QTLY 600 (2013).

27 See, generally, JOHN MILLER, THE WOLF BY THE EARS (1977), and HENRY WIENCEK, MASTER OF THE MOUNTAIN (2013).

28 For Lincoln's thoughts about the resettlement of freed slaves, see PHILLIP MAGNESS and SEBASTIAN PAGE, COLONIZATION AFTER EMANCIPATION (2011).

29 For historical perspectives on this trend, see TORRIE HESTER, DEPORTATION (2017), and HIDETAKA HIROTA, EXPELLING THE POOR (2017).

30 See, generally, KENT WONG, DREAMS DEPORTED (2013); ALFONSO GONZALES, REFORM WITHOUT JUSTICE (2013); and CECILIA MENJIVAR et al., IMMIGRANT FAMILIES (2016). The quote comes from Paul Lewis, *A Wall Apart*, GUARD. (Mar. 29, 2016).

31 See, generally, Jordan Grossman, *Hidden in Plain Sight*, 8 HARV. L. & POL'Y REV. 195 (2014).

32 These state policies were discussed in: Joelle Hong, *Illinois Joins Three States in Granting Driving Privileges to Undocumented Immigrants*, 26 GEORG. IMMIGR. L. J. 713 (2012); Jagdish Bhagwati and Francisco Rivera-Batiz, *A Kinder, Gentler Immigration Policy*, 92 FOR. AFF. 9 (2013); and John Goodwin, *Legally Present, But Not Yet Legal*, 46 COLUM. HUMAN RIGHTS L. REV. 340 (2014).

33 See, generally, TRAUX (2015); Adam Cox and Christina Rodriguez, *The President and Immigration Law Redux*, 125 YALE L. J. 104 (2015); Bianca Figueroa-Santana, *Divided We Stand*, 115 COLUM. L. REV. 2219 (2015); and Austin Kocher, *The New Resistance*, 16 J. LAT. AMER. GEOGR. 165 (2017).

34 For the fate of DACA and DAPA, see Christine Bealer, *The Uncertain Future of Immigration Policy*, 29 GEORG. IMMIGR. L. J. 313 (2015); Mae Ngai and Daniel Kanstroom, *Executive Justice?* 62 DISSENT 35 (2015); Julie Rheinstrom, *Deferred Dreams Denied?* 31 GEORG. IMMIGR. L. J. 135 (2016); and Ming Chen, *Beyond Legality*, 66 SYR. L. REV. 87 (2016).

35 The case appears as *Texas v. United States*, 787 F.3d 733 (5th Cir. 2015).

36 For a discussion of these tensions, see Michael Gerhardt and Richard Painter, *Majority Rule and the Future of Judicial Selection*, 2017 WISC. L. REV. 263.

37 For the erosion of manners during the Obama years, see Robert Rowland, *Barack Obama and the Revitalization of Public Reason*, 14 RHET. & PUB. AFF. 693 (2011). For Joe Wilson's speech and its aftermath, see Kate Phillips, *Carter's Racism Charge Sparks War of Words*, N.Y. TIMES (Sep. 16, 2009).

38 Meghan McDowell and Nancy Wonders, *Keeping Migrants in Their Place*, 36 SOC. JUST. 54 (2009); Seth Stodder and Nicolle Rippeon, *State and Local Governments and Immigration Laws*, 41 URBAN L. 387 (2009); Nik Theodore, *Policing Borders*, 38 SOC. JUST. 123 (2011); and Terry Carter, *The Maricopa Courthouse War*, 96 ABA J. 42 (2010).

39 See, generally, LATINO POLITICS AND ARIZONA'S IMMIGRATION LAW SB 1070 (Lisa Mangana and Erik Lee, eds., 2013). The *Journal of American Ethnic History* published a special collection of essays (volume 35, 2016) about the rules in Arizona, Alabama, and other states. See, specifically, the essays by Raymond Mohl, Kevin Johnson, and Lisa Mangana.

40 For a preliminary view of Donald Trump, Jeff Sessions, and the travel ban, see Bradley Wendel, *Sally Yates, Ronald Dworkin, and the Best View of the Law*, 115 MICH. L. REV. ON. 78 (2017).

9 The Great Divides

1 For an amusing account, see ROBERT GUEST, BORDERLESS ECONOMICS (2013). Sea turtles and wild geese are common within Asian countries: see YASEMIN SOYSAL, TRANSNATIONAL TRAJECTORIES IN EAST ASIA (2016).
2 MARI YOSHIHARA, MUSICIANS FROM A DIFFERENT SHORE (2008), and GRACE WANG, SOUNDTRACKS OF ASIAN AMERICA (2015).
3 AMY CHUA, BATTLE HYMN OF THE TIGER MOTHER (2011). The Asian music mom appears in WANG (2015).
4 See, generally, Mehera Nori, *Asian/American/Alien*, 27 HASTINGS WOMEN'S L. J. 87 (2016).
5 Tyler Grant, *Made in America*, 22 VA. J. SOC. POL'Y & L. 159 (2015). See, also, *LA Targets "Birth Tourists,"* KOREA TIMES (Feb. 4, 2013). On policies like the visa waiver program, see Mahmut Yasar et al., *Bilateral Trade Impacts of Temporary Foreign Visitor Policy*, 148 REV. WORLD ECON. 501 (2012).
6 On the disinvestment in public higher education, see NEWFIELD (2011); CHRISTOPHER NEWFIELD, THE GREAT MISTAKE (2016); and MICHAEL FABRICANT and STEPHEN BRIER, AUSTERITY BLUES (2016).
7 See, for example: CECILIA MENJIVAR, FRAGMENTED TIES (2000); ABREGO (2014); and ROBERTO GONZALES, LIVES IN LIMBO (2015).
8 GONZALES (2015). On the strangeness of cancellation of removal, see Margot Mendelson, *Constructing America*, 119 YALE L. J. 1012 (2010).
9 These themes appear in DREBY (2015), and in FRANK BEAN et al., PARENTS WITHOUT PAPERS (2015).
10 See, generally, Michael Fix and Wendy Zimmerman, *All Under One Roof*, 35 INT. MIG. REV. 397 (2001); Mary Romero, *The Inclusion of Citizenship Status in Intersectionality*, 34 INT. J. SOC. FAM. 131 (2008); and Laura Enriquez, *Multigenerational Punishment*, 77 J. MARR. & FAM. 939 (2015).
11 For an overview of regions that cluster the highly skilled, see MANUEL CASTELLS, THE RISE OF NETWORK SOCIETY (1996); SASSEN (2001); THE HUMAN FACE OF GLOBAL MOBILITY (Michael Smith and Adrian Favell, eds., 2006); and RETHINKING INTERNATIONAL SKILLED MIGRATION (Micheline van Riemsdijk and Qingfang Wang, eds., 2016).
12 For how globalization has impacted low-wage workers across a range of industries, see, generally, RHACEL PARRENAS, SERVANTS OF GLOBALIZATION (2002, 2015); ANNA GUEVARRA, MARKETING DREAMS, MANUFACTURING HEROES (2009); RHACEL PARRENAS, ILLICIT FLIRTATIONS (2011); and LAAVANYA KATHIRAVELU, MIGRANT DUBAI (2016).
13 See, generally, NADIA KIM, IMPERIAL CITIZENS (2008), and CHUNG (2007).
14 SHARMILA RUDRAPPA, ETHNIC ROUTES TO BELONGING (2004). See also Sandhya Shukla, *Locations for South Asian Diasporas*, 30 ANN. REV. ANTHRO. 551 (2001), and VANITA REDDY, FASHIONING CULTURE (2016). For a story about Mr. Shah, see Rashmi Menon, *Marine Drive to Chicago Penthouse*, ECON. TIMES (Feb. 6, 2015).
15 See, generally, RACHAEL WOLDOFF, WHITE FLIGHT / BLACK FLIGHT (2011) and ROBERT SAMPSON, GREAT AMERICAN CITY (2013), for studies of contemporary residential segregation. For studies of class divisions among South Asians, see: RUDRAPPA (2004); Monami Maulik, *Our Movement Is For the Long Haul*, 4 RACE/ETHNICITY 455 (2011); and MONISHA DAS GUPTA, UNRULY IMMIGRANTS (2016). For a demographic profile of the

South Asian American population in and around Chicago, I relied on the SOUTH ASIAN AMERICAN POLICY RESEARCH INSTITUTE, SOUTH ASIAN AMERICANS IN ILLINOIS (2013), and IRVING CUTLER, CHICAGO (2006).
16 XIAOJIAN ZHAO, THE NEW CHINESE AMERICA (2010).
17 PATRICK KEEFE, THE SNAKEHEAD (2009). For additional background, see KO-LIN CHIN, SMUGGLED CHINESE (1999).
18 See also LINDA ZHAO, FINANCING ILLEGAL MIGRATION (2013).
19 ZHAO (2013).
20 Corey Kilgannon and Jeffrey Singer, *A Smuggler of Immigrants Dies in Prison, But Is Praised in Chinatown*, N.Y. TIMES (Apr. 27, 2014).
21 For scholarly work about Chinatowns, urban and suburban, see, generally, Min Zhou and John Logan, *In and Out of Chinatown*, 70 SOC. FORCES 387 (1991); Min Zhou and Mingang Yang, *Community Transformation and the Formation of Ethnic Capital*, 1 J. CHIN. OVERSEAS 260 (2005); Kenneth Guest, *All-You-Can-Eat Buffets and Chicken and Broccoli to Go*, 1 ANTHRO. NOW 21 (2009); and Jennifer Fang, *"To Cultivate Our Children to Be of East and West,"* 34 J. AMER. ETH. HIST. 54 (2015). For stories about John Liu, see Jennifer Lee, *Victories Across City Resonate in Chinatown*, N.Y. TIMES (Sept. 16, 2009), and Thomas Kaplan, *Liu Announces Bid to Unseat Queens State Senator*, N.Y. TIMES (May 24, 2014).
22 PETER KWONG, THE NEW CHINATOWN (1996); KWONG, FORBIDDEN WORKERS (1999); and PETER KWONG and DUSANKA MISCEVIC, CHINESE AMERICA (2005).
23 See, generally, ASIAN AMERICANS (Pyong Gap Min, ed., 2005), and Taeku Lee, *Koreans in America*, 13 ASIA POL'Y 39 (2012). For stories about Koreatowns in New Jersey, see Richard Perez-Pena, *As Koreans Pour In, a Town Is Remade*, N.Y. TIMES (Dec. 15, 2010), and Richard Morgan, *A Korean Spa Offers Saunas, Bibimbap, and a Taste of Home in New Jersey*, N.Y. TIMES (Jan. 2, 2017).
24 For articles about the South Asian community in the New York region, see Richard Perez-Pena, *New Jersey's Ethnic Makeup Shifts*, N.Y. TIMES (Feb. 4, 2011); Vivian Lee, *At Madison Square Garden, Chants, Cheers, and Roars for Modi*, N.Y. TIMES (Sep. 29, 2014); and Acantika Chilkoti, *With Trump Set to Meet Modi, Many U.S. Indians Are Hopeful*, N.Y. TIMES (June 26, 2017).
25 For studies of South Asian Americans, from a range of perspectives, see A PART, YET APART (Lavina Shankar and Rajini Srikanth, eds., 1998); RAJINI SRIKANTH, THE WORLD NEXT DOOR (2004); PAWAN DHINGRA, MANAGING MULTICULTURAL LIVES (2007); NITASHA SHARMA, HIP HOP DESIS (2010); PAWAN DHINGRA, LIFE BEHIND THE LOBBY (2012); ASIAN AMERICA (Pawan Dhingra and Robyn Rodriguez, eds., 2014); and TAMARA BHALLA, READING TOGETHER, READING APART (2016).
26 See Thomas Curwen, *How the Wilshire Grand Center Was Born*, L.A. TIMES (Aug. 10, 2014), and Christopher Hawthorne, *The Wilshire Grand Center*, L.A. TIMES (June 24, 2017).
27 For an overview of that transformation, see KAREN BRODKIN, MAKING DEMOCRACY MATTER (2007). For a pre-history of this moment, see LAURA PULIDO, BLACK, BROWN, YELLOW, AND LEFT (2006).
28 See generally, Daisy Ha, *An Analysis and Critique of KIWA's Reform Efforts in the Los Angeles Korean American Restaurant Industry*, 8 ASIAN L. J. 111 (2001).
29 For scholarly discussions of workers' centers, including KIWA, see: JANICE FINE, WORKER CENTERS (2006); WORKING FOR JUSTICE (Ruth Milkman et al., eds., 2010); and NEW LABOR IN NEW YORK (Ruth Milkman and Ed Ott, eds., 2014).

30 For more about this dispute and labor activism in Los Angeles, see Edward Park, *Labor Organizing Beyond Race and Nation*, 24 INT. J. SOC. & SOC. POL'Y 138 (2004); Victor Narro, *Impacting Next Wave Organizing*, 50 N.Y. L. SCH. L. REV. 465 (2005); Daniel Widener, *Another City Is Possible*, 1 RACE/ETHNICITY 189 (2008); and Angie Chung et al., *Reinventing an Authentic "Ethnic" Politics*, 13 ETHNICITIES 838 (2013).

31 Some of the other leading works in this field would include JENNIFER GORDON, SUBURBAN SWEATSHOPS (2007); GLEESON (2016); and VANESSA TAIT, POOR WORKERS' UNION (2016).

32 For a detailed discussion of this dispute, see Eli Naduris-Weissman, *The Workers Center Movement and Traditional Labor Law*, 30 BERKELEY J. EMP. & LAB. L. 232 (2009), and Narro (2005).

33 See, generally, Yungsuhn Park, *The Immigrant Workers Union*, 12 ASIAN AM. L. J. 67 (2005).

34 For reporting about this dispute, see Tiffany Hsu, *Urasawa, Home of $1,111 Sushi Bill, Faces Labor Violation Fines*, L.A. TIMES (Mar. 14, 2013), and Jennifer Medina, *At an Upscale Beverly Hills Restaurant, Claims of Underpaying Workers*, N.Y. TIMES (July 20, 2013). For scholarly articles about "wage theft," see Nicole Taykhman, *Defying Silence*, 32 COLUM. J. GENDER & L. 96 (2016); Elizabeth Fussell, *The Deportation Threat Dynamic and Victimization of Latino Migrants*, 52 SOC. QTLY 593 (2011); and Annette Bernhardt et al., *All Work and No Pay*, 91 SOC. FORCES 725 (2013).

35 For an overview of these debates and reforms, see ROBERT POLLIN et. al., A MEASURE OF FAIRNESS (2008), and RICHARD ANKER and MARTHA ANKER, LIVING WAGES AROUND THE WORLD (2017). For discussions of minimum wage ordinances in American cities, see Richard Schragger, *Mobile Capital, Local Economic Regulation, and the Democratic City*, 123 HARV. L. REV. 482 (2009); Candace Kovacic-Fleischer, *Food Stamps, Unjust Enrichment, and Minimum Wage*, 35 L. & INEQ. 1 (2017); and Clayton Gilette, *Local Redistribution, Living Wage Ordinances, and Judicial Intervention*, 101 NW. U. L. REV. 1057 (2017). A few scholars have proposed weaving egalitarian commitments into urban design and planning; see, for example, SUSAN FAINSTEIN, JUST CITIES (2011).

36 For a story about Senator Harris and her path to the Senate, see Matt Flegenheimer, *Senator (Un)Interrupted*, N.Y. TIMES (July 6, 2017).

37 For a discussion of this parallel, see Sam Kamin, *Prosecutorial Discretion in the Context of Immigration and Marijuana Law Reform*, 14 OHIO STATE J. CRIM. L. 183 (2016).

10 The Future of American Migrations

1 The phrase comes from AIWHA ONG, FLEXIBLE CITIZENSHIP (1999).

2 For studies of remittances, see MANUEL OROZCO, REMITTANCES AND DEVELOPMENT (2013); SARAH LOPEZ, THE REMITTANCE LANDSCAPE (2015); and THE WORLD BANK, MIGRATION AND REMITTANCES FACTBOOK 2016 (2016). For stories of migrants fenced in by immigration rules, see FORCED OUT AND FENCED IN (Tanya Golash-Boza, ed., 2017).

3 See, generally, Anming Zhang and Hongmin Chen, *Evolution of China's Air Transport Development and Policy Towards International Liberalization*, 42 TRANS. J. 31 (2003); Pengfei Ni, *Cities as the New Engines for Sino-Indian Cooperation*, 64 J. INT. AFF. 143 (2011); and Qiang Zhang et al., *Market Conduct of the Three Biggest Airports in China*,

47 J. TRANS. ECON. & POL'Y 335 (2013). For work about air travel in Mexico, see Juan Torres-Landa, *Opening to Private Investment of the Mexican Airport Network System*, 32 INT. LAW. 405 (1998), and HOLIDAY IN MEXICO (Dina Berger and Andrew Wood, eds., 2010).
4 See, generally, Malcolm Beith, *A Broken Mexico*, 22 SMALL WARS & INSURG. 787 (2011); Robert Bonner, *The Cartel Crackdown*, 91 FOR. AFF. 12 (2012); and NATHAN JONES, MEXICO'S ILLICIT DRUG NETWORKS AND THE STATE REACTION (2016).
5 For a single volume just about cocaine in the United States, see DOMINIC STREATFIELD, COCAINE (2003). For estimates of cocaine use in the United States, see Abiy Mohammed and Jim Anthony, *Social Rank and Cocaine Dependence*, 156 DRUG & ALC. DEPEND. 155 (2015), and CENTER FOR BEHAVIORAL HEALTH STATISTICS AND QUALITY, BEHAVIORAL HEALTH TRENDS IN THE UNITED STATES (2015).
6 See, generally, Tomas Kellner and Francesco Pipitone, *Inside Mexico's Drug War*, 27 WORLD POL'Y J. 29 (2010); Melissa Wright, *Necropolitics, Narcopolitics, and Femicide*, 36 SIGNS 707 (2011); Paul Gootenberg, *Cocaine's Long March North, 1900–2010*, 54 LAT. AMER. POL. & SOC. 159 (2012); and Nathaniel Flannery, *Calderon's War*, 66 J. INT. AFF. 181 (2013).
7 T. W. WARD, GANGSTERS WITHOUT BORDERS (2012).
8 MARAS (Thomas Bruneau et al., eds., 2011). See also, ELLEN MOODIE, EL SALVADOR IN THE AFTERMATH OF PEACE (2012).
9 For a study of persistent family migrations in the context of immigration rules, see DEBORAH BOEHM, INTIMATE MIGRATIONS (2012).
10 Diana Negroponte, *The Surge in Unaccompanied Children from Central America*, BROOKINGS (July 2, 2014); Muzaffar Chishti and Faye Hipsman, *Increased Central American Migration to the United States May Prove an Enduring Phenomenon*, MIG. POL'Y INST. (Feb. 18, 2016); and Katherine Donato and Samantha Perez, *Crossing the U.S.–Mexico Border*, 3 RSF: J. SOC. SCI. 116 (2017).
11 Julia Preston, *U.S. Continues to Deport Central American Migrants*, N.Y. TIMES (Mar. 9, 2016).
12 See, generally, Matt Ford, *Trump's Travel Ban Returns*, ATLANTIC (June 29, 2017).
13 For accounts of the wars in Iraq and Afghanistan, see STEPHEN COLL, GHOST WARS (2004); DEXTER FIGGINS, THE FOREVER WAR (2009); and DANIEL BOLGER, WHY WE LOST (2014).
14 VICTOR CHA, THE IMPOSSIBLE STATE (2013); ANDREI LANKOV, THE REAL NORTH KOREA (2014); and NORTH KOREA AND NUCLEAR WEAPONS (Sung Chul Kim and Michael Cohen, eds., 2017).
15 See, generally, NAOMI KLEIN, THIS CHANGES EVERYTHING (2015); ELIZABETH KOLBERT, THE SIXTH EXTINCTION (2015); and JEREMY DAVIES, THE BIRTH OF THE ANTHROPOCENE (2016).
16 FOUAD HERBERT and JANE DWIGHT, THE SYRIAN REBELLION (2012); CARSTEN WIELAND et al., THE SYRIAN UPRISING (2013); SAMER ABBOUD, SYRIA (2016); and MARK THOMAS, THE RELIGIOUS ROOTS OF THE SYRIAN CONFLICT (2016).
17 See ABBOUD (2016). For a survey of changes in climate in the Middle East, see ECONOMICS OF CLIMATE CHANGE IN THE ARAB WORLD (Dorte Verner et al., eds., 2013).
18 See, generally, JOBY WARRICK, BLACK FLAGS (2016); JESSICA STERN, ISIS (2016); and LAWRENCE WRIGHT, THE TERROR YEARS (2016).

19 See, for example, DAVEED GARTENSTEIN-ROSS and LAURA GROSSMAN, HOMEGROWN TERRORISTS IN THE U.S. AND THE U.K. (2009).
20 See, generally, Francesca De Chatel, *The Role of Drought and Climate Change in the Syrian Uprising*, 50 MID. EAST. STUD. 521 (2014); Caitlin Werrell et al., *Did We See It Coming?* 35 SAIS REV. INT. AFF. 29 (2015), and Colin Kelley et al., *Climate Change in the Fertile Crescent and Implications of the Recent Syrian Drought*, 112 PROCEED. NAT. ACAD. SCI. U.S.A. 3241 (2015).

Epilogue

1 For history and background about the Ghost Dance, I've relied on LOUIS WARREN, GOD'S RED SON (2017). For studies of more contemporary forms of nostalgia, longing, and politics beyond the hard social sciences, I would recommend BOYM (2002); SARA AHMED, THE CULTURAL POLITICS OF EMOTION (2004); and PAULA IOANIDE, THE EMOTIONAL POLITICS OF RACE (2015).
2 For studies that point away from hard international borders, and toward domicile, residency, and belonging, I would recommend JOSEPH CARENS, IMMIGRANTS AND THE RIGHT TO STAY (2010); BRIDGET ANDERSON, US AND THEM? (2015); and CATHERINE DAUVERGNE, THE NEW POLITICS OF IMMIGRATION AND THE END OF SETTLER SOCIETIES (2016).

INDEX

adoption, 39–42, 47–8
African and Afro-Caribbean immigrants, 8, 104
African Americans, 8, 12–20, 23, 25–6, 50–2, 61, 64–7, 73, 107, 137–8, 144
American Constitution, 11, 17–19, 25, 29, 54, 71, 78, 111–14, 126–7, 138, 140–1
Anti-Terrorism Act (AEDPA), 122
Arab Americans, 57
Aristide, Jean Bertrand, 87, 109
Arizona v. *United States* (2012), 142–3
Arpaio, Joe, 142
Assad, Bashar, 174–5

Bentley, Robert, 131, 143
birthright citizenship, 113–14, 147–8
birth tourism, 147–8
Black Codes, Slave Codes, 14, 25
Bracero Program, 42–6, 75–6, 80, 88, 106, 108–10
Brennan, William, 110–12
Brewer, Jan, 142–3
Breyer, Stephen, 132
Brown, Kathleen, 118–19
Brown v. *Board of Education* (1952), 25, 29, 51
Buchanan, Patrick, 114–15
Bush, George H. W., 66, 86–7, 89, 109, 114–15, 117, 120, 154

Bush, George W., ix, 6, 102, 130, 135–7, 142, 169

California Dream Act, 128–9
cancellation of removal, 150–1
Carter, Jimmy, 79–81, 87
Castro, Fidel, 23–4, 62, 81
Central American civil wars, 62–3, 80–1
Central American immigrants and refugees, 62–3, 79–82, 84, 87
chain migration, 37–8, 92–4
Chavez, Cesar, 46, 76–7, 110, 117
Chinese Americans, Chinese immigrants, 98, 101–2, 107, 109–10, 121, 154–7
Chinese emigration, 94–5, 109–10, 146–8, 167–8
Chinese Exclusion, 19–21, 50, 73, 77, 97, 107
City of San Diego v. *Viloria* (1967), 77–8
Civil Rights Movement, 25, 29, 48, 52, 54, 105, 153
Civil War, 20, 26, 39, 70, 72–3, 106–7, 138
climate change, 8, 172–7
Clinton, Bill, 102, 115, 120–3, 128
Clinton, Hillary, 144, 171
Cuban Revolution, 23–4, 79, 109
cultural defense, 57–60

Davis, Gray, 127–9
De Canas v. *Bica* (1976), 110

Deferred Action for Childhood Arrivals, Deferred Action for Parents of Americans (DACA, DAPA), 140–1, 143, 171
deindustrialization, 62, 88–9, 103, 116
Deng Xiaoping, 41–2, 95
Dream Act bill (US Congress, 2001), 128–30, 140
Dreamers, 129–31, 150–2
drug cartels, 168–9
Durbin, Richard, 128, 130, 140

Edwards v. *California* (1941), 71
Eisenhower, Dwight, 26
El Monte slave case, 132, 162
employer sanctions, 83, 111, 116
Ethnoburbs, 101–4, 154–6
European immigration, 20–1

failed states, 172–3
family reunification, 37, 41, 45–7, 87–8, 92–3, 98–9, 108, 121–4
Firebaugh, Marco, 128–9
Ford, Gerald, 41
Fugitive Slave Act of 1850, 19–20, 26, 106–7

Gentleman's Agreement, 21
Ghost Dance, 181–2
Golden Venture, 154–6
Great Depression, 22–3, 26, 34, 43, 71, 90
Guantanamo Bay, 109, 121

H-1B visas, 88–9, 102–3, 156
H-2 visas, 108–9
haigui, "sea turtles," 146–7
Haiti, Haitian immigrants, 24, 87, 109, 121
Hanigan case, Arizona, 52–3, 55
Hatch, Orrin, 128, 130, 140
hate crimes, 52–7
Hoffman Plastic Compounds v. *NLRB* (2002), 131–2
Holt International, 40–1
homosexuality, as ground for exclusion, 87

Immigrant Responsibility Act (IIRIRA), 121–2, 127–8
Immigration Act of 1952, 29–31, 45, 103, 108
Immigration Act of 1965, vi–x, 11, 28–31, 37, 46–8, 51, 77–8, 93, 98, 103–4, 108–9, 115, 146, 181

Immigration Act of 1990, 86–90, 99–100, 102–3, 114, 153
immigration federalism, 11, 125, 163–4
Immigration Reform and Control Act of 1986, 82–4, 110–11
Indian emigration, Indian immigrants, 59, 95–7, 103–4, 153, 157–8, 173
Indian Institutes of Technology (IIT), 96–97
interracial violence, 14–16, 50–1, 61–2
Iranian immigrants, 79–80
Islamic State (ISIS), 175–6

Jackson, Andrew, 17–18, 39, 51
Japan, Japanese immigrants, 21–2, 23, 38, 90–1
Japanese American internment, 51, 75, 98
Jefferson, Thomas, 17, 137–8
Johnson, Lyndon, vii, 25, 29–30, 51, 78, 84, 98, 108–10

Kennedy, Edward, 30, 79, 83, 87–9
Kennedy, John, 30
Khrushchev, Nikita, 23–4
Kim, Jay, 67, 120–3
King, Rodney, 64, 66–7
Korea, North, 7, 30, 92, 172–3
Korea, South, Korean immigrants, 6–7, 23, 31, 36, 40–1, 47, 58–9, 63–4, 90–2, 99–101, 120, 153, 157–61
Korean Immigrant Workers Advocates, 158–61
Ku Klux Klan, 55–6, 101

Latasha Harlins case, 64–6
Lee, David, 100
Lincoln, Abraham, 20, 138
Los Angeles riots, 1992, 66–7, 115, 117–18
Loving v. *Virginia* (1967), 25, 48

mail-order brides, 37–8
Mao Tse-tung, 94–5
Mara Salvatrucha, 169–70
Mexico, Mexican immigrants, 2, 5, 9, 19, 30–1, 42–7, 51–4, 60–3, 67, 75–7, 84, 106–10, 123–4, 134, 139, 167–9, 170–1
Mill, John Stuart, 49
minimum wage ordinances, 162–3
model minority myth, 98–102
Monterey Park, 64, 101–3

national origins system, 21–2
Native Americans, 12–20, 26, 39, 50–1, 181–3
Naturalization Act of 1790, 17, 25
Nazis, Nazi Germany, 22, 28, 34, 73–4, 80
North American Free Trade Agreement (NAFTA), 115, 121

Obama, Barack, ix, 104, 113, 123, 125, 130, 136–44, 171
Operation Wetback, 45–6, 76–7, 83, 108

Park Chung-hee, 93–4
Patriot Act (2001), 136, 139
People's Republic of China, 23, 31, 41–2, 87, 94–7, 104, 154–6, 168
Philippines, immigrants from the Philippines, 22–4, 30–3, 38, 86, 90–4, 124
Plyler v. *Doe* (1982), 111–14, 119, 126–30, 140, 142, 147
Proposition 187 (California, 1994), 118–23, 127–9
public charge provision, 73, 77–8

Rao, Narasimha, 96
Rawls, John, 72
Reagan, Ronald, 63, 80–5, 87, 110, 114–17, 137, 165, 169
Refugee Act of 1980, 79–81, 98, 101
Rehnquist, William, 131–2
remittances, 123–4, 167
removal, deportation, 11, 13–15, 17–18, 26, 87, 122–3, 139, 150–1, 168–70
rental ordinances against "illegal aliens," 133–5
retaliatory reporting, 160–1
Roosevelt, Franklin, 44, 71–3
Russia, Soviet Union, 7, 23, 28, 38, 41–2, 62, 79, 81, 98, 116, 173

sanctuary movement, 81–4, 109, 118, 139–40
Secure Communities (2008), 135–6, 139–40, 142
Sessions, Jeff, 143–4
Simpson, Alan, 80, 82–3, 88
Sister Ping, Cheng Chiu Ping, 154–6

slavery, law of slavery, 13–14, 17–20, 25, 50–1, 59, 65, 126, 137–8
Su, Julie, 162
Syria, Syrian Civil War, 174–6

Taiwan, Republic of China, 23, 31, 47, 89–94, 97, 145, 156
taxation, as "coercive redistribution," 72–3
Tea Party, 136–7, 140–1
temporary protected status, TPS, 86–7
terrorism, 57, 122, 135, 143–4, 172, 175–6, 180
Texas proviso, 45, 108–10
Truman, Harry, 29, 75
Trump, Donald, 38, 67–8, 112–13, 125, 137, 143–4, 151, 166, 171–2
Trump, Melania, 38
Tydings–McDuffie Act of 1934, 22

unaccompanied minors, as immigrants, 170–1
United Farm Workers, 46, 110–11, 133
United States v. *Texas* (2016), 140–1
University of California, vi, 4–5, 92, 97, 101, 117, 127–8, 148–9

Vietnamese fishermen case, Texas, 55–6
Vietnamese immigrants, refugees, 79, 98–9
Vietnam War, 23–4, 32, 41, 55, 94
Vincent Chin case, Michigan, 53–4, 91
visa waiver program, 148

wage theft, 159–62
Wallace, George, 52, 115
war brides, military brides, 24, 34–7
War Brides Act, 35, 53
Warren, Earl, 51
Waters, Maxine, 67
Watts riots, 51–2, 61
Welfare Act (PRWORA of 1996), 122–3
Wilson, Joe, 141–2
Wilson, Pete, 67, 116–21, 131, 136
World War II, 4, 7, 22–4, 26, 28, 31–2, 34–7, 42–3, 47, 53, 74–5, 90–1
Wounded Knee Creek, 61, 182
Wovoka, 181–2

Xi Jinping, 94